REGGIE

A Season with a Superstar

REGGIE

☆ *A Season with a Superstar* ☆

by
Reggie Jackson
with Bill Libby

ᑫᔦP

A Playboy Press Book

For those who would like to know.

Acknowledgments

The authors wish to thank all members of the Oakland A's organization for their cooperation with this project.

And they wish to thank the dedicated ladies who transcribed the tapes, Wilma Robinson and Margaret Sullivan.

Finally, they wish to thank Matt Merola and Paul Goetz of Mattgo Enterprises, who conceived the book, and Bill Adler, Bob Gleason and the others at Playboy Press who made it a reality.

CONTENTS

1.	MARCH	1
2.	APRIL	26
3.	MAY	54
4.	JUNE	81
5.	CONVERSATION WITH CHARLIE	119
6.	JULY	130
7.	AUGUST	161
8.	SEPTEMBER	187
9.	OCTOBER	215
10.	NOVEMBER	266
11.	FEBRUARY	270

REGGIE

A Season with a Superstar

1 ☆ MARCH

My name is Reggie Jackson and I am the best in baseball. This may sound conceited, but I want to be honest about how I feel. There are others who hit more consistently or harder, who run faster, field better or throw better. But there is no one who does as many things as well as I do. I have a fair average, I hit with great power, I run with surprising speed on the bases and in the field, I won't miss many balls within my reach and I can throw. I can do it all and I create an excitement in a ballpark when I walk on the field.

I like that just fine.

I was born in May of 1946, so I will be 28 during this coming 1974 season. I am approaching my peak and I was a long time getting there. I turned pro in 1966 and made the majors the tail end of the following season. I came up to Kansas City where the A's were that season and moved with them to Oakland the following season.

I had a lot of dreams about being a baseball star. For a long time I had cigar boxes full of baseball cards at home. Sometimes I'd take them out and look at them. All those great players, come and gone. They didn't get much time, but they left a mark. That's what I want to do, make a mark to leave behind. I really love baseball. I love life, and baseball is part of my life.

At first, I loved going to the park, putting on that tapered uniform and going out on the field in front of all those people. The sound of that ball smacking into my glove was a sort of music to me. I loved to throw the ball on a line from the fence to the plate and see the catcher take it and put it on a sliding runner and see the ump's arm jerk up in an "out" sign. There was nothing I liked better than hitting a ball hard. The feel of it, the sound of it. And hearing the cheers of the crowd. Some people never get cheered. Seeing a look of respect in the eyes of my peers, the other players, did something to me. I wanted to be respected. I wanted to be a leader.

But some of the magic has gone out of the game for me.

I am still excited just watching the great stars perform. I admire ability and talent. I have come to admire professional play. I see things I didn't used to see in players. I see things that don't show in the statistics and on the surface. I see the things that make some men winners and some men losers. I see who can execute the plays that have to be made under pressure. At first, all I could see was the stats.

I hit .250 and I drove in 79 runs in my rookie year of 1968. I hit 29 home runs. I was on my way. The first half of my second season, I tore up the league. I was way ahead of Babe Ruth's pace the season he hit 60 home runs. I went for it. I took the superswing on every pitch. I struck out a lot, but I figured if I hit 65 home runs, no one was going to ask me how many times I struck out. I wound up leading the league in strikeouts four different seasons and I never have hit those 65 home runs. I thought I was a stud who could stand up to pressure, but I found out I was human.

At first I ate up that spotlight. There were stories on me in every newspaper and magazine, and my picture was everywhere. After a while, the spotlight started to burn me. All those writers and all those broadcasters asking the same questions over and over again, and pretty soon the same answers stopped satisfying them. They wanted something more from me and I didn't have anything else to give 'em. I was used up. The phone never stopped ringing. I never had a moment to myself.

I stopped being a person. I became a trophy. I got to hate it and I just wanted to get the hell away from it. I started arguing with my wife and my marriage went sour. There was a lot of temptation out there on the road and I wanted to be free. I was too young to be married and I wasn't ready to settle down. I just wanted to get what I could out of life.

I was playing for 20 grand. I tailed off at the end, but still finished with a .275 batting average, 47 home runs and 118 runs-batted-in. It was still a helluva year and I expected a hell of a raise from Charlie Finley. I had held out the previous spring without winning him over, but I felt I had proven my point and established myself. I wanted 60 grand. He offered 40 grand. He reminded me that he paid me 95 grand to sign originally. I reminded him that that was then, and this was now. I remembered I had wanted 100 grand, so he had given me 95. I figured Finley out. He was never going to give you what you wanted. I was young and defiant and I stuck to my guns almost all of the spring. When I could see the season getting away from me, I caved in. It took a lot out of me.

I had a lousy season. I was out of shape. I started slow. Finley started to ride me. He told the manager, John McNa-mara, to bench me. He benched me. Finley told the writers he might send me to the minors. They told me. I told them not to tell me that shit. He wanted to send me, but he was afraid it would make him look bad. He asked me to go volun-tarily. He said it would be good for me. I couldn't see how it would be good for me. I refused. He was furious. McNamara played me, I hit a homer, Finley benched me. If I struck out, I stayed in. He even pinch-hit for me. He was punishing me. He wanted to break my spirit. He almost did. The players started to kid me about being a fifty-grand pinch-runner. I took it. I tried to make a joke of it. I caught the pitchers when they were warming up. I offered to carry Sal Bando's bag at the airport. He offered me a tip. It was a long season.

Baseball was not for me what I expected it to be. It is not all hitting home runs and running around the bases and tipping your cap to the cheers of the fans, then drawing a fat paycheck and going out funning. It's striking out, too. It's throwing one away. It's heaving your helmet. It's trying too hard and making a mistake and getting fined for it. It's being booed. It's getting so mad at yourself you can't see straight. It's riding the bench when you should be out there breaking out of your slump. It's seven hours a day at the ballpark, seven days a week, seven months a year. It's riding those planes and living out of suitcases and sitting around hotel lobbies and clubhouses and beginning to bitch about bad things and squabbling with your teammates. It's having to hustle every minute of every inning even when you're worn down and worried. It's the pressure of producing and having every move measured in those long lists of statistics. It's the writers asking you questions you don't want to answer and the fans coming at you when you want to be alone. It's having friends you don't want to have. It's having a man own you and having to take whatever he wants to pay you and accept whatever he wants to do with you, or go dig a ditch for a living. It's not what I thought it would be.

An owner like Finley puts it to you whenever he wants to. It's legalized rape. He almost broke my spirit. I got to where I didn't want any more big years. I got to where I just wanted to have good years, not great years, do my job, help my team win, go home and get a little raise every year without anyone noticing me or hassling me. I spent several seasons just playing the games as if I was working at a job, without enthusiasm for it. But it wasn't me. My mind was messed up at that time.

It was a humbling experience. It may have been good for me. It may have been the Lord's way of testing me, of making me a better man. I'm not that religious, but I know who Jesus Christ is. And He apparently knows who I am. I got too high and He took me down. I was taught that life was sweet *and* sour. I decided that life was too short to let some sonofabitch spoil it for me. People told me to take all the crap, be nice and humble, don't rock the boat. Well, I'm a ballplayer, not a flunky. I have the ability to perform in a profession and I won't waste it.

I decided I was cheating myself, my family, my friends, my teammates, the fans and even my owner, if I didn't make the most of what I had in me. I had to get myself together. I even started to see a psychiatrist. He helped me. He made me look at myself and what was inside of me. He made me see that R-E-G-G-I-E doesn't spell J-E-S-U-S. He made me see that I am just a man with weaknesses to overcome. I had to get the meanness out of me. I had to control rage. He made me see that I had strengths, too, that I could use. I had to become the best ballplayer I could be. I felt if I could be the best I could control my destiny. If I got to be big enough, even The Man couldn't control me.

Finley made money in insurance. He bought a ballclub. Before the draft he went out and bought the best bonus babies he could. He put together a talented team. It took awhile for it to mature. He was impatient. He must have had nine or ten managers. He fired them as fast as he hired them. This team has only one manager—Finley. But finally he landed a manager who could deal with him—Dick Williams. Dick just took the crap Finley fed him and ran the club as much as he could. He taught us to take crap from Finley and play the games as well as we could. He taught us fundamentals. He taught us how to use our talent to win. We had our disagreements, but he disregarded them. Winning was all he wanted out of us.

Winning was what Finley wanted, too. But he wanted to win his way. He wanted to be the one who won with us. He screwed around with the roster, so that Williams didn't know who would be in the dressing room when he went in there. Williams had a team he could win with, so he took it as long as he could. We won the division in 1971, but we weren't ready to go any further. Just winning that one thing was enough for us that year. We acted afraid of Baltimore. We blew it and when it was suddenly over I couldn't believe it. I lay on the dugout steps and I cried.

The next year we won the division and we won the playoffs and we won the World Series. And Finley was out front taking all the bows. And I was in the background, slipping through the shadows. I tore up a leg muscle sliding in the playoffs and I didn't even get to play in the Series. I didn't feel a part of it. I wanted to be a part of a championship team.

I made up my mind last season would be my season. It was.

I became the best. I hit close to .300. I led the league with 32 home runs, 99 runs scored, and 117 runs-batted-in. Not only was I voted Most Valuable Player in the American League—but it was unanimous. We won our division again, we won the pennant again and we won the World Series again. I got the big hits and I was voted Most Valuable Player in the World Series. All of a sudden I was considered as good as the best in baseball.

It gave me confidence in myself, not only as a ballplayer but as a person. I had overcome my obstacles to make the most of myself. I feel a responsibility to my talent and my image now. The spotlight is still hot and I hope I can handle it. The pressure pounds at me now, but I don't want to be broken by it. I want to be equal to life.

The chance has come to put one season of my life into a book, so I am taking it. I am told all I have to do is talk into a tape recorder every day or so and tell what's going down and what I'm thinking, so I'm going to do it. An L.A. writer, Bill Libby, will put it into shape, but I'll make sure it's me.

I am torn between being my own man and looking good. I am still trying to find my way. But I know how to find it now. I know I have to look at myself and everyone else and everything else in life objectively. I know I have to try to see through the surface of things to the truth. But I am moody. I am maturing and I still ride a rollercoaster of emotions. I am happy sometimes and sometimes I'm sad. I am satisfied sometimes and sometimes I am dissatisfied. I try to control my temper, but I am a perfectionist and a passionate person. I am learning to live with myself and with others. I am just learning what my life is like.

I live off-seasons in a condominium in Tempe, where I went to college at Arizona State, and I live in-seasons in an apartment in Oakland, where I do my job. I'm still in Tempe now and it's about time to start a new season.

I'm alone now. I go home to an empty house. Well, hell, I could have people around all the time if I wanted. Sometimes I want and sometimes I don't want. I was married for two years or so. I was married in 1968 and divorced in 1973, but I was separated from her for two years. Her name was Jenni and she was the nicest girl I ever met, but I wasn't ready to be married to any girl. She was a smart girl and she made me feel stupid at times. I'm smart, not stupid, but she had more polish. She liked foreign films and I liked cowboy movies, you know. And she read and I didn't.

I came from a broken home and I didn't know how to make a marriage work. All I knew was to try to be a good ballplayer and make money and buy a nice house and put food on the table. I wasn't ready for the responsibility of living with a lady and making my way of life fit with hers. When I had my first big year in 1969, everyone was telling me how great I was and I figured I was and I got carried away and got to strutting around. I guess I got to be insufferable. The broads are always coming after a ballplayer, too, you know, especially a big ballplayer, and they make it easy for him. It's hard to resist, harder than anyone who's never had it that way realizes.

She tried to make it work. Jesus Christ, she tried. But I tried, too. I just didn't realize what was happening to me and to her and to us. She wasn't able to make me see it, and she didn't have the patience to wait for me to get the whole scene into the proper perspective. I was wrong because I was unaware, but I won't whip myself for it. We've all got to grow and she wouldn't wait for me to grow up. She was hard on me, too. She just kept kicking me. She just couldn't handle our relationship. I tried to express to her how I felt but she wouldn't listen, she just saw it her way and it didn't matter if it was the right way. Finally, I felt we'd tried enough, you know. So we split.

I loved her even after we split up. I still care about her, but not the way I once did. There was just too much that went down wrong between us, you know. She lives in L.A. now. I see her sometimes, but not often. I call her sometimes, but not often. She doesn't want to hear me. She says, hey, you're a big ballplayer now, you must be making a lot of money now, you must be happy now, because that's all you care about. She thinks I'm the same stud I always was. I'm not, but if that's

what I am to her then there's nothing I can do about it.   Maybe
someday she'll see it differently.

I want to be happily married and to have a family of kids.
That's one of my ambitions in life because without a wife and
kids life is incomplete.   I want a wife and three kids, maybe
four or five or six.   I want to have people I can share my life
with.   I mean *really* share.   Everything.   I think I've met the
girl I'm going to marry and have as my wife the rest of my
life.   But I'm not ready to marry again, yet.   My life isn't right,
yet.   A ballplayer's life isn't right for a wife.   Most are married,
of course, but most run around a lot, too, and that ain't right.
And you're away half the time, which is no way to raise kids.

I'm young yet and I want to go out with different girls right
now.   I don't say I'm going to go into town and get me a piece
of tail.   I don't hustle ass.   Girls come at me, but I never met
one that way that I wanted to stay with.   I kid around with them.
I pick up the girls.   But the ones I see a lot are the ones I've seen
something in, and sought out for myself.   I can tell if I can
trust a girl, if I mean more to her than just being Reggie Jackson, big ballplayer, big stud.   And although I'm generous with
them, I won't let them pick my pockets.

I like looks in a girl, but looks only last so long, you know.
Once you've had her, there has to be something else to her.
She has to be able to see inside of things and talk about different things.   She has to have interests and be interesting.   I'm a
moody man and she has to be woman enough to handle my
moods.   I want to be man enough to handle hers, too.

I don't run with most of the other ballplayers, because most of
them are married and they lead different lives than I do.   And
because I don't want to be part of any running around they
do.   Some do, some don't.   I don't date married women.   I
have, but I don't want to.   I don't want to be breakin' up no
marriages.   I don't need the trouble, either.   I was dating a
girl in Arizona at one time who was married but separated
from her husband before I ever met her.   Even so, her husband sued me for alienation of her affections.   It cost me
$1200 to dig out from under it. I think I could have won the
case but my lawyers told me it would be cheaper to give the cat

a grand and give his attorneys something instead of fighting. A big-money ballplayer is a target and I'm not going to stick my neck out where someone can shoot my head off.

I lead a decent life. I date decent girls. I'm a bachelor now and I'm entitled, but I don't dissipate a lot and risk my future. And some day when I'm settled down I'll get married and have me a mess of kids and try to raise them right, the way my daddy raised me. I'll try to give them the sort of life my parents didn't provide for me.

I love kids. I got nieces I go ape over. They're always on the lookout for Uncle Reggie because they know they can get anything from me they want. Which is the way I want it. I care for them and I want them to know it. If I got something that can make life nicer for them, that's what I'm here for, that's one of the reasons. There isn't anything I wouldn't do for those kids. And some day soon I'm gonna do for my own. I'm gonna have a wife and kids to share my life, who I can take care of, who will take care of me. But I want it to be right. And the time's not right, yet. I'm not ready, yet. So I'll go my own way for a while yet.

I have something to fall back on now. I am a partner in a real-estate firm in Tempe with my closest friend, Gary Walker. He is a former insurance salesman and from my old school. He is white and I am black, but that plays no part in our partnership or our friendship. I try not to see color, although some people keep showing it to me. I would trust Walker with my life. I do, because United Development Company is my future. Much of what little land is left in this country is in Arizona and there is a future for a lot of people here.

We sell land to players and to just plain people. We have holdings worth 30 million dollars, which makes me a millionaire on paper. I could quit baseball now if I wanted to and live a good life, but there is still too much I can get out of the game for me to go yet. I may own a team someday. They talk about how we're going to have the first black manager, but I look for the day I'm the first black owner. I'll buy Finley and sell him to Trenton. I almost bought his basketball team from him this winter. We offered him a fair price and we were going to take it from Memphis to Tucson, but he laughed it off because he didn't want to sell out to one of his slaves.

We were ready to build an ABA team around Bill Walton. We were going to let poor people in free. Walton talks about wanting a free life-style and wanting to do for others. We said if he'd sign for us, we'd give him a house in the mountains if he built it himself, and a million-dollar loan, provided he'd spend 20 hours a month working with delinquent kids in the ghettos. I don't think he took us seriously.

I give away a lot of money to black, Indian and Mexican-American groups in Arizona and I back a Boys' Club to help troubled kids, but I haven't found the best way to make use of my money yet. I've never had much money and I'm fortunate enough to have ability in a business where a man can make a lot of money for a little while. I want to make the most of it first and enjoy it for a while.

This season baseball put in an arbitration board to settle contract disputes. Finley had more disputes go to the board than any other owner. We had a big year and he offered his best players raises of five or ten or fifteen grand to try to keep them humble and hungry. He made us sweat. Contracts have to go out by the fifteenth of December—and that was the day he sent them out. I had played for 75 grand last season and he offered me 90. I know he figured I'd settle at 100.

There's method to his madness. He wants to keep his players competing against each other for the top dollar. He tried to screw us, so we decided to stick it to him. I talked to him but he was stepping on my manhood, trying to deprive me of my dignity. To him, I'm just a piece of flesh, a commodity. I didn't ask for the moon. I know I'm not a Henry Aaron. But treat me fair. I talked to him twice on the telephone, and my partner acting as my advisor talked to him and he went to $100,000 and held the line. So I took him to arbitration, along with a lot of my teammates.

We read the rules of arbitration. I called my managers in New York, Matt Merola and Paul Goetz of Mattgo Enterprises, and we gathered up all the stats that showed the sort of per-

formance I'd produced.   I called top players and we got letters
of testimonial from them.   I called every MVP of the past ten
years to find out what kind of raise they had gotten from it and
what kind of money they were making.

Johnny Bench told me the MVP was worth 40 grand to him
each of the two times he won it.   Our stats were comparable,
but he was making 125 grand and going to get more and I was
making 75.   Pete Rose was MVP last year and he jumped 40
grand, too.   Tom Seaver said he was making $140,000 last
year and he was going up to $172,500 this year.   Forty
seemed fair, so I asked for 60 because Finley hadn't been fair.
The way it worked, the board heard the arguments and they
voted for his figure or your figure, they didn't compromise.
His figure was $100,000 and mine was $135,000.

Finley laughed off arbitration.   He underestimated it.
Players came with advisors and lawyers, and Finley came with
his wife.   Other players were heard before me and I sat in.
Finley tried to have me thrown out, but I was allowed to stay
because I'm our player rep.   I watched everything that went on
and I took notes and I got together with my advisors and I
planned our attack.

My turn came and I went in with my advisors and my stats
and graphs and charts and testimonials from Frank Robinson
and Jim Palmer.   And with Dave Duncan in person.   We'd
flown him in to testify for me.   And Finley fucking walked in
with himself and his brain.   He was unprepared to perform.

All he wanted to do was put down his players, and the board
wouldn't buy it.   He put us all down and he put me down
worst of all.   He said I was always hurt and a troublemaker
and I didn't perform to my talent and the only reason I was
voted MVP was it was the sort of year where there wasn't anyone who was any good.   He said he had won it, not us, and
they were turned off him by this.   We were in there three
hours, and three days later the board voted on my behalf.

I got the biggest single boost of any player who went to
arbitration.   Of the players who went from our team, Ken
Holtzman won at $93,000, Rollie Fingers at $65,000, and Darold
Knowles at $59,000.   It's wrong, but Joe Rudi lost and got

$55,000 and Gene Tenace lost and got $45,000. And a few lesser players lost.

Catfish Hunter should have gone, but settled for $100,000 a year for two years. Sal Bando also got $100,000 for the year, Campy Campaneris $68,000, on the second year of a two-year contract, and Vida Blue $75,000.

That was the middle of February. Now it's March and I'm on my way to training, which is not far from here, in Tempe. We have a new manager, Alvin Dark, who has been here before. But we have pretty much the same team we've had through two straight world titles. It is a tremendous team, the best-balanced ballclub in baseball.

Gene Tenace at first, Dick Green at second, Campy Campaneris at short and Sal Bando at third make up a fine-fielding infield. Greenie is the glue that holds our defense together. Joe Rudi in left, Billy North in center and Reggie Jackson in right can go for the ball, catch it, and throw it. Rudi is the best left fielder in baseball. When Tenace catches, Rudi plays first. Ray Fosse is our regular behind the plate, a capable catcher.

We don't hit for high average, but we hit with men on. Reggie, Rudi, Bando and Tenace have power and produce runs. Deron Johnson is a powerful designated hitter, though he is coming off an injury. Reserves Angel Mangual and Vic Davalillo are clever hitters. Campy and North are clever hitters who steal a ton of bases.

We have super pitching. We have three of the best starters in the game in Catfish Hunter, Ken Holtzman and Vida Blue. We will have to find extra starters from among veterans like Blue Moon Odom, Chuck Dobson and Dave Hamilton, or a kid like Glenn Abbott. This is our only weakness. We have a superb bullpen in Rollie Fingers, Darold Knowles and Paul Lindblad. We have depth behind us on the bench. We have it all.

We fight among ourselves and pop off, but we produce on the field and under pressure. We are the best and we are just approaching our peak. I look forward to another winning season. I feel sure we will win it all again. And have a lot of fun along the way. But it is a long way to go.

Saturday, the 2nd. I got permission to get here late because my ex-wife had a back operation and I wanted to fly to Los Angeles to see how she was before beginning the baseball season. I saw her and she was all right. The visit was okay, but it wasn't what I wanted it to be. I try not to think of her because I know it is finished. But I still feel for her and I want her to be all right.

I no more had got in here with the team than the shit had hit the fan. Our World Series rings arrived and they were trash. They were the same as last year's, only they didn't have diamonds like last year's. That may not seem like so much, but Finley had promised us more for this year if we won again, and he welshed on us. All the players were burnt up. Catfish called him "cheap." Charlie was quoted in the newspaper as saying he was dumb, not cheap. He pointed out he'd made money loans to the Cat in the past. He gave him money to buy a farm. He didn't point out that he hassled Cat so much Cat sold part of the farm and paid off the loan. Cat hates him now. So do most of the guys because they've all been down a hard road with him and been hurt by him.

Finley is reneging on the rings because we didn't back him in the last World Series against the Mets. Mike Andrews made errors at second that cost us the second game. I was disappointed by him, but I felt for him. But Finley had been frustrated by the Commissioner and by the Mets in his efforts to get an extra player, Manny Trillo, into the Series. Now he saw another opportunity to try. He was like a fan who gets mad at a player who makes mistakes and wants to get rid of him. Andrews had hurts and Finley called him together with the team doctor and asked the player to sign a statement that he was too injured to perform and was resigning from the Series. It was an old tactic of his. He hammered at Andrews at a time the player was low and the poor guy gave in. It was dehumanizing and when we found out about it we were raging. It could have been any of us, you know. That's the way Charlie treats people. There are times I feel he's a good old guy who's just eccentric, and then times when I feel he's a miserable man, or is corrupted by his power.

Mike had headed home and we talked among ourselves and thought about refusing to play unless he was returned. But that's as far as the idea got. Some of the guys wore black arm-bands to a workout. But we worked out and we played. We didn't have the guts to go through with it. That hurt, too. But the Commissioner jumped on Charlie, and Andrews was restored to the team and to the lineup. He returned and he even played. But something had gone out of the games for us.

Williams earlier had told some of us he'd had all he could take from Finley and was leaving. After the Andrews incident, he announced he was retiring at season's end. That hurt, be-cause Finley had fucked us out of the best manager in baseball.

We won the Series, anyway. We're winners, no matter what. We thrive on rhubarbs. We've been toughened by tough times.

During the 1972 season Finley figured out a promotion where we'd grow mustaches and he'd have a "Mustache Day" and every guy who wore a mustache would be let in free. He offered a hundred bucks to each of us to let our mustaches grow and most of us went along with it. We liked it. Now we have the longest hair and more mustaches than any team in baseball. I even have a beard. It's just something I want to wear for a while. I think it makes me look mean. We're a team of mean men.

We look any way we want to look and act any way we want to act. Once we started to shoot off our mouths, speak our minds and punch each other out when we lost our tempers, we found we could get away with it. Williams couldn't have cared less as long as we won. And Finley didn't dare interfere as long as we kept winning. I had a fuss with Blue Moon Odom and a fight with him at our victory party after the World Series, for God's sake. Forgive and forget. Live your life any way you want and play the game the way you've found out wins for you, and you'll be all right.

It's become a business with us. We have jobs to do and we do them. We want the money that's there for the winners. Finley took all the fun out of it for us, so we take our fun any way we can find it. We have a reputation to live up to and we seem to like maintaining it. We swagger through life, the world champs—and we're cocky about it.

After last season the team got death threats on my life in the mail. At first I felt like a star, but then I felt afraid. After all, a kook can do this. And he said he'd snipe me from the stands if I played in the playoffs and World Series. I played—with protection from the FBI and a friend, Tony Del Rio, who is big and acted as a bodyguard. I didn't tell about it until after we had won it all. And I was proud that I had performed so well under that sort of pressure.

I used to dream about how good it would be to be Willie Mays or Mickey Mantle. My dreams have died. I still want to be as good as them, but I know now it won't be as good as I thought it would be. Even the rotten rings aren't what they're supposed to be. Screw the rings. I'll buy my own diamonds. I can afford it now. No one gives you anything, you've got to get it for yourself.

Tuesday, the 5th. There's not much to break up the monotony of spring training, but the other day I played golf with Vice President Ford. I got a telephone call from someone who said it was the White House calling. I thought a pal was putting me on, and I said, "Man, Reggie Jackson ain't here and who the fuck are you?" The man said that it really was the White House and Vice President Ford really would like to speak to Mr. Jackson. Somehow the tone convinced me and I said, "Wait a minute, I'll put him on." I was embarrassed, you know. And then they put Ford on. I'd met him at a banquet in Columbus, Ohio, in January and he reminded me I'd agreed to play golf with him when he was in Phoenix. He was going to be there over the weekend and asked if I would play a round with him. I said I sure would, then I went to Dark and was given permission to take the afternoon off.

I'm not much for politics. I don't want my name used. And I'm under the impression that Nixon is a crooked cat. I don't respect politicians in general. But this man had come across as a decent, down-to-earth guy, a former football player at Michigan who understood athletes, and I have to admit that

I was awed that the Vice President would call me at my house and ask me to play golf with him.   He's just a man, but he seems more in that office.

He invited me to bring anyone I wanted, so I brought Ralph Earle, my shrink.   I asked Alvin and Sal and some of the other players, but Dark didn't think Finley would like it if any of the others went.   We played at the Paradise Country Club in Scottsdale, where a lot of the area wealth is.   I wore a T-shirt and Puma shoes.   I don't know why, except I was wondering how many niggers had played that club and I guess I wanted to show I took it in stride.   Ford didn't seem to notice.   He had about 30 Secret Service men with him and some of them had machine guns.

When word got out he was there, about a hundred people turned up to see him and he treated them with a lot of respect.   It was the first time I was ever with someone who was asked for more autographs than I was.   I shot a 90 to his 97 and took ten bucks off him.

Afterwards, we went into the clubhouse and visited.   I had an iced tea and he had a scotch-and-water and he invited me to go on to Denver with him, but I declined with thanks, thinking I didn't want to lend myself to anything political.   I invited him to stop by my house any time he was in town.   He smiled and said I was welcome at his pad any time, too.

Cool cat.   I mean, I'm not judging him as a politician, but as a person.   There isn't much joy in his job, either, and the pressure has to be heavy.   His life is a hell of a lot heavier than mine, that's for sure.

I also went to a dinner in honor of the Angel manager and my old coach at Arizona State, Bobby Winkles, in Phoenix the other night.   A lot of players were invited and I was one of the few who showed up.   It was embarrassing and I felt bad for the man.   I donated a thousand bucks to the boys' home he is sponsoring there.   It was giving something back to a community which has given me so much.   I told him I was going to give him a gold watch and he laughed and said he'd be waiting. Well, he'll be fooled because I'm going to give it to him.   I've already ordered it to be inscribed on the back, "To Bobby

Winkles from Reggie Jackson." The night was made nicer by a dynamite date, a girl named Lois Anderson.

Thursday, the 7th. I'm living at home and commuting to the ballpark. Billy North comes over mornings and I cook him breakfast and we go to the ballpark together. He's a good guy and we ran around a lot this winter, but once spring training starts you stop running around for awhile. After a week of working out I'm glad the exhibition schedule starts tomorrow.

Exhibition games mean nothing, but they're a chance to get your stuff together. We have to do it on our own this season. We are going to miss Dick Williams. It's hard to tell how much Dark can do for us. That's what a player cares about in a manager, what he can do for you. And how he hurts you. If he fucks up, he fucks you up. Dark played the game and managed a couple of clubs, including this one in Kansas City. He's not the first man Finley hired and fired and hired back. But he's been out of baseball a few years.

No one wanted him because he had a bad reputation. He'd made some statement that suggested blacks and Latins were lazy and hard to handle. We have blacks and Latins on this team. I'm both, as far as that goes. Some of us are looking at him hard. He says he didn't say it. He says he's changed. He's gotten religion. He quotes from the Bible all the time. He has said to us we needn't worry about him quoting psalms to us from now on, but he's still doing it. I'm willing to give him a chance. I'll wait and see what he is. Finley manages this team anyway.

Finley fucked Williams. When Williams said he was leaving, Charlie wished him well. But when Williams went to sign with the Yankees, Finley refused to release him from his contract. So the best manager in baseball is selling insurance in Florida and it's a shame. We feel for him, but we feel he didn't have to sign a new contract with Charlie when he already knew what Charlie was, so he dug his own grave.

You wonder why a man will sign with The Man, but Dark didn't have any other offers. Finley wanted someone he could handle easily, anyway. In this organization, Charlie O. is God.

He treats people like trash. He has the smallest front-office staff in baseball because he's always firing people or they're always quitting on him. He keeps his office in Chicago, and when he flies in to his office in Oakland, the hired help starts to sweat. Finley puts them to work at midnight stuffing envelopes.

He's as close as the nearest telephone anyway. He calls everyone on his payroll all the time to tell them what to do. They're afraid to do anything until he tells them to do it. So they don't do anything and nothing gets done. It's no wonder we don't draw in Oakland. It's a bad baseball town and we have a bad baseball park and a scared organization. We don't even have TV or radio contracts right now. We have one announcer, Monte Moore, who everyone suspects of being Finley's informer. He has a different partner every season. Finley hires and fires them as fast as he does managers.

Finley is trimming our roster now. Andrews was the first to go and no one took him.

Al Dark was saying the other day that Chuck Dobson looked like he could help us. The next day, Finley phoned Dobson to tell him he was released. Dobson told us Finley told him he hated to do it, but he was having his problems with his divorce and all. Dobson was getting released and Finley was telling him *his* problems! Amazing!

Finley is having problems but the players don't feel for him too much. He lost a lot at arbitration. The Internal Revenue is suing him for a half-million or so in back taxes. We hear the AMA, his main customer, may take their insurance away from his company. He's making money in Oakland, but not what he should, and he may be short a little cash.

He had his second or third heart attack last season. His doctors want him to retire, but he doesn't want to sell his team. It's all he has left and he loves doing whatever the hell he wants with it. Only he's stuck on a long-term lease in Oakland, and he can't move it to Seattle or Washington or New Orleans or Toronto or some such place. He sets a price and when someone meets it, he ups it. He may sell, but he doesn't want to. He may not move, but he wants to.

His wife is suing him for divorce. They've been married 30 years or so and have six or seven children. She's living at the family farm in Indiana and she wants more than a grand a week from him. Good luck, lady. We're rooting for her. We hear she hired a bodyguard to protect herself from her husband, which the players felt was funny. Who's protecting us?

Friday, the 8th. We won our opening exhibition game from San Diego in Yuma, 13–3. It doesn't mean much, but it was nice to get going that way. We hit a lot of home runs. I hit one. I am going to hit a lot of home runs this season. I love to hit. I'd rather hit than have sex. I'll still be having sex when I'm no longer hitting. It's the catcher and the pitcher against the batter. They try to outwit you and overpower you. I go to the plate with a plan. Concentration is a lot of it because it's a long season and it's easy to lose your intensity. You hit one out and you can be satisfied. I'm never satisfied because I always want another one. I am ready for whatever the pitcher has. And I know how to get what I want. If I want a fastball, I move up in the batter's box as if I'm expecting a curve. He sees it and tries to blow a burner by me, but I have backed off and I blast it.

I don't guess, I anticipate. I'm looking for something, but I'm prepared to deal with something else. If it looks good, I'll go for it hard for two strikes. I'll take the big cut until I have two strikes on me. Then, unless we need a long one, I'll cut down on my stroke and just try to meet the ball. Lots of hitters could be better hitters than they are, but they're easily distracted, they're not always thinking, they've got lazy bats and they're afraid. I'm confident. I fear no pitcher. There are pitchers who are harder to hit than others, but I always feel I'm going to hit them. I don't always do it, but I do it enough so I feel I can.

My main asset is my strength. I am 6 feet tall, I weigh 204 pounds. I have 17-inch biceps and 27-inch thighs. I put all my body against that ball. I don't use a great big bat, about 36 ounces, because I want to whip it fast, with speed. I'm hard. Johnny Summers, a kid with this club, says I'm one big callus.

I have a working man's hands and body.   I am a working man. This is a physical job I do.

But my muscles are a problem for me.   My legs are so heavy I've pulled the hamstring muscles behind my thighs eight or nine times.   I'm fast for a big guy.   I can steal.   But it's a risk any time I run hard because my muscles are easy to pull.

Actually, I'm a physical wreck.   I have an arthritic spine. I'm near-sighted and astigmatic and have to wear glasses to see good.   I'm always pulling muscles and playing in pain. But I want to play the whole game.   I want to be a complete player.   Some of my teammates call me "Buck" because that's what Willie Mays was called and they know how much I admire Mays.   I admire a Mays and a Mantle and an Aaron because they could do it all and beat you a lot of ways.

I admire a Frank Robinson because he is such a great player and such a great man.   When I was at my lowest, I went to him in winter ball and he dragged me up out of the depths.   I admire a Pete Rose because he hustles all the time for all he can get.   These guys are living definitions of the word "determination."   They can go to a movie and stand out with the lights out.   They look good licking an ice-cream cone.   They walk by a bench and other ballplayers watch them.   That's what I want for me.   Hitting has to be my best way, but the other things count too, and the way I conduct myself counts as much as anything.

I won't pretend to be anything I'm not.   I'll just try to be myself.   In this book I'll say what I'm thinking.   I'll use words I wouldn't use with ladies around because I do use them when ladies aren't around.   And I'll apologize to any ladies who read this when it is put on paper.   The thing is I want it to be me on paper.

Tuesday, the 19th.   Bando got on Billy North about the beard he was growing and asked him who the hell he thought he was, Reggie Jackson?   Blue Moon Odom said Bando was a wop who couldn't tell Billy North from Reggie Jackson because all niggers looked alike to him.

Wednesday, the 20th. We have played ten exhibition games and we have lost six. We have had days when we were awesome and other days when we were rotten. I have had days when I swung the bat good and days when I didn't. When you have won as much as we have it is hard to get up for games that are meaningless, but I am beginning to worry that we will build bad habits. I've been bitching about this and that. Rollie Fingers started to get on me yesterday, asking me if all my bats had arrived and my helmet fit right, and if I was about ready to play ball. I told him I was tired of carrying him, and the pitchers on this team were just lucky they had hitters behind them.

Rollie's been riding everyone. He hollered at Bando, "Hey, you damn dago, you're so fucking fat you make the fat-ass manager look thin!" Sal told him he'd been hanging around with the Jew Holtzman so long, he was beginning to think he was smart, too. When he said it, it seemed pretty funny. Fingers got roughed up that day and we said in the dressing room he was the sort of fireman who started fires in the other guys' bats.

There just aren't many breaks from the routine. We play not only at our base but at other teams' bases all over Arizona and California, and the daily hopping around depresses you. You're not going to have many days off once the regular season starts, so you'd kind of like to lay out some days during the preseason. But Dark says Finley ordered him to play his regulars at least six innings every day, so that's what he's doing —every fucking day.

The other day I had a lady in the stands waiting on me and I was happy as hell when I got hit on the ankle by a pitch and got to leave early. I told the team I was sorry but I wouldn't be fit to make the game in Tucson the next day and they really got on me about that because it's a fucking 45-minute bus ride.

I did go to Tucson, though. The wind was blowing in so bad, Greenie said no one was going to hit one out—so I hit one out. I felt like a fucking hero and let Greenie and the guys know about it. Everybody loved it.

The ride back was bad because we got into the subject of Jerry Adair's wife. He's our coach and his daughter died of cancer about three years ago and now his wife may have cancer. She has to go into the hospital for an operation and we took up a collection to buy her a gift and some flowers and a card. I'll have to take care of it as the player rep. I'll probably buy her a robe or something she can wear in the hospital which might cheer her up. I don't know how to cheer him up.

Dark had told Adair to go home and be with her as long as she needed him. Some of the guys said Finley would fire him for letting the guy go, but we kidded if he did we'd go on strike. It's sad, but you think of those things when you live with Finley—and he can't be *that* bad.

I've had some dealings with him as player rep recently and he seems sincere. You have to kid with him, but he does take an interest in what happens on the team. It's just that he has this motto: "Sweat Plus Sacrifice Equals Success." He spiels it all the time, and he won't accept anything that interferes with winning. Well, life interferes sometimes. Adair has a job to do and he does it well, but I'm sure at this minute other things matter more to him.

Wednesday, the 27th. We had lost four straight before we won yesterday. We've lost ten out of sixteen. I went into Dark's office and talked to him about it because I believe we better begin bearing down or we'll go into the season with bad habits.

I don't know about Dark. He may have been away too long. Several times this spring he's talked to us about certain ballplayers on certain teams we have to play—and they haven't been with the teams for a couple of seasons. Some of them aren't even in the league anymore! It's embarrassing.

For instance, he was talking about the Twins' pitching staff and mentioned Jim Kaat. Someone said, "Alvin, Kaat was put on waivers and picked up by the White Sox last August." Dark mumbled, "Oh." Now he's asking us about the players and teams instead of telling us, and it's awkward.

He held a meeting and told us we have to get going. I had hoped he'd have more to say; maybe be a bit tougher.

I got on the guys, but they already were getting on me. It was in Phoenix and I drove over in my own car and it stalled. I couldn't get it going and I had to get help. By the time I got to the ballpark, the guys welcomed me with open arms and open mouths: "Hey, here he is, The Superstar, nice of you to take the time to come visit us"—and that kind of crap. I don't blame them but it shows I got to keep my act clean now that I'm in the position I'm in.

After the game, a lot of fans mobbed me, and two of them turned out to be girls I've been dating. They didn't know one another and it was embarrassing as hell. I really don't want to embarrass anyone. It just happened and I hated it. I felt bad. Then I met a little boy who had been brought to the ballpark on a stretcher, in a cast from his waist up. I gave him my hat and my shoes and I think I would have given him everything I had if he'd wanted it. There are worse things than woman trouble.

Speaking of shoes, I signed a contract last winter with Puma Shoes to advertise and promote them for three years for $30,000, and then it turns out Charlie O. signed a contract with Adidas for his players to wear them exclusively. When my picture appeared in an ad for my company, Charlie called me to complain. I worked with Puma's engineers, telling them what a player wanted in the way of a shoe. They turned out a super shoe and I have a stake in it more than money. I told Charlie that, but he didn't want to hear about it. Charlie said I'll wear his shoes and so will the other players or we'll be benched and docked a day's pay for every day we're out. Then he threatened to fine me $1000 a day. I said I'd think about it and hung up. I wish I had told him off. I intend to wear my shoes. We'll see what happens.

We now have the fastest thing in any kind of shoes on our side—Herb Washington. Charlie got the designated hitter into our league and now he wants a designated runner. He says Herb will pinch-run and win ten games for us. Charlie's imaginative and an innovator. He asked for things like night All-Star games and night World Series games long before baseball figured the sense of this out for itself. He put us in our fancy green and gold uniforms and kangaroo white shoes and we all hated them, but now everyone wears something like them.   Baseball won't buy everything he wants, like three-ball walks and orange baseballs, and the other owners hate him for hustling them all the time, but some of his ideas have turned out to be outstanding.

But I don't know about this one.   The guys are bitter because Herb isn't a baseball player, he's a former sprint champion.   They figure he's taking a job away from a baseball player. Someone said, "He's a race horse, not a ballplayer." Dick Green ran up to him and said, "If you break a leg, we'll have to shoot you."   When I almost hit him with a line drive during batting practice, Bando said, "I hope it kills the SOB!" The thing is, Herbie's going to have to show us something and he doesn't know anything about baseball.   He's going to know what it's like to be ridden by professional needlers before long.

Wednesday, the 3rd of April.   We lost five in a row before we won another one.   Then we lost the last one to the Dodgers in Mesa.   That may be the team we'll play in October in the World Series.   We've gotten through March and we're into April and the exhibition season is behind us and we're headed into the regular season.   We won 8 and lost 16 of our 24 exhibition games.   That's one out of three—we were terrible.   But I don't want to make too much of it.   We know what we can do and I'm confident that as soon as we get to the games that matter we'll show our stuff.

I haven't hit much.   None of our big hitters have hit much. But I can't concentrate in exhibition games so I can't blame the other boys for not bearing down.

A friend of mine from Oakland, Everitt Miss, flew in to drive my World Series car back so I can fly with the team.

I've been getting a lot of last-minute things in order at my place and my office, talking to my tax man and my attorney and my partner.   One good thing about leaving is that this is a small town and everyone knows me here and everyone knows my phone number no matter how many times I change it.   It'll be good to get away where I can get some peace.

I look on the season as a time of peace, when I'm at work, doing my job, tending to business, with something to look forward to every day. But I don't know who the hell I think I'm kidding. There is no peace in playing ball. Once the real season starts, there is no rest. You look at the schedule and you see 162 games over six months with very few days off—and you know it's going to be tough. You wonder what the hell will happen this season. Every season it's something else. But this is the season we can win a third-straight World Series so it's something special.

2 ☆ APRIL

Thursday, the 4th. It's opening day—opening night really—and before the game Finley felt he had to talk to me about this business of the shoes. He said he understood that I had a contract and a commitment to wear Pumas, and it was to my financial interests to promote Pumas, and he didn't really care what kind of shoes I wear and all he cared about was winning—which I felt was the way it should be.

But he couldn't leave it at that, he had to add that he had a contract and a commitment and a financial interest in having all his players wear Adidas, and that he could be in breach of his contract with Adidas, and I could be in breach of my contract with the team to be in proper uniform if he cared to call me on it—which I felt was his way of showing he still had the muscle. Well, I'll wear what I want to wear.

It was a distraction, but I don't give a damn about that; I'm used to distractions before the games and after the games. I don't get distracted in games. Once the game starts I am in my element. I don't care if the sun doesn't shine, or if it snows. I don't care what Charlie Finley does. I don't care what Alvin Dark does. I don't care if Richard Nixon jumps off a bridge. I don't want to know what else is happening in the world. As far as I'm concerned, nothing else is happening, nothing else matters but the ball game and what I'm doing out there on that field. When I'm playing, baseball is beautiful. I don't care if we're in Oakland or Texas or anywhere else. I don't mind opening on the road. I don't even mind if I'm booed. I expect to be booed on the road. The better I do, the more I'm booed. I'm stimulated as much by boos on the road as I am by cheers at home.

I did good today. So did a lot of our guys. And we did it against a good pitcher, Jim Bibby. He no-hit us last year. I got the first hit off him today. It was a double down the right-field line, and it could just as easy have been foul as fair, but it got us going. I got two doubles and a home run, even stole a base and scored four runs, and it felt just fine. Rudi and Green each drove in a couple of runs. We drove Bibby out in the fifth and finished with seven runs. They got two off Catfish and Fingers, but we looked good as a team.

I figured once we got to the real games we'd be fine—and I guess I figured right. We looked like the real A's, especially when the bitching began. We were kinda slow getting started, but we started to stir things up in the seventh when Dark took out Rudi to have Herb Washington pinch-run, and Rudi bitched about it. He said he wanted to be a nine-inning player, not half a ballplayer, for which I don't blame him. I figure it's Finley's orders Dark is following and we'll just have to see how it goes. If we weren't raising hell one way or another among ourselves it wouldn't be us, so no one takes it too seriously.

After the game Finley came over to me. There were some writers there and they asked us about the shoes and the stuff that goes on on this team. They even had the guts to ask me, right in front of him, if it was true that a lot of the players didn't like Finley. I said that Mr. Finley says what he feels and he lets us say what we feel and it helps us because we don't keep any bitterness bottled up. I said dissension didn't build up because of this and we liked Finley for it and for not carrying grudges when we had differences. I said we'd work out our differences over the shoes. Finley laughed and said as long as I hit the way I had in this game I could go barefoot. He said he had no problems with his players.

Well, that's what he said.

Saturday, the 6th. Yesterday was an off-day, but we worked out at noon. I've got a sore finger so I didn't do much, but some of the guys who wound up camp in batting slumps—North, Campy, Tenace and Johnson—asked me to hang around and watch them hit, to see if I had any help to offer them. That made me feel good. I think I helped some with some tips. After dinner, Finley asked me to have a drink with him and talk, so I had a beer and we talked. He said since I was the player rep he wanted to talk to me a lot during the season because he wanted to build a better relationship with the players. He wanted to know when they had gripes, and he wanted them to know what he was doing and why. I said this was good.

He said he hadn't done some of the things he'd planned on doing if we won another championship because we hadn't expressed any appreciation for the things he'd done last year and wound up treating him badly. He said he wanted to be all business, he wanted to be professional in the way he treated his players, but he also wanted to be fair. He talked like a father to me. He said he was proud of the way I presented myself to the public, but thought I could do even more, such as tipping my hat to the fans after hitting home runs and keeping my cool more. I told him it made sense. He's given me a lot of good advice.

I guess he wasn't finished talking because he suggested we meet for a late lunch today, too. It was my pregame meal and although they weren't serving in the dining room at the time, he got them to serve us a couple of steaks, which he can do. He let me talk this time. I told him about a few things I knew the guys wanted—like free baseballs to give away. He said he couldn't give 'em away because he didn't have a television or a radio contract. Said he was on a low budget and didn't have the dough to spare. I pointed out that the guys would wind up stealing more than he might give them for free, but he wouldn't listen to that.

I also asked if the guys could have single rooms on the road, especially the veterans. He said they could, but they'd have to pay the difference. I asked him if I could have a single room because it was customary for player reps. He answered that it

might be customary but it would be breaking club rules so I'd
have to pay the difference, which is what I do. You know, he
can say he wants you to ask for what you want, but that doesn't
mean he's going to give it to you. He doesn't give much.

We got to talking about the team and I said the one thing I
thought we needed most was a fourth starter. He noted that
Milt Pappas was available, but that he was trouble. I said I
could see that, to an owner, Pappas spelled trouble. But as a
player, he looked to me like a pitcher who might help a team.

I told him I thought he'd made a mistake in releasing Dobson. He said he'd given Dobson a couple of years, but that he
hadn't been willing to pay the price to make a successful come-
back. I agreed that Dobo didn't take care of himself the way
he should, but I liked the guts he brought to every game.
Charlie explained that he was going to try Odom for the
fourth starter, and if that didn't pan out, they'd try Hamilton,
and if that didn't pan out they'd try Paul Lindblad, and if that
didn't pan out they'd bring Glenn Abbott up from the minors
to try.

So they are grabbing at straws and Blue Moon will be the
first one out of the box. If he doesn't make it maybe he'll hang
around because Charlie likes him or maybe he'll be gone. This
can be a cruel game.

It was only a few years ago that Blue Moon was sitting on top
of the world, and then his arm went bad. Now he's down in
the dumps trying to dig out. He's lost his confidence and he's
concerned for his future and it's made him touchy, which is
why he gets in so many fights. He's not a mean man. He's a
good guy. I feel for him and root for him, and I wonder what
the hell he'll do with his life if he's bounced out of baseball,
because baseball's his life.

I had to go play a game. Fergy Jenkins gave us something
to bitch about in the game. He was just a master, putting the
ball where he wanted and where we couldn't handle it. I could
see why he's won 20 six times. If he can keep pitching like this
he's going to win 25 or 30 this time. The only hit we got was a
bunt single by Campy in the fourth. The Rangers only got two
runs, but that was all they needed. They only got one off

Holtzman before he was lifted in the fifth. Kenny cut up Dark later about his quick hook.

In Atlanta, Henry Aaron hit his 715th home run to break Babe Ruth's record. He has been a remarkable player. I don't know, maybe about the best I've seen. A lot goes into being the best. Willie Mays did more things better. And there have been others. But Aaron has been remarkable because he is remarkable both physically and mentally. He has played 20 years without breaking down and he has been incredibly consistent, which counts more than anything.

He never hit 60 homers. He never even hit 50. But he hit 30 or 40 year after year after year, and he never let the pressure get to him. Some sneer at his feat because he had so many more times up than Ruth, but if durability isn't part of such a record, what is? The fact is, it is a hell of a lot harder to play night after night than it is day after day. Aaron played almost all night games, while Ruth never played any. As far as I can see, Aaron rates the record. And no one I know is gonna break it.

I'm mentioned as one of the guys who might break it some day. No way. I average 30 a year and I have to average 40. If I just went for homers, maybe, but I don't. If I'm not close near the end of my career, I'm not going to go on. Anyway, if I played that long and got that good they couldn't afford to pay me!

Sunday, the 7th. We had our first Sunday religious service this morning. Watson Spoelstra, a Detroit writer, has set up a chapel program for the ball clubs. He asked me if I would represent the A's and I accepted. He's going to arrange to have someone speak to us whenever we're on the road on a Sunday. I'm told who and I tell the guys and get a place for him. Well, I arranged a place at the hotel and I'd told the guys two days before, but no one showed up.

With Dark's help we switched it to eleven at the ballpark. Since the players were there by then, about ten or twelve turned out, which was all right. A man named Burke had some interesting things to say. All I ask of the guys is that they listen.

I don't care what faith they are. This is a nondenominational thing, although the man who speaks may be a minister of one faith or the other.

I personally am a Christian. I may not always do as I should do, but I do believe. I realize it is not money that'll make me happy but the life I lead, and I need my faith to tie everything in my life together. It is only through my faith that I feel any peace. So I hustle the guys to get them to come and at least listen because I believe in it, you know?

I have a picture of Jonathan Livingston Seagull at my place. I read the book and I believed in it—it was almost a religious experience. I know you can do what you believe you can do, if you have a talent for it and are willing to sacrifice for it. Well, I did something special today that not many have done: I hit two homers with two men on and a single. And I drove in seven runs—and we beat Texas, 8–4. After the game Finley came out of the stands to shake my hand and congratulate me on my day and my great start. And I thought that was nice. He doesn't get to many games, but he's gotten to the three in Texas that have started our season, and he said he'd be at the home opener in Oakland, of course.

We should have been happy, but there were some unhappy A's, as usual. For the third straight game, Dark took out a starter who might have been permitted to finish. For the second straight game, the pitcher got the quick hook in the fifth inning—after giving up only one run. Holtzman was unhappy yesterday and Blue was bitter today. Holtzman said Fingers would be the only 20-game winner on the team. Blue banged his bat against the clubhouse wall a couple of times. In the bus he hollered that it was all right this one time, but if Al did it another time he was going to be hit with the worst words in the book and get his office ripped up.

We got guys who like to get this sort of thing going and after they needled Kenny and Vida awhile both of them were really steaming. I told Vida, "Hey, man, look, you two guys don't have to bullshit about something like this. You're big enough to go up to the man and say, 'I'm a twenty-game winner, and if you want me to help you this year the way I helped the other

guy last year, you don't take me outta games unless I get
knocked out.'   I don't need guys playing catch in the bullpen
behind me."   Vida liked what I said; so did Kenny.

Tuesday, the 9th.   I don't know if it was my advice, but when we
got to Kansas City, Vida and Kenny had a meeting with Dark
and the pitching coach, Wes Stock, at the ballpark before our
workout yesterday and talked it out.   I think the pitchers feel
they made their point and I think they'll be given a little more
leeway from now on.   I don't *know* this because Dark doesn't
make all these decisions, Finley does—by telephone if he's not
at the ballpark.

Dark used Washington as a pinch-runner in each of the first
three games of the season and admitted later that this was on
orders from Finley.   This just weakens the manager's position
with us.   There are places where a pinch-runner can help you,
and maybe Washington will learn enough to help us.   But if
there's some sort of rule that he replaces a regular someplace
in every game whether we need it or not, he's gonna hurt us.

Dark says Finley is not only the owner but the general manager and so has a right to give advice to the manager.   That's
bullshit!   Finley doesn't give advice; he gives orders.   Even a
general manager has to let his manager manage the games or
the games get screwed up.

Last night in the lobby, we were jivin' around and had a good
time with a guy who said he was a Giant fan and who tried to
tell us how much better the San Francisco team was, position-
by-position, than the Oakland team.   I laughed and said maybe
the players are, but the results aren't.   He couldn't argue with
the numbers in the won-and-lost column the last few years.

But we have a good time with guys like this.   He went down
our lineups and about the only place he wouldn't insist the
Giants are better—at least, not while I was there—was in right
field where Reggie Jackson plays for the A's.   He insisted
Garry Matthews was better than Joe Rudi, which shows you
how underrated some of our players like Rudi are.

Tonight Rudi hit three doubles to help us beat the Royals,
6–4, even though Hunter didn't have it. I had a double, too, and

Bando had a homer. I enjoy beating Kansas City. They have a cocky club. They finished second to us in our division last season, and they think they're gonna finish first this season. Well, they're not that good. They're not any better than Chicago or Minnesota or even Texas, which is getting tougher. Kansas City has some real good players like John Mayberry, who's as strong a hitter as there is in baseball, and Amos Otis. I enjoy cutting up with these guys. But most of all, I enjoy beating them.

Wednesday, the 10*th*. They beat us tonight. Steve Busby beat us, 4–1, despite three more hits by Rudi. I've seen Busby better. He's thrown harder and with better stuff. But he was good enough to get us out tonight. I was blanked. And Mayberry hit one out of sight. That's the way it goes. Now we go home to open the season in Oakland.

Friday, the 12*th*. We've been home with two off-days in a row before the big game that starts the season in Oakland on Saturday. Home here for me is an apartment in a high-rise in downtown Oakland adjacent to Lake Merritt. It's a nice apartment in an expensive building. Finley used to have an apartment here. Huey Newton does now. A lot of athletes like Nate Thurmond live here or have lived here. I originally took an apartment here to stick it to Finley when he agreed to pay for a place for me during the season as part of our contract hassle a few years ago. It costs $400 a month, which outraged the old man. Then I got it for free because it'd become a black neighborhood and there'd been a lot of trouble on the streets—and they wanted to have me here as a selling point. Now, however, they want to start charging me. If I'm going to pay a lot of money I might as well have my own house. I spoke to my business partner in Arizona about it. He said I might as well because I spend most of every year here, and we can also use it as an office and write a lot of it off on taxes. We agreed I'd go for 60 or 65 grand if I can find a condominium I like. We can afford it.

There's always talk Finley will take the team to another town.

He brought it here from Kansas City so I suppose he could take it from here and put it somewhere else. He denies it publicly, but he has admitted it privately. After the 1972 World Series he told me, Catfish, Vida and Tenace, while we were driving to his house in Indiana for a party, that if we didn't draw a million-three in 1973 there was no way he would stay. He has a lease that runs through 1988, but he seemed to feel he could get out of it. He warned us not to buy homes here. Well, we drew a million, but we didn't draw a million-three. We didn't even make a million-one, which is terrible for a team that won its third straight divisional title and second straight World Series championship.

A lot of it is Finley's fault. I think the people like the players and the team, but not Finley. A lot of people want us to lose because they don't want Finley to win. He has done a lot of things that antagonize the press. He won't feed them, and I think the worst thing you can do to a writer is get him in the stomach. Now he's cut their passes way down, and they love those freebies. Well, what the hell, we don't get anywhere near the coverage we would in another town. Ron Bergman of the Oakland newspaper is the only guy who travels with us regularly. He's a good reporter maybe, but always stirrin' up shit.

Finley's doing a lot of things that look like he doesn't want a lot of attendance. He never has had a front office, and now he has less than ever. He just put a guy in charge of cash who was a bank clerk a few weeks ago. He's cut off the fireworks and fired the ballgirls, who were the only thing dressing up the ballpark. He's knocked off the special deals and discounts to season-ticket holders and cut way back on the half-price family nights, which accounted for about a third of our attendance last season. He has a rotten radio setup and no television at all.

He won't give the ballplayers a break. Things other clubs do—like providing postage stamps and mailing for photos to the fans—we don't get. Alvin Dark sent up for some pictures the other day and they charged him thirteen cents for a fucking black-and-white photo. They charge us for every baseball we take. You can't get a cap for a kid. They give away 20,000 bats on a special day, and the ballplayers get two bats. You got 40,000 empty seats in the ballpark, and if you ask for seven tickets for your friends instead of the six you're allowed for every game—you hear about it. Well, if you let him bother you, you're letting him beat you.

Maybe the people in Oakland don't deserve any better, anyway. No matter what Finley does or doesn't do, the team still deserves better support than it's gotten from the town. Oakland has one of the biggest black populations of any town in the country and the average black man still can't make the sort of money he needs to support a baseball habit. The wealthy whites go so far out of town into the suburbs at the end of the working day that there is no way they're going to go to the ballpark very often.

A ballplayer, black or white, can't make a buck in this town outside of the ballpark. I've gotta go to the ballpark today to shoot a commercial for General Mills, but if I was playing in New York or Los Angeles I'd be making ten times what I'm making in side money.

And the ballpark itself is a bad one. We call it "The Mausoleum." There's no color to it. Empty and dead. Most of the time it's windy and cold and foggy, and it hurts your body—and has to shorten your career. It's just plain uncomfortable. The air is heavy and it's hard on hitters. I've learned to live with it. I don't care if we stay or go. I play for pay. I do whatever I got to do wherever I am. If I want a house, I'll buy me a house. If we move I'll get me a house wherever we land. I gotta live and I live a lot of my life beyond the ballpark.

I lead a quiet life here. I eat out a lot. I like good food. I go to Lois the Pie Queen's for a late breakfast most days. Soul food, there. She has a place on the Oakland-Berkeley border. Just a little place, but she's good people and treats me nice. She's like my second mother. Has my picture on the wall and all. Has other players' pictures, too. I hang around the Del Rios' some afternoons. They're brothers and run a place where they fix up cars. It's like an amusement park for me. I'm hung up on cars. Good old cars. Foreign cars. Fast cars. When I

meet my maker it will be behind the wheel of a car someday.   I
drive too fast—too fucking fast.   But it gets something out of
my system driving fast.   It relaxes me to be around cars, working on cars.   And the cops cool it with me.

I don't go out as much in Oakland as I do on the road.   I'm
too well known here.   I have a good image and I want to keep
it.   I like music and I like to dance.   Soul music.   I have a lot
of records I play all the time at home.   I turn the sound way
up loud and get lost in it.   It's an escape.   I'd just as soon be with
a girl at my place or at her place, listening to music and talking,
as out on the town.   Yeah, talking.   I like sex.   And I think a
regular sex life is healthy for a man.   But I don't overdo it,
because I'm a ballplayer and my body is important to me and
I'm not gonna abuse it.   I go with different women, but not a
lot of women.   There's a girl named Susan who lives in L.A.
and goes to UCLA—and I like being around her.   And there's
a girl named Mary I'm dating in Oakland.   She cooks for me
sometimes.   And I can talk to her.   She was one of the ballgirls
and she's beautiful.   I'm also seeing a girl named Traci.   She's
a fox and has the brains of an Einstein.   But I'm not going with
any one girl right now.   And right now I gotta go to the ballpark.

Saturday the 13th.   Well, it felt good to be back at home in our
own ballpark.   Not that this is home for me, really, or that the
ballpark isn't bad, but it's what we're used to.   But the game
went bad.   We were bombed, 10–3.   Jeff Burroughs hit a
three-run homer.   Although he is young, Burroughs has the
best home run swing in baseball and he is going to hit a lot of
home runs and drive in a lot of runs.   I almost hit one.   Two
on, too, in the first inning.   Everyone in the ballpark thought it
was out.   The wind held it up and it was caught at the warning
track.   Despite the final score, I think the game might have
gone differently if it had been out.

Bibby wasn't bad, but he could have been beat this time.
Gene Tenace hit two home runs off him.   Gene doesn't hit for
average, but he hits for distance and he drives in runs.   He is
becoming a good first baseman, too.   Gene doesn't like to catch
and he complains when he has to catch.   It takes away from his

hitting.   But he only complains when he has cause.   He busts his ass on the field.   Personally, I respect him and I feel he respects me and we get along great.   I consider him a winner.

So we blew the ball game and already a lot of people are bitching about Alvin.   I think it's bush.   A lot of people thought he shouldn't have been hired in the first place, and they're looking for reasons to fire him before he has a chance. The other day he wrote Vic Davalillo on the lineup card as the designated hitter and had to change it at the last minute when Finley told him to use Deron Johnson, who has not been hitting and is hurt.   Alvin admits Finley tells him to do things.   Well, hell, what's new about that?   Finley told Williams what to do a lot of times, too.   When Finley's your owner you have to have a manager who can get along with him.   I don't know if Dark is that man or not.   I don't know about Dark as a man or as a manager.   Not yet.   He's made mistakes.   But it's bad business to be jumping on the guy just because he's the underdog.   I'm gonna back him up and give him all the help I can, man, because he rates a break.

Sunday, the 14th.   I hit a home run in the first inning of the first game today, but Texas came back to get two runs and they led, 2–1, most of the game.   Still, Catfish was pitching super—he is a super pitcher, a super competitor.   You can count on Catfish and so he is a pitcher you give something extra because you want to back him up.   When I struck out with a man on I felt shitty.   And then I came up in the eighth with men on second and third after North singled and Bando doubled and I wanted it real bad, but I figured they'd walk me because there were two out with first base open.   Well, they pitched to me and it pissed me off.   I mean it was embarrassing.   I feel I have proved myself a player you do not pitch to in a spot like that, but I guess you have to prove yourself over and over again.   Steve Hargan was pitching and he got two strikes on me and I fouled off pitch after pitch until I saw one coming I thought I could connect on with a big cut.   I cut and hit the sonofabitch right out of the ballpark.   It was my second home run of the game, the second time Billy Martin has had his pitchers pitch to me in that situation this season, and the second time I have hit a three-run homer. I'll tell you it was a good feeling!

The fans loved me for it. There were less than 12,000 there, but they gave me a standing ovation, so as I went back to the dugout I tipped my cap to 'em, just like Charlie said to do. Charlie was there, so he musta liked that. When I ran back out on the field for the ninth they gave me another ovation, so I stopped and tipped my hat again. I guess most people never have moments like that in their lives, which is too bad because it's beautiful. My hit won it for us and the Cat, 4–2.

We still had to play a second game. A lot of guys don't like doubleheaders: If you win the first one you tend to let up, although if you lose it you tend to try harder. Myself—it don't make no difference to me. But I coulda lived without this one. I got a single and a double, but we got blasted, 10–2. Odom didn't have it and they got an early lead and we fell apart. You give a guy like Ferguson Jenkins an early lead and he has a lock on it. As the lead built up, he was just coasting. But it is a pleasure to be beaten by him. If you like this game, you have to like watching him. He is so graceful and he performs with such poise. He is the only pitcher we face who can overpower you with control. Catfish is like that, too. Fergy is the master of all of his pitches and he puts them where you can't hit them, just like the Cat. They can win 25 or 30 games any year.

It was payday, but it was Sunday so the guys couldn't cash their checks. I didn't even accept mine because an attorney is working on a plan to defer my income over a period of years and invest some of my money for me to protect my future. But some of the guys needed dough. Manny Trillo had a check for $650 he wanted to cash and he had the clubhouse man take it up to the office for him, but they wouldn't cash it because Finley wasn't there to OK it. They have to get his OK to buy a bat or a paper clip. It really is rotten when a club won't cash its own check for a player on a Sunday. It murders morale.

Thursday, the 18*th.* Right after the ball game Sunday, I flew to Phoenix to do my taxes and some other things. You're not supposed to do it, but I did it, round trip in eight hours. And Monday I flew to Reno to look at a new Ferrari a guy was going to give me a deal on. I didn't go for it. On the way back a girl on the plane asked me for my autograph and I told her to listen to the game that night because I'd hit a home run. I knew Wilbur Wood was pitching and I hit more home runs off him than any other pitcher I face. Sure enough I hit another off him. I don't mean he's a bad pitcher and won't get me out some time when I want a hit badly, but there are pitchers certain batters make look bad and Wilbur's been my man. He throws a knuckler that moves miles, but I'm able to time it somehow. I have confidence against him, which means a lot. They work him too much because he wants to work. It takes something off his stuff. Oh, he wins his 20, but he loses his 20, too, or damn near, and I don't care how many a pitcher wins, if he loses almost as many he is not helping his side a lot.

We went thirteen to beat the White Sox and Jim Kaat, 4–3, on Monday night. Ray Fosse hit a two-run homer and Tenace knocked in the winner. Fingers bailed out Holtzman. My sixth homer and Bando's homer helped us whip Wood by the same score Tuesday night. Fingers saved us again. I stole two bases. I think I can steal more bases and be thrown out less than almost any player around. But I keep pulling muscles, so every time I run I'm risking that. Wednesday night I was rotten. I hit a double and a single to help us to a lead, but loused up a couple in the field to help them tie. Brian Downing, a rookie catcher, hit a homer to win it for them off of Darold Knowles, who was booed. Well, he looks bad, to tell you the truth. He was a hero in our World Series win last fall, pitching in all seven games, but he seems to have lost something.

Fingers is a key guy for us. We have strong starters, but you have to have strong relievers to be a strong team. And Fingers is the best right-handed reliever—maybe the best reliever, period, in the American League, if not in all of baseball. I don't know about Mike Marshall in the National League. I know he works too much and it may take more out of him than he will admit. I know Fingers and I know he's going to be as good in the World Series as he is on opening day.

He has two super pitches, a great fastball and a great breaking ball, and the hitters can't set themselves for both. He pitches with such rhythm I'd rather watch him work than any pitcher I know. The greatest single pitch I ever saw him make was a 3-and-2 slider he threw to Johnny Bench in the World Series, striking him out. Maybe he didn't know it was Bench: he was pitching to Brooks Robinson one time and afterwards he was saying things about it that made you realize he thought it was Frank Robinson. Brooks is white and Frank is black; but it don't make no difference to Fingers, they're all the same to him. There's no point in his going to the meetings when they go over the hitters, because he doesn't know who the hell is hitting anyway. We call him "Buzzard" because he's off in his own world. Nothing bothers him. Him and that handlebar mustache of his—he's cool.

I had one great experience in the Series. I was on first base, and for the first time in my career I felt qualified to give some advice to Richie Allen. I said, "Hey, man, you've probably forgotten more about hitting than I'll ever know, but you're not a pull-hitter and it looks to me like you're lousing yourself up by trying to pull the ball right now." I didn't know how he'd take it. But he thanked me for it, and it was a pleasure realizing he appreciated advice from me, because he's given me a lot of good advice. Rich is not only a super player, but a super person. He may have been bounced from team to team because he goes his own way and does his own things. But he produces on the field and he is respected by all players, especially black players. He is a boss man among blacks. He is a high-salary player, and he's made a lot of money for other players and, again, especially for blacks. When he got to 250 grand a year, he got everyone's salary up.

When I was breaking in he told me to be my own man but to keep my cool. He told me not to let anyone fuck with my ability and to get my money from them. He said I had ability, but I had to show him performance. He told me not to speak with my mouth, but with my bat. He held up a bat like it was a torch and said that with it I could speak to the world. Well, we're different people. I respect rules more than he does and mouth off more. But what he said has stuck with me and restrained me and inspired me. And the other day he congratulated me. He said I'd shown him something; I was doing it on the field and was a credit to my race off the field. Coming from him that was as fine a compliment as I've ever had.

I tried to help him because I want him to do well even if he can hurt us. He is my friend and I want a friend to do well. I can see him only on the field. But I still think of him as a friend. He is a fellow ballplayer. I want ballplayers to do well. I want to beat them, but I want to beat them at their best. I want to be a good friend and a bad enemy. If someone crosses me, I don't care about him. But if someone is with me, I'm with him. I try to do for my friends, whether it's money or just a kind word. Even if it's someone I don't know well, if I can do something for him, fine. I figure if I can leave someone a little better off for my having been with him, then I have done something.

Billy North has one hit in 25 or 30 times up. He is off to a terrible start. He is really down in the dumps, and he is letting his lack of hitting hurt his other things. We have run together. I feel for him and I spoke to him before the Chicago series. I said, "Man, you got six hundred more at-bats coming, you hang in there and you will get your hits." I told him the way he can run he could hit .250. I told him to keep his cool. I think it encouraged him. He gets down on himself and on the world. I see the way I used to be. I see a lot of me in him.

Today was an off-day and I did a lot of things I had to do to get organized, like pay bills. But I have a secretary now. Her name is Marlaine Lucchesi and she's a nice lady. I need someone to sort out and answer my mail and answer the phone and keep my bills straight, and she'll do that for me. Nothing personal. I just pay her and let her do things for me. I have attorneys. I have managers, like Merola and Goetz. They get me deals and manage me as much as I let anyone manage me. My life is fucking complicated, man.

I looked at a new condominium up in the hills. I liked it. It costs 85 grand, however. I looked at another Ferrari. I checked over my old cars. I visited my friends Don Doten and Ed Dohnt at Doten Pontiac. They give me a free car every year. More important, they give me friendship. I visited with Vida at his place. Knowles was there. And Bob Moore of the Raiders. And Clyde Lee of the Warriors. And one of the Seals' hockey players. We had agreed to go to an auction set up to help pay hospital bills for a paper boy, Ronnie Hansen, who was damn near beaten to death by somebody.

Vida's jersey sold for $90. One of my bats sold for $50 and one of my gloves for $100. George Blanda's helmet sold for $150. That sort of thing. I was happy to be a part of it and I think it's nice to know that in our country people will get together and contribute to help someone when they're down and out. It's an out-of-sight feeling when your prominence pays off in a good way like this. The thing was organized by a Bay Area sportswriter, Sam Spear, who is one of my favorite people.

Afterwards I was gonna stay for dinner, but people hassled hell out of me. I know I'd be pissed off if these people didn't recognize me, but there are times they get to be a real pain in the ass. It was Reggie, Reggie, Reggie until I cut out. I try to be nice to people. There are guys who can do it all the time. I like that in a guy. I just can't. I know I'm better with the fans and the writers than most players, but it is tough not to be able to go out in public without ever being left alone. You got to have a private life, too. You got to have some peace.

Sunday, the 21st. Dave Duncan called to point out to me that he had five home runs and I had six and he was breathing down my neck. He used to be our catcher but he told off Finley when we were celebrating a victory on the airplane during the 1972 World Series. Since he wasn't critical to the club Finley traded him for Ray Fosse. Dave's a good guy and we're buddies. While he's not going to hit the home runs I will, he's gonna make the most of those he does hit. We kidded around about it, and he said he was in Boston with Cleveland and was good for two or three more that weekend. I said I'd make him a little bet: The next one of us that hits a home run buys the other guy dinner the next time we're together—a complete dinner, steak to wine, first class. He said I had a deal. Well, I knew I had my back to the wall because the Angels were in town and I figured to face Bill Singer, Nolan Ryan and maybe Rudy May, and they don't come much tougher. He was shooting for that short fence in Fenway. But I was aroused. The next night I took on Singer and the second time up I hit a low-and-in slider, I mean almost on the ground, up into the seats, and as I was running around the bases I was grinning and I thought, "Ha, Dave, I gotcha!" I was just happy to have been lucky. We coasted behind Catfish, 5–1. Good ol' Catfish. I called Dave to give him the bad news.

Saturday afternoon we knocked out Ryan early, but they came back to hit Holtzman and tie it up. We won with a single by Bando to score Campaneris from second in the tenth. Mike Epstein, another ex-teammate who got into it with Finley—and with me too one time—had hit the three-run homer to tie it. That must have made him happy, but we had the last laugh. I had two hits Friday and two Saturday and two more today, Sunday, but they won a wild one, 9–5, today.

I sat next to Vida every time we were on the bench and I talked to him until I was tired of talking, but I don't think he listened. He has all the talent in the world, but he felt Finley fucked him over his salary a few years ago, when he had his big year, and he lost interest in the game. Finley can do that to you. He treats you bad and you let it bother you. He treated me bad and I let it bother me for a couple of years. I grew up. I told Vida he had to grow up.

I said, fuck Finley, you're not doing this thing for him, you're doing it for you. I told him he wasn't being Vida Blue; he wasn't bearing down; he wasn't concentrating; he didn't give a damn whether he won or lost. He wasn't about to turn it on until he got close to 20. Hell, he could win 30.

Well, we built a lead and he had 'em and he let 'em get away from him. He didn't bear down. He lost a game he should have won and he tore up the goddam bat rack to show he cared, but it came too late. He's a good-looking stud and he'll go out with some good-looking gal tonight and have a good time, but he should be doing it with a win in his hip pocket.

I blew my cool today, too. In the ninth inning Skip Lockwood threw at me and I had to go down to avoid getting hit in the head and it made me madder than hell. I told him, "Throw the ball over the plate, goddammit, before I have to come out there and hurt you." And I pointed at Bobby Winkles in the Angel dugout and I told him I wasn't going to forget it. I was so goddam mad I struck out, not because I was scared, but because I'd lost control of myself physically and emotionally.

They say it's part of baseball, but that's a bunch of bullshit. They can throw the ball at us twice before they get the business, but we only have to throw the bat at them once and we're suspended. I think I've earned the right not to be thrown at. They know they can't scare me. I may have struck out this time, but I'll hit a home run the next time. I mean I've done it and I'm doing it, and I'm gonna keep on doing it. So what the fuck are they gonna knock me down for? They tryin' to hurt me? Well, I don't try to hurt them and I don't expect them to try to hurt me. I know damn well Winks called for it and I called him on it.

In college Winks taught me a lot, but I'm not sure he's a major league manager. I like him personally, but I don't know if I'd want to play for him in the majors. Before one of the games I was talking to Johnny Roseboro, who's coaching for the Angels, and he told me Winks had made a lot of rules for the players: short haircuts, no sideburns, no mustaches, no informal clothes, you gotta wear ties and jackets, no tape recorders on the bus, no music in the clubhouse. It's a lot of crap that can only keep the guys from being themselves, and they're pissed off about it. They're all uptight about it, moaning and bitching.

It's stupid. In the majors a manager is managing men, not boys. They've got to play 162 games. If they aren't loose, they're gonna lose. Short haircuts don't win games. A bed-check isn't going to keep a guy straight.

Whatever the rules are, I'll live with 'em, but I don't have to like 'em. Dick Williams let his players be themselves and try to enjoy the baseball life instead of making it misery. The manager has a right to expect performance on the field. If he doesn't get it, the player has a right to expect to be sent on his way. Winks knows baseball, but he doesn't know major-leaguers. His team is off to a fast start, but it'll fold. Except for pitching, it doesn't have much talent.

Dark is having his troubles, too. The second game, Holtzman was taken out and Fingers, who has been brought in too much, got blasted. The guys were bitching. Fingers got a garbage victory, so today we loaded up his locker with garbage: dirty socks, broken bats, every piece of trash we could find. We hung a sign over it, "Garbage Collector." Fingers thought it was funny.

Darold Knowles, who isn't being used much, told some writers that Alvin didn't know anything about handling a pitching staff. Naturally it made all the newspapers, and everyone was saying the fighting A's were right in form, fighting among themselves and so sure to win a lot of games. I guess it's true up to a point, but everything we do is blown up out of proportion because we're the champs. You're not going to get 25 guys and a manager together for six months and not have some fights and some unhappy guys, but if you're a bad ball club no one cares and no one ever hears about what happens.

You gotta learn to live with the writers and with the publicity. The writers like me because I'm not afraid to tell it as it is, but they don't always put it in the way I give it to them, and I'm always afraid of that. The other day I had breakfast with a writer from the L.A. *Times,* Jeff Prugh. I heard he was a ripper, but I like to decide these things for myself.

He asked me about baseball and a lot about how I feel about life, and it was enjoyable. I like talkin' about life. He asked me if I was going out that night. I told him, hell, no, I was going home to get my rest because Nolan Ryan was pitching the next day—and you don't face Ryan without your rest. He's the only guy I go against that makes me go to bed before midnight. The article was OK. It had some depth to it. I'm off to such a good start I gotta expect a lot of interviews and I just hope the articles are all right. I worry about my image. I don't mind being presented as I am, but I hate it when I look like something I'm not.

Wednesday, the 24th. Back on the road. We lost Tuesday. Christ Almighty, it was cold! But Gaylord Perry was hot. We had beaten him nine or ten straight times over the years, but he beat us this time, 2–1. Ray Fosse hit a home run for the only run off him. They got only three hits off Hunter, but won with them. Alvin moved the defense around and screwed it up some. He also called for a curve to Charlie Spikes with two on in the seventh, which a lot of players thought was the wrong pitch for that situation. Spikes hit it for a triple and both their runs. A lot of players threw that loss on Alvin. That night I collected my dinner from Duncan and he asked me about Alvin. I said I thought he was a good man and trying hard, but he was losing the respect of the team by letting them mouth off about him without calling them on it. We need to feel the guy in charge *is* in charge.

Today we won, 9–2. Bando batted in five runs with a homer, double and sacrifice fly. He does not hit for a high average, but his hits bring in runs. He is probably the toughest out in the league in a tight spot. While I am the player rep and like to think of myself as the team leader, Sal is the captain and a manager for us on the field. He is as smart about baseball as anyone around. He is steady, on and off the field. I have as much respect for Sal as for anyone in this sport.

Thursday morning, the 25th. We're in Baltimore and I'm really looking forward to tonight's game. They're probably the best team in their division and we're the best in ours and we'll probably meet in the playoffs. They have Jim Palmer pitching against us tonight and he has as much stuff as any pitcher. We have Vida Blue going. I really look forward to a game like tonight's. It should be a helluva game!

Thursday night, the 25th. Shit! What a sloppy game! We lost it, 6–5, after leading. Palmer went nine, but he was struggling all the way. We had him, 4–1, in the eighth. Any time the A's have a three-run lead with six outs to go we ought to be able to shut the door. We didn't play like the A's. Vida got beat. No, I shouldn't say he got beat. We lost. There's a difference.

They got three runs on two hits to tie it. Then I hit my second homer of the night to put us ahead in the twelfth. But they got a run to tie it again in their half, on a walk and two hits. Blue started the inning and then Fingers came in and then Knowles and then Mike Hooten—four fucking pitchers pitching to one batter at a time and they couldn't get those guys out.

With one out in the twelfth and Lindblad pitching, Don Baylor hit a flyball to North in center. Billy made a long run for it. Then he dropped it, and Baylor wound up on third. We walked the next two guys to load the bases in hopes of getting a double play. But Andy Etchebarren popped a pitch into short center—so short it should never have scored the run. But Billy charged the ball and threw it over the catcher's head, and that was it. Two errors on two batters. Billy can catch and he can throw and I guess these things happen, but I can't help thinking they are happening to him because he is thinking about not hitting and not thinking about fielding.

We are the World Champions but we don't look like it right now. Our defense stinks. Dick Green has been hurt since the second week in April with a bad foot, and everyone we put in for him at second base seems to get hurt. I don't care if Greenie never gets a hit, our whole defense seems to come apart when he's not a part of it. But the other guys got to do it, too. The guys tried to blame Alvin afterwards, but this one was ours. I had four hits but I've seldom felt as frustrated by a game as I did after this one. I'm glad we got a day off tomorrow because I got to go somewhere—to forget.

Sunday, the 28th. Saturday was another rotten game. But it didn't frustrate me because we did win it, 11–5. We got twelve hits and Campy had three of them. Neither their starter, Mike Cuellar, nor ours, Hunter, had it.

This morning, Elvin Hayes spoke at chapel and I thought he

was one of the most interesting speakers we've had.   He keeps
control of his religion.   He doesn't try to talk anyone into
Christ, he just lays out his philosophy of life for you and lets
you take what you want from it.   It lasted about twenty minutes and about fifteen guys turned out.

Dark turns out.   You know, chapel is the place for religion,
but Alvin is always laying quotes from the Bible on everyone
when it *isn't* the place for it, and it ticks the guys off. You gotta
live your life the way you feel is right for you, but you don't
lay your way on everyone else.

This afternoon, we lost, 4–3.   Holtzman lost to Ross Grimsley, but neither was dominating.   What's worse, I got hurt
again.   I was on first with two out and the game tied in the
ninth.   Joe Rudi was up.   It was the spot to steal so I could be
where a single would drive me in.   I stole the base, but Rudi
couldn't get the hit so it was wasted.   I slid headfirst and
somehow hurt a nerve in my leg.   It just went numb and I
came up cursing.   I am always hurt.

I am supposed to be a stud but I am a wreck.   I do exercises to
try to keep loose.   I wrap up my legs a lot.   What can I do, not
run, hold back?   It is so fucking frustrating to never know when
you're gonna come up crippled—maybe a couple of times a
year.   I feel if I'm ever healthy a whole season I'll tear up the
league.   But I don't know if it'll ever happen.   Well, this was a
freak.   I'll be OK this time.   Fuck it.

Wednesday, May 1*st.*   New York, the big town.   I'd be big in this
town.   Nat Tarnapole, a friend of mine who owns Brunswick
Records and is a multi-multimillionaire, got with me to ask if
I'd be interested in signing with the World Baseball League,
which is the latest league they've dreamed up.   It may get off
the ground, but I doubt it.   He never got around to talking
dollars, but I did.   I told him I was making a lot of money, I
dug being one of the best playing against the best and it would
take a helluva lot of money—like maybe two million for four
years—to make me even think of making a move to a new
league.   He said that *sure* was a helluva lot of money—but he
kept talking to me.

We met the next day, too. He admitted to me the World Football League might get going, but was going to get in trouble because a lot of the people that were taking teams in it weren't that strong, backbone-wise, and didn't have the dough they had to have to ride out rough times. All the talk about the other league, the baseball league, came to nothing.

We had an off-day our first day in New York and we had a workout scheduled, but Dark canceled it. The guys were kidding about it, saying it was because Alvin's wife was in town. The kidding was in bad taste, but the guys kid about bad things, about each other's wives and girl friends and so forth. That's the way guys are in baseball, and I have to admit I laughed. Dark admitted to a writer the other day that he wasn't doing a good job. So far he isn't.

I hit my tenth homer Tuesday night, but we lost, 4–3. Rudi hit one tonight, but we lost, 4–3, again. My leg hurt like hell, so I was designated hitter in both games.

In one of the games, Campy Campaneris took a throw in front of second base on a steal. A lot of the guys felt that if he'd been at the base, he'd have gotten the runner. They felt he was afraid to take the throw there. I hate to question Campy's courage. Hell, he takes a lot of throws at base. I agree with the guys that he protects himself too much sometimes, but we can't all be gung-ho guys. It's not in Campy's nature. But he puts a lot of money in our pockets.

In the second game, Dark went out to the mound to instruct Fingers to pitch to Thurman Munson with a man on second and first base open. I thought he should have walked Munson with a weaker hitter, Horace Clarke, up next. That's what Fingers felt. That's what Fosse and Bando thought. They were still standing on the mound talking it over after Alvin left. So Fingers walked Munson on four pitches, and then got the side out. Later, Fingers said it was strictly unintentional. But when he was saying it he was doing his W. C. Fields imitation. I guess you can get away with this if you're good enough.

I went walking the sidewalks of New York and had a good time.

I met a New York madam by the name of Blanche. I had a

ball talking to her. She was trying to hustle me. She said she had a stable of stallions. Tremendous-looking ladies, she said. She said she would have me taken care of for a hundred bucks. I told her I wasn't used to paying for it—that I didn't have to, you know. In fact, I told her I was thinking about selling myself for a hundred dollars a day. It was fun for me. I like people and I don't care if they're pimps or pushers, madams or nobodies, they interest me.

Billy North and I missed the bus to the ballpark and took a taxi together and it turned out to be a hell of a head trip. I've been on him a bit because he hasn't been going good, and he said that he and a lot of the black ballplayers on the club were convinced that I was pulling against them instead of for them. He said I got on them and I didn't get on the whites. He said I ran with whites and not with blacks. He said the blacks didn't feel I was their friend. It took me by surprise and hurt me inside.

It was a bunch of bull, but it goes to show you what bigotry can do to your mind. Blacks can be as guilty of it as whites. I'm guilty of it, too. On ball clubs blacks are set apart from whites, even today. We may run together a little, but not a lot. A few years ago I roomed with a white player, Chuck Dobson, and everyone made a big deal about it. I guess I try to lead the blacks, not the whites, as if that was the way it should be. I'm not afraid to tell a black player off, but I don't try that stuff on a white player; I leave that to other whites. So I guess the blacks believe I'm picking on them.

I didn't try to argue with Billy, but I did say some things to him. I said that if I went out with Joe Rudi it's because I dig Joe Rudi, not because he's white. I pointed out that I had gone out with Billy North a hell of a lot all winter—and not because he was black. I said if I got on him it was because I had been down the same road he was going down now, and I felt I knew how to overcome the obstacles. I wanted him to be all the ballplayer he could be. I said the black ballplayers seldom invited me out with 'em and now I saw maybe this was because they thought I wasn't with them. I said they were wrong. I don't know if I got through to him. He's moody and if he gets something in his mind it's hard to get it out. He made me feel bad about being black.

I wouldn't know what color I was if whites didn't make me feel black and blacks didn't make me feel blacker. I happened to be raised in a neighborhood where race wasn't an issue and I didn't know anything about prejudice until I was 18 and at Arizona State and the white coaches got on me about dating a white girl. I do date white girls. I date black girls, too. I date girls, period, regardless of their color.

I go out with guys like Gene Tenace and Sal Bando because they're good guys, not because they're white. But somebody on the ball club told me they were talking about me behind my back about this. That hurt me, and when I told them about it, I think it hurt them. I got a letter from a guy who said I was an Oreo cookie—you know, black on the outside and white on the inside. He said he was a friend of Billy North's. Maybe North is talking against me. I don't like to think so. I don't get much hate mail—maybe one in a thousand—but it's hard to take anyway.

A guy on the team I know is my friend, Cookie Mangual, is black. He's also level-headed. He told me that a lot of guys hang around me because of who I am, but put me down behind my back. He said a lot of white dudes hate niggers, but will buddy up to a big guy. Well, hell, I know that. But I have to find out for myself about anyone, white or black, and I'm gonna give them the benefit of the doubt before I push 'em away. I live in a country of 200 million people and 180 million of them are white. If I'm friends only with black guys or go out only with black girls, I'm cutting myself off from a lot of the people in my world.

I don't care what a guy looks like. Tony Del Rio looks like a hoodlum, but I'm not going to quit hanging around with him because of it—I like him. I have a friend who looks like a junky, but he's my friend. If he wants to smoke pot when he's with me, cool. I won't, but he does what he wants to do. Some of my friends are straight and some aren't.

You know, when a guy grows up in a ghetto he doesn't look down on guys who do what they have to do to survive. And

I've been around guys like this and it's rubbed off on me. It may be wrong for a guy to steal or a gal to whore, but if that's the only way you can get by, that's the way you go. I found another way. I was lucky. A kid in a ghetto looks up to a pimp or a pusher as much as he does to me because we got the big bankrolls, the fancy clothes, the nice car and the pretty ladies—and that's what the kid wants when he grows up.

If you think something is a sin, well, you don't do it. There are things I won't do, don't do. But there are things I do because I don't think they're wrong. The biggest thing God gave us was the power to reason, and I reason my life out for myself. One guy wears a cross and another wears a mezuzah. Some believe in Christ and some don't. Some worship cows. Do you think one's gonna go to heaven and the rest to hell? Forget it. Whatever there is out there for us, a guy's only gonna get the best of the bargain if he does right as he sees it. Well, for me it would be wrong to pick my friends because of the color of their skin.

Because I am black I've made a special effort to help my own kind. I've given money to black causes. I'm not out there fronting for these causes because that's not my way. Maybe I should make sure that what I do is out front, but as I see it that spoils the sincerity of it. Just talkin' about it now spoils the sincerity of it, but I'm tryin' to tell what's in my head. And my head is all mixed up right now. I've been bending over backwards to help the blacks on my ball club and it's being taken in the wrong way. Maybe I should quit trying—and just look out for me.

Before the game the other night I was kidding with Graig Nettles of the Yankees because he hit eleven home runs in April, which was even more than me. Maybe I shouldn't have been kidding with him because he's not black, but I give a ballplayer respect because of the player he is, not the color he is. Graig is a good ballplayer, but there is no way he should hit eleven home runs in one month and he knows it and I was teasing him about it. I asked him if he was trying to make me look bad. He said he would if he could. I think I like this part of being a ballplayer as much as anything—being a member of an exclusive fraternity, being able to kibitz guys who go out and do my thing so damn well. This other shit, this black-white crap, that's for the birds. We're all the same under the skin. I wish to hell I could just do my thing and forget the other things. I can't. I'm good at what I do, but I gotta be more, too. Something inside of me makes me that way.

It's tough enough being good at what I do. It seems easy right now because I'm going good, but it's going to get tougher. I know, because I've been through it. I'm coming out of the first month of the new season hitting .400 with ten home runs and 29 or 30 runs-batted-in. I'm attracting a lot of attention because it looks like I'm going to take this league apart, but the league will still be standing when the season's old. I'll get hurt or something. Something always happens to screw a season up. There's no way I'm going to have a bad season. I forgot how to have bad seasons. But those great ones are hard to get. I'll slow down. I can see that, even if the rest of the world can't. I'm human. I'm just me. I shouldn't play God.

3 ☆ MAY

Friday, the 3rd. The flight back to Oakland was a busy one and came to a bad end. Vic Davalillo is a good guy who goes bad when he drinks. He doesn't drink much, but when he does he can't handle it. The guys tend to drink a little on the long air rides. The guy who handles the charter flights for United came to me on this flight and said Vic had had too much to drink and maybe I might do something to settle him down. He said in other years he could go to Dick Williams with things like this and Dick would take care of them. But he said that since Dark doesn't drink, he didn't understand and didn't seem to want to be bothered. He said he didn't know who else to go to except to me. If I didn't do something, he said he'd land the sonofabitch and boot us all off because he was responsible for what happened on the plane—and if it got to Finley, there'd be hell to pay.

Well, I went back and tried to control Vic, but there was no way to keep him in check. He'd been hassling the stewardesses. He was hassling the other players. He almost got in a fight with Odom. He almost got in a fight with Mangual. He almost got in a fight with Heidemann. He almost got in a fight with one of our coaches, Vern Hoscheit. He almost got in a fight with Dark, when he finally did look into it. Vic was unhappy when anyone blocked his way to the bar and unhappy when he wasn't given another beer. There was some scuffling, some almost-fights. I picked him up and carried him away. No damage was done, and I know he didn't mean harm to anyone. But it is bad for a ball club.

Today when we got to the ballpark, we heard that Finley had found out and had released Vic. John Summers, a left-handed hitter, was called up from Tucson. And no one could say Charlie was wrong. I doubt that anyone will pick Vic up, though they may. He has played for five or six teams for four-teen or fifteen years in the majors. He can play. He is a hit-ter. He can help us. He has helped us. But he is out of a $40,000-a-year job with the World Champions and maybe out of baseball because of booze. Not because he's a boozer but because he liked to take a drink or two on a plane ride. I don't know what fucking good it does to drink.

Before the rhubarb on the plane, we were talking and de-cided to have a meeting of the players—no coaches, no manager—to decide what we're going to do about Dark. There was no way we were going to talk to Finley about him or try to have Alvin fired or anything. But we decided we have to come up with some way of handling him. When we told Dark we wanted to meet among ourselves, he insisted he wanted to talk to us first. The meeting was held after batting practice before tonight's game. Dark said he'd been on teams that had players' meetings before, and he'd learned from them that if we were too hard on our teammates, it would create hard feelings. We felt it was a bunch of bullshit and we didn't even want to take the time to listen to it. We got into it after he was gone.

I spoke, and so did Sal, Catfish, Knowles, North, Odom and one or two others. Knowles and Vida and Holtzman said how the man was messing them up and bothering them. But we knew that—that's why we were there. Sal said the most significant things. He admitted he bitched about Alvin as much as anyone did. And he said he probably would go right on doing it, because the man was going to go right on doing things he shouldn't do. But, he said, if Alvin fucks up he isn't going to be here long.   In the meantime, if we wanted to be around, we'd better accept his moves, and do the best we could.

I said we'd all love to have Dick Williams here, but he wasn't gonna be here, so why cry over spilt milk?   We have to learn to live with the manager who is here, whether it's Dark or someone else.   We better just play ball the way the World Champion A's can, and the hell with everything else and with everyone else.   We all know Dark isn't the man in charge, and we have to give him a chance to do the best he can.   So what if he brings in the wrong pitcher or puts the bat in the wrong guy's hands or puts the wrong man in the field?   If you're that man, you can still strike out the batter or hit the home run or make the catch, and the hell with management.   I told the guys there are things we can't control, so fuck 'em—let's play ball!   They seemed to agree with this, though living with it is something else.   Meetings like this sometimes help.   Sometimes they don't.

Sunday, the 5th.   Our meeting didn't make any miracles.   We split four games with Cleveland.   We won the opener Friday night, 3–1, topping Jim Perry.   Holtzman was sharp, but Dark got him out of there in the eighth for Fingers, who finished up. We were feeling pretty good Saturday afternoon, ready to rip Gaylord Perry right off.   But Billy North led off by hitting the ball back to the pitcher and didn't run it out, and it bothered me. I mean, he can beat out infield hits.   And if he'd beat out this one we woulda had a man on, with the thumpers coming up. Here we'd just had a meeting and agreed to bust our asses and this guy is going bad and can't be bothered to give it his best.

When he got back to the dugout I said, "Hey, man, what's wrong, you don't feel good or what?"

He said he felt fine.

I said, "Well, shit, man, then why the hell didn't you run that ball out?" "What business is it of yours?" he asked. "Who the hell are you?   I've seen you not run balls out."

Which was true, but it just made me madder.   I know it's no goddam good, I learned you got to give your best on every ball. So I said, "I'm the man who's tellin' you you had no business doggin' it on the play.

"Look, we had a fuckin' meeting here yesterday just because we been fuckin' around and we made up our minds we were gonna bust our butts on every ball. Then you come out here and the first ball you hit, you loaf on it. I want you to know if you're not going to do your job, we don't want you out there with us."

By then everybody on the bench was watching us and listening to us, and he was mad as hell. "Look, man, I don't see no number five on your back. [Number five is Dark's number.] Until you have M-G-R after your name, you just stick to R-F and butt the hell out of my business." And he stormed off.

Well, hell, I felt bad about it, but if I didn't do it, the manager sure as hell wasn't going to do it. And he didn't back me up on it either. He stayed the hell out of it—as if it wasn't any of his business. And I can't say the other guys got on Billy, either. But, afterwards, a lot of the guys—Bando, Rudi, Fosse, Tenace, Hunter, Fingers, Knowles, a lot of the guys—came to me and agreed with me and told me I had done the right thing. But I was alone in it. I felt bad about it. I dig the guy, really. But I want to win and he wasn't helping us win. And we didn't win that day. We got beat by Perry, 8–2. And the World Champion A's are in last place, five games under .500.

Today, Sunday, Billy comes up to me before the game and tells me he never wants to speak to me again. He said he thought I was his friend and he thought I respected him but now he knew otherwise and he didn't want to hear from me anymore. He told me to go fuck myself. And I said, well, all right, if that's what he wanted. But I felt bad about it. I still thought I'd done the right thing and it had been my place to do it, but I was sorry it had happened.

Billy's a funny guy. A good guy. A very good guy. He likes people and he's concerned about them. He has some depth to him. He's sensitive. Maybe he's too sensitive. He's very moody. He's up and he's down. Before I ever met him, I heard he was moody—that he can turn people on and off. He can't stand to be crossed. I heard from Billy Williams that when he was with the Cubs, Ernie Banks lied to North one time and North never talked to Ernie the rest of the season. I don't

know what the story was. I know Ernie's not much for lying to
people. Ernie's straight. But Billy felt Banks had betrayed
him. And he turned on him.

We traded Rick Monday to the Cubs for North. Billy had
trouble getting started with us last season and he was throwing
his bat and throwing his helmet and in general acting up. The
guys were getting on him, and it was getting to him so I got
between him and the guys. I befriended him and was a sort of
shield for him. You know, like no one would give him too
much heat because the big guy was his friend.

I remember when I was in his position. In college ball
Bobby Winkles raised hell with us if we raised hell. He
wouldn't let us throw anything or kick anything when things
went wrong. I learned to hold it in. When I got to the majors
some of the guys said I acted like I didn't care if I made an out or
made an error. So I started to throw things and kick things
again. And then they said I was acting like a spoiled kid
throwing temper tantrums. Sometimes you can't win. Once I
saw that, I said the hell with it, no one's gonna tell me what to
do, I'll do what comes natural. So I didn't bawl Billy out for
his behavior. He found his own way. And he started to play
the way he can.

During the off-season, we got real thick. In January, they
had an affair in his honor in his hometown of Seattle.
Hometown boy makes good, you know. I guess he told them
I was his friend so the people putting on the thing asked me to
come. He was home by then, but I flew in, and he picked me
up at the airport and put me up at his place and we had a good
time. Then when spring training started we were thick as
thieves. I don't usually let anyone get that close to me. It's a
mistake. You can be hurt that way. When the season started
and he started slow again, I tried to talk him into keeping his
cool. He wasn't doing it. Finally, I got on him. I guess I
should have let him find his own way. But he might not, you
know.

I talked to Alvin about it. Alvin told me Billy had come to him
and apologized about not running out the ball.

I said, "Well, hell, Alvin, if he knew he was wrong, why

didn't he admit it to me? Why did he jump down my throat?"

Alvin said, "It would have been a hard thing for him to do," and added that maybe I should be a bit more diplomatic. I guess so, but it wouldn't be me.

We won the first game easily enough, anyway, 3–0, as Catfish collected his first shutout of the season. But we blew the second one, 9–3, as they blasted Blue Moon and Holtzman.

The new player, John Summers, is a nice guy. I took him home with me and let him move in with me. He didn't have a place to stay. He had a room at the hotel but that was costing him fifteen, sixteen bucks a day and he isn't making big money. So, hell, I'll let him live with me and save a little money for a week or ten days until he sees if he's going to stay. He's got good ability and a good attitude, but I don't know if he's got it all together yet. I figured I'd give the dude a break. I got to do something good for someone.

Thursday, the 9th. Baltimore came to town and beat us two out of three, but it wasn't so bad because there weren't any phone calls from Finley and there wasn't any real bitching about Alvin and I didn't tell anyone off. North's still not speaking to me, but I can't do anything about that. I talk to him, but he doesn't answer. They beat us, 6–3, Monday night. We went with Paul Lindblad, but he got bombed. I hit a home run, my 11th of the season and 200th of my career. I read that somewhere. I keep track, but not that close.

My home run came off Mike Cuellar. He got off to a slow start and it was his first victory, but it won't be his last. He's a tough pitcher. There are tougher, but he's tough. He throws a screwball that screws you up. But he didn't throw me a screwball. He threw me a fastball and I hit it back faster than he'd thrown it. It's funny, but most pitchers pitch me differently than they do our other hitters. If they're throwing fastballs to most of the hitters, they curve me. If a guy like Cuellar is throwing screwballs to the other guys, he throws me fastballs. I don't know why, but maybe it's because I'm more of a threat than the other guys and they're trying to trick me. They figured I'm reading them, and they figure they'll fool me.

Tuesday night, Holtzman didn't have it and Odom didn't have it and the Orioles got 21 hits. They won easy, 9–3. Ross Grimsley pitched for them and I got two hits off him in three times up. Wednesday night I went two-for-three again, off Jim Palmer, who didn't pitch like Palmer, and the relievers, and we won, 7–3, behind Blue and Fingers. I drove in a couple of runs. I'm going good, no doubt about it. I can tell because the writers are all over me.

A guy named Phil Taubman from *Time* magazine has been with me for about a week. I haven't had a date for six days —like it would be a bad thing to do. So he tells me he'd like to get me with a girl, you know, he wanted to get a rounded picture of my life—just like the guy who's doing this book with me—always bugging me to pour my private life into it. I don't feel like it, you know, but I guess you got to give in to it. It is a part of my life.

So, anyway, I went over to the Playboy Club with the guy. I know some girls over there. I date one. And I just kidded around with them awhile and the magazine took some pictures. Then a gal I date in Phoenix flew in for a couple of days and the writer tagged around after us. I took her, the writer and a photographer to Scomas, a seafood restaurant.

I don't know why the hell I do things like this except it is *Time*, after all, a magazine that doesn't do big stories on ballplayers too much. The writer said this would be a cover story.

Now I got a guy named Roy Blount picking me up to do a cover story for *Sports Illustrated*, so my life will be screwed up some more. Let's face it, up to a point I eat it up, but now I'm going to have a guy living with me for another week or so and it really screws up my life. I just hope to hell the stories come out all right.

Time had a picture of me in their "People" section that really brought me razzing. I guess you call it beefcake. You know, stripped to the waist, muscles bulging, big smile on my face. Hell, I didn't even know they were going to take it. I was sitting in front of my locker, stripped down, and when they said to smile, I smiled. I was sorry later. *Sports Illustrated* ran one like that the year I made a run at Ruth's record, and I still haven't heard the last of it. Now this one and the guys are asking me who the hell I think I am. The fact is, I turned down a nude centerfold for that magazine *Playgirl*. Could have gotten a couple grand for it, too. But that's not me. I'm no male model. When you're going good, that's what you get in this business.

Sunday, the 12*th.* Minnesota came to town. I looked up Rod Carew to tell him I was going good, in case he hadn't noticed. It isn't often I can cut it up with the high-average guys. I'm hitting .390 or so and I won't be there long, so I got to make the most of it. Different hitters have different standards. My standard is 30 homers and 100 ribbies. Carew's is 200 hits and a .350 average. He wins the batting title every year, it seems like. He'll win it again this season.

He handles the bat beautifully. He hits the ball where it's pitched and he hits it everywhere. He doesn't take a big swing, just a quick one. He can hit a ball a hell of a lot better than he can catch it at second base. He shouldn't be in the infield. He should just be at bat, hitting that ball. I'm hitting more than him right now and I wanted to remind him of that fact.

I said, "Hey, Carew, I don't want you to get nervous or mad at me. I'm not trying to show you up. I'll let you have the batting title. So don't you get seven or eight hits this series. This is my ballpark and my spotlight. Save your hits for when you're home. I'll let you have them there. You can kill us there."

He laughed and said something about taking it easy on us, that he was no glory guy like some guys he knew, but I should remember to look at the top ten when the season was ended. I said I would—and I will; I know what I'll see there, too.

He only got a couple of hits in the series. He's just getting started. He'll be there at the end. That's this game: Swing the bat enough; throw enough pitches—and in the end you'll wind up with what you're supposed to have. This is a 162-game season. I'll walk up to the plate 600 times. I'm hot now. I'll cool off. In the end, I'll get what my talent is.

I got a double in the first game, another in the second. I didn't play the third. We won all three, 4-2, 4-1 and 9-2.

Hunter, Holtzman and Hamilton pitched. Fingers relieved in two of them. Deron Johnson hit homers in two of them. It was the first hitting he's done for us as our designated hitter this season. Mangual filled in for me the last game and hit a homer.

I got hurt, goddammit. We were ahead, 4–0, in the fourth inning of the second game, Saturday. They say now it wasn't the spot to steal. The hell with that. If I don't steal when I can, I'm shortchanging myself, my family, my peers, the owner, the fans and the Man Upstairs. Does Henry Aaron *not* swing for a homer when he's way ahead? Does Lou Brock *not* steal when he has the chance? Forget it. So I went. And halfway there I felt the muscle go. Whack! Like someone hit me in the back of my thigh with a knife. The right hamstring. It hurt like hell. I had it before and I knew what it was without anyone telling me. I got the hell off it as soon as it happened. The doctor checked me and said I'd be out maybe a couple of days. I knew that was wrong. I went to the hospital and another doctor told me maybe ten days or two weeks. That's wrong, too. I been down this road before. Maybe a week, then I'll be able to bat at least.

Wednesday, the 15*th.* Billy North is talking to me again and now I wish he'd stop. He's bitter and he won't let it go. He keeps making wisecracks about what a hot dog I am. Sometimes he says things as if he was speaking to himself, but loud enough for me to hear. Sometimes he says things to me, needling things, but not in fun. The needle's digging a little deep. I've tried to make up to him, but he won't have any of it. I'm trying not to let it get to me, but it's getting to me.

Thursday, the 16*th.* The team is hurting. Dick Green's been out with a foot injury since the first week of the season. His sub at second, Manny Trillo, pulled a muscle. Ted Kubiak took over, but he was hit by a pitch on the leg. Finley took to the telephone. He's traded away John Donaldson twice, but he brought him back from Tucson. Johnny had been hanging on hoping to get back up because he needed 50 to 60 days more in the majors for the fours years he needed to qualify for a pension. All players aren't rich, you know. John waited four or five years in the minors hoping to get back to the majors. He got back and three days later Billy North ran into him on a pop to short center. John hurt his shoulder and Charlie sent him back to Tucson, still short his time.

Finley found another former A's player, Dal Maxvill, who had been dropped by the Pirates and was sitting home drinking beer. Charlie called and Dal came. He's a good guy and we were glad to see him. His second game back, the same game I got hurt in, he got spiked and it took 23 stitches to sew up the wound. How many second basemen is that we've used—four, five? Finley phoned Tucson for Phil Garner, but found out he had a bad back. He called up Gaylen Pitts instead. Pitts played second, but not very well. One game. Turns out he's a third baseman. So he went to third and Kubiak went back to second. Kubiak got four hits his first game back. The next night Pitts drove in two runs with two doubles. A catcher, Larry Haney, wound up at third one game and started a double play. Somehow, we make do.

I think the team can least afford to lose me and Bando, but they can win without us for awhile. Not for long, but for awhile. We won two of three from Kansas City. Monday night we whipped them, 11–2, behind Blue, who won his second after losing his first four. We got nineteen hits. Kubiak got four and Campaneris got three. Tuesday night we had a twi-night double-header. They snapped our five-game winning streak in the opener, 4–2. North got two hits and stole two bases. Maybe he's breaking out of it. We bounced back to win the second game, 2–1. Glenn Abbott shaded old Lindy McDaniel in ten innings on Pitts's second double. The Royals are in first, but it won't last. They'll fall back and we'll blow right on past. They're not that solid.

Before one of the games, I was rapping with big John Mayberry. He didn't want to talk because there's supposed to be a fine for fraternizing with your foes on the field. I asked John what $50 was to him? He asked me how come Texas pitched to me with first base open. I don't know how, but we all know these things—and we re-mem-ber them. I pointed out I'd put the pitch in the seats to show them their mistake. He said he understood I wasn't reaching the seats much any more. He said I was getting con-sis-tence instead of dis-tance. I told him I was keeping 'em down to 400 feet or so. He asked me if I was using a light bat these days. I said not exactly. I handed him my 288RJ and warned him not to swing it lest he sprain his wrist on it. He just laughed. Hell, that horse could use it for a toothpick.

Going back to the dugout a few fans called to me. There's so few of them in our ballpark, I get to know the regulars by sight. I asked one if he was enjoying his hot dog. He said I was the hot dog he enjoyed most. A boy asked me for a ball I had in my hand. I told him I didn't give anyone anything but a hard time. He begged for the ball. I told him he was here every day and I bet he had a hundred balls at home. He said, "I ain't got none at home, honest, Reggie. I sell 'em before I ever leave the park." That made me laugh. Such honesty deserves a reward, so I threw him the ball. Fuck Finley! The funny thing was it was a ball I was going to steal myself to take home for someone.

I got nothing to do these days except chat with the fellows and the fans and talk about myself to the fellow from *Sports Illustrated*. One day I spent the day in a T-shirt and Levi's, washing my car, fucking around with some guys—beer-drinking, hell-raising guys, and that night I duded up and went with this writer to speak to some auto dealers at the Silverado Country Club—rich guys drinking cocktails. The contrast really got to me. As we were walking in I said something about the only niggers they had here before were the ones that cut the grass.

The other afternoon a beautiful, beautiful girl asked me if I would sign an autograph for a black girl. I said, "Honey, I don't give a damn what color you are, I'll sign." I said, "Hey, I dig the fact that you're black, I dig the fact that you're beautiful, and I dig meeting beautiful black women, but why make a big deal of it?" She gave me her telephone number. Maybe I'll use it. But not because she's black.

Sunday, the 19th. We're on the road. The writer wanted to fly with us to Chicago. I said I'd call Charlie, but I couldn't get him. And no one else would OK it without Charlie's OK. We had a charter with 95 seats and half of them empty and I couldn't get this guy on it. It's not as if he wasn't going to give the money back. He met me in Chicago and he couldn't get a room at our hotel. I said I'd get him in, I'd use my influence.

So I call down and I say, "Hey, this is Reggie Jackson, you know, of the Oakland A's. My parents are coming to town and I need an extra room."

The guy said, "Well, Reggie, we don't have anything. But I'll see the manager, and you stop by the desk later and I'll see what we can do."

We went out to eat. We got some rotten ribs at the Playboy Club. I told the bunny they were o-for-four with a couple of strikeouts thrown in. And a pop-up to the pitcher. All the time this guy's pen is scratching on his pad. When I told him how I'd handled the room bit, he pointed out he was one person, white, and only a few years older than me. He wanted to know how the hell he was supposed to pass for family. I told him I'd say I was adopted. We got back to the hotel and he got his room. They always save some for VIPs. And their adoptive parents.

We're in Chicago and we're all wondering how Alvin's gonna act in Finley's town with Charlie sitting in the stands. The first night, we found out. Alvin stood at the corner of the dugout, didn't move, didn't make a sound. Wilbur Wood was pitching and I was sorry I wasn't hitting because I hit good sets against him. But we were beating him, 2–1, in the third. Ken Holtzman was pitching for us and he gave up a couple of hits and Alvin went out to talk to him—at least that's what we all thought.

And that's what Kenny thought, but it turned out Dark had gone to take him out. Kenny just flipped the ball and walked away. The ball hit the back of Alvin's hand and fell to the ground. He had to bend down to pick it up; it was embarrassing. Kenny walked into the dugout and then into the clubhouse and took off his uniform and sat there steaming. We found him that way when some of us went in while we were at bat. He was *mad* and none of the players blamed him.

While we were there Finley poked his head in the clubhouse door, then ducked out again. We wondered what the hell he was up to. A few seconds later he was back with Wes Stock, one of the coaches. Charlie started to scream, "Goddammit, the next time something happens to one of my ballplayers and the others don't at least offer him a word of confidence, I'm gonna get rid of you sons-of-bitches!"

Then he turned to Stock and asked, "Is that right, Wes?" Wes was sort of startled and he said, "Yes, sir, that's sure right, sir."

Then Finley turned on him and yelled, "And that goes for you and all the other fucking coaches, too! And that goes for Dark, too!" And then he started to chew out Dark—with Alvin ain't even being there. He was out in the dugout trying to win a ball game.

Charlie walked over to Vida and looked like he was gonna chew out Vida. But then it seemed to me that Charlie saw that if he said one wrong word to Vida, Vida was gonna be all over him. Vida ain't gonna take no shit from that man. So Charlie shifts gears just like that, and says, "The next time they take you out with a big lead, I'm gonna have their asses. Is that all right with you, Vida?"

And Vida laughed and said, "Yeah, *that's* OK with me, Charlie."

I wish Charlie hadn't done that. He can't get in between the players and the coaches and the manager and expect peace on the team.

We blew that game, 4–3. We got the tying run in the eighth, but then it started to rain. After we waited an hour and a half, the game was called and the score reverted to the seventh and we lost. Even the gods were against us that night.

After the game, I went to Stock and asked him, "Howareya? You know, are you okay?" And he said he was. I said I was sorry for what happened but not to feel bad because it brought us closer together as men.

And he said, "Thanks, Reggie, just a hell of a lot, I really appreciate it." And he shook my hand. He's doing his job. As much as they'll let him. So are all the coaches. But Dark's suspicious of them. He thinks they're Finley's men and he doesn't trust them. So he isn't speaking to them. Can you imagine a manager and his coaches not conversing? He asked Finley to fire them, especially Irv Noren. Finley refused. He didn't want to pay them off. He asked Noren to quit. Noren refused. He wasn't going to go without his dough. So that's the way it stands, with Finley fucking up both sides.

Friday night, Fosse hit a triple with the bases loaded in the first inning to get us off to a 10–4 win. It was the sixth straight game I'd missed. Saturday was my birthday. Twenty-eight years old. Old man. I felt old. I was due to be designated hitter, which is a helluva thing the other league doesn't have. It's good for old guys and injured guys who can still swing the bat, and it gets a *batter* up to bat instead of some pitcher that doesn't know one end of the bat from the other and couldn't care less. It rained during the day and I was kinda hopin' it would keep up so I could get one more day's rest, but it stopped and I played that night.

I had a hitting streak of six straight games still alive, and I stretched it to seven with a single. I also got a walk. And I went out once. But the next time I was due up, Alvin walked up to me and told me he was gonna pinch-hit for me because they had a left-hander pitching, Terry Forster, who was a little wild and he didn't want me to have to make any quick moves to get out of the way.

I said, "Well, I'm okay, ya know. I can hit. I had a hit."

And he said, "I know, but I don't want to take any chances with you."

Well, I've only been pinch-hit for once before in my career, when Finley was trying to embarrass me in 1970, but this seemed reasonable, so I said okay. I went in and changed. Then later the situation came up where I should have been up with a man on second and nobody out. But I wasn't there. We did get the run—and we lost by a run.

Later the guys were bitching about Finley. They figure he called it. Bando told me I should talk to Dark to make it clear

I wouldn't want it to happen again. Greenie said the same thing. But I said, "Well, he wouldn't have done it if I hadn't gone along with it, so I can't gripe about it."

Then Finley went flying into Dark's office and started to shout so loud everyone in the dressing room could hear him, including some writers.

"I don't know what the fuck you're in this game for," he said to Alvin, "but I'm in it to win. And if you don't get your fucking ass in gear, you're gonna be gone! We won two straight without you and we can make it three without you, too. All you got to do is write the fucking names down on the piece of paper and let them play. We got the best goddam team in baseball, goddammit, and if you can't win with the talent we got, you can't win!"

Then he said something that really surprised us. "You got Washington on this ball club. And in the ninth you got a chance to use him with a man on first and a run behind. You needed a steal to get the run in scoring position, and you didn't use him. You were the one that wanted him. I got him for you. I'm paying him forty grand a year—and you don't use him. If you don't use him in a situation like that, what good is he?"

We thought all along Washington was Finley's idea. He'd always talked about a designated runner. He'd had guys around before just to pinch-run. Maybe Dark suggested him because he thought it would appeal to Finley. But it was interesting that Herb was Dark's idea, not Finley's.

The fact is, Finley can take the heat. He didn't say it was Dark's idea when the idea was ridiculed. The guy does go out and get what he thinks we need to win. He wants to win so bad he blows up when we lose. I admire his wanting to win, even if I don't admire the way he goes about it sometimes.

Anyway, he was hollering, humiliating his manager. Alvin knew everyone could hear every word. Alvin was speaking real soft, like he didn't want to be heard, but we heard him anyway. He said, "I was gonna run Herb for Mangual, but Mangual runs real good."

"Mangual got four hits. Mangual did his job! You can't ask

any more of him," Charlie hollered. "But you can put Washington in to do his job."

Well, Washington wasn't doing his job. He wasn't able to do it. He was working at it. He was a good guy and he was getting along with the guys despite all the needling he'd been taking. But he had as much business playing baseball in the majors as I had running the 100-yard dash in the Olympics. I was helping him. A lot of guys were helping him. And he was gonna get to where he could help us, but he wasn't there yet. He was getting picked off and thrown out, and Alvin was afraid to use him. Dark said so to Finley—real soft.

Finley answered—real loud, "He ain't ever going to learn if you don't use him! If you don't want to use him, get rid of him. And maybe you ought to get rid of about twenty-five pounds off that fat ass of yours and maybe you'll be able to think better!"

That did it. I just started laughing and walked out of the clubhouse. I mean it was funny. But after awhile it didn't seem so funny. I felt for Dark. Everyone was watching him when he got on the bus, but he didn't look at anyone, he had his head and his eyes down. It was sad and you had to feel sorry for him. Well, he could quit.

But you know something? Guys don't quit in situations like that; so why feel sorry for them? Finley's not the only owner that meddles with his manager or his coach, who embarrasses them—but these guys go on, they take it. Well, if they want the job that bad, they can have all the crap that goes with it. The funny thing was, Finley took Dark to dinner that night. And I hear he treated him like royalty. How unbelievable can a cat be?

Naturally, it was all over the papers the next day, Sunday. Dark was quoted as saying, "Great peace have they which love Thy law, and nothing shall offend them—Psalms 119:165." He's unbelievable, too. I sometimes think we are run by madmen. We're surrounded by them. They've escaped the booby hatch and taken over.

We won today's game, anyway. It was given to us. Stan Bahnsen walked three men in the first inning and Mangual hit the first grand slam of his career. I hit a double and a single and scored two runs. We were ahead, 8–0, after eight innings and Hunter had a four-hit shutout, but Dark put in Paul Lindblad to pitch the ninth. He gave up a home run and three runs before we got out of it. I know what the papers will say tomorrow. They'll say we won because we were bawled out by Finley.

Wednesday, the 22nd. As I expected, the headlines when we got to Minnesota were that the A's won after Finley told Dark they better win. His timing was perfect, and it made him look like a genius. I guess you are a genius when you can get the pitcher on the other team to walk three men and then serve up a grand-slam home run in the first inning. Well, we did win, and we won three straight here. We took over first place and I think we'll be there the rest of this season. We can screw around all we want, there isn't anyone in our division who's in our class. When someone acts like they mean business, we get down to business. We are the best team and the rest of the teams know it, you can tell by the way they play us. They don't play to win; they play not to lose, which is no way to win. We are not playing well, but we don't have to be at our best to win.

I was designated hitter all three games. I got a single in the first game. We led, 5–0, but had to hold on to win, 5–4. Mangual, Fosse and Rudi all hit triples to build us a big lead. Then they got one in the seventh and three in the ninth, and we almost blew it. Carew got three hits—he's now hitting .418. I meant to tell him I was only kidding him when I said he could kill us in his own ballpark. I hit a home run in the second game, we got fourteen hits and we breezed, 8–1. Dave Hamilton pitched real well most of the way. I hit a home run, a double and a single in the third game and drove in five runs in the last game, and we won it, 7–4. I now have thirteen home runs, I've hit in eleven straight games and we have won eleven out of fourteen and are five over .500.

I was busy off the field. I really had to play the part of a player rep. We're still short in the infield and Finley called up Phil Garner, whose back was better. Pitts has been doing a good job at third, but he happened to make a couple of errors and right away Finley wanted to replace him. Well, when Garner arrived it turned out he was playing without a contract. At the start of the season he had asked for $1700 a month and Finley had offered him $1400. Garner had agreed to play in the minors for $1400, but he had not agreed to sign a contract for the season. He felt that he would be a free agent at year's end and would sign with someone else.

The reserve clause binds a player to his team for life. Because other sports have option clauses in their contracts and players can play out their contracts and become free agents, it is something that he might be able to win in court. Finley said it was illegal to play in the majors without a signed contract. Finley said he'd pay him the major league minimum of $15,000 if he signed a contract, but it would have to contain a clause that he'd have to revert to $14,000 if he was sent back down. Garner refused. Finley told Phil since his bags were still packed, he could go right back.

The players brought Garner to me. I tried to reach the Players' Association lawyer, Marvin Miller, on the phone, but failed. I talked to Finley. He didn't want to listen. He was emphatic that he would not let Phil play without a signed contract. He said it was illegal. I knew it wasn't and I told him that. He said, well, it was club policy. I said it would be a shame if he deprived the player of a chance to prove himself in the majors. He said he didn't know if the player was a major-leaguer, that he wasn't acting like one. I said if he hadn't thought he needed him, he wouldn't have called him up. He said he didn't need him that much, that he wasn't going to let a minor-leaguer blackmail him. He also said the kid had demanded that he be kept up top at least two months. He said to phone the kid to find out for myself if I didn't believe him.

I put the questions to Phil. He said he wanted more money if he signed to play in the majors. And he said if he played in the majors without a contract, he had asked to stay long enough at the major league rate to move his season salary up. Phil's answers satisfied me, and I told this to Finley. He started to get angry. I told him not to get excited, to hear me

out. I said he could do whatever he wanted in the end, but I
might say something that made sense to him. I pointed out
the player might prove he was worth more money if he gave
him a chance. I told him if he didn't give the player a chance,
the kid was going to go back down and when they asked what
had happened, he would tell them and it would make Finley
look bad. He started to listen a little. I said it would be sad if
he put a block up between himself and the kid so the kid's
career could be ruined. I said he was too big a guy to do something like that for spite over a few thousand dollars. He smiled
and said he would think about it and let us know.

I told Phil his fate was under consideration and went out to
warm up. About ten minutes later I was called to speak to
Finley on the phone. He said he had decided to give Garner
what he wanted if he would sign. Garner thanked me and
signed. Dark and the players all approved of how I'd handled
it. I felt like I'd done something good that went beyond
baseball. I'm player rep and I was able to do something for a
player. I feel Finley didn't want the reserve clause taken to
court for a test. I only hope he doesn't take it out on the kid,
who could be buried.

The writer is still with me. We walked around downtown
Minneapolis the other afternoon. He was pumping me for my
feelings about ladies. As we went along I rated ladies, like a lot
of ballplayers do, on a scale from one to ten. Just in jest. Eight
and above, I'd stop and chat with them. He was scribbling
away. I didn't want to look bad so I even stopped to talk to a
one. But she didn't want to talk to me. A *one* and she didn't
want to talk to me! I went back to the eights. One was in a
health club. She was willing to talk, but only about business.
She wanted to sign me up for some exercise. I told her I didn't
need none. I finally found a nine in a department store. I
told her, "You're the best-looking lady we've seen so far. You're
a superstar!"

She told me I had a date.

Thursday, the 23rd. In San Diego, Ray Kroc, the McDonald's
hamburger king, said he'd pay a million bucks to buy me from

Finley for the Padres. Finley says he wouldn't sell me to anyone at any price. He loves me too much. He wouldn't want to
spoil me by making me happy. Hell, I'd pay a million, myself,
for myself. And I'd be getting a bargain.

Friday, the 24th. We got to Anaheim for a series with the
Angels. Before the first game tonight, Bando told me his leg
felt good and he felt ready to return to the lineup. He said
Dark had asked him to say when he was ready. I told Sal to
tell the man he was ready. And apparently Alvin told him he
was in. But then a little later, when Alvin posted the lineup,
Sal wasn't on it. He argued angrily about it with Alvin. Alvin
just said he wanted to be sure he was healed before he put him
back in the lineup.

Sal asked me what the hell I thought he should do. I told
him I'd tell Alvin I could go back to right field, I felt good
enough. Bando could at least be the designated hitter. Sal
said to go ahead.

I told Alvin what I thought he should do. I said Sal knows
better than anyone else what he can and can't do. I said it
didn't do him any good to have his captain angry at him. And
Alvin said he wanted to play Sal, but he just felt he couldn't
afford to take a chance; he might hurt himself again, even as
designated hitter.

And I said, "Well, hell, Alvin, I'm coming back from an injury, and you've been using me as a designated hitter."

Alvin said, "Well, look, I can talk to you, you understand.
Just between you and me, we know black boys heal faster
than white boys."

I was stunned. I just stood there, looking at him. I guess I
nodded and stammered something about all right, Alvin, whatever you want, and walked away. I couldn't believe it; but
there it was. I thought about it. Well, he'd said it to me and it
was no secret to him I was black. He looked on me as a leader
of the team and a go-between with the players and he sure as
hell wasn't about to offend me if he knew he was offending me.
He didn't know.

To him, there is a difference between black and white. It's the way he thinks. He doesn't think. I was mad at myself for not calling him on it. But what good would it do? All that lousy publicity he got that time he rapped Latins and blacks didn't change him, so why would something I say change him?

There's no changing him. He grew up this way and this is the way he is. He meant it as a compliment to the physical prowess of blacks, or something. He was confiding to me what he considers to be truth. If it was bigoted, I'm not sure he knows he's a bigot. If he does harm, he doesn't mean to. He hurt me, but he didn't mean to. I can't respect him for it, but it's hard to hate him for it.

Sunday, the 26*th.* We lost two out of three to the Angels, but it was no big deal. Several of their players, Dave Sells especially, were quoted as saying the Angels and A's had a big rivalry. The two California clubs in the league and all that crap, you know, and how they wanted to beat us more than any other team. But it is crap; there's no real rivalry. They're just another team, and not a real good one at that. If we took them more seriously we wouldn't lose one out of three to them.

They had lost eight straight to Hunter, but they beat him Friday night, 4–3. They batted out Holtzman Saturday night, 8–2. Dick Lange and Frank Tanana, a couple of pretty good young pitchers, pitched the two games for them. We knocked out a better pitcher, Bill Singer, Sunday afternoon and hung on to win, 6–5. Bando got back in the lineup at third Saturday night, and he drove in the winning run with a fly ball Sunday afternoon. I got a hit in each of the first two games and two hits in the third game. I went back to right field and strained the muscle a little more, so I went right back to designated hitter. My streak is up to fourteen games now, so I want to keep swinging that bat.

The thing I like best about playing the Angels is getting together with Frank Robinson. Ever since he managed me in winter ball one year when I needed straightening out—and he straightened me out—I have really respected Robinson, more than any man in this game. He is more man than anyone I've ever known. He is more respected by ballplayers than anyone

I know. He has been a helluva ballplayer. He has been MVP in both leagues and he has led more teams to the top than anyone. But it is more than that. He is smart and he has a super personality and he can communicate with anyone. It's what makes one man a better manager than another. Frank would make a marvelous manager.

Every time I'm in Anaheim I go over to Frank's house and have dinner with him and his wife. It's something I want to do. I look forward to it. I've been called his other son. This time he talked about wanting to be a manager. I told him he'd make a helluva manager, but it was something that maybe wasn't going to happen. If it was going to happen, why hadn't it happened in Oakland when Williams left, before Finley brought in Dark? Frank was from Oakland. It's a black town and he's a hero there. Finley does things others don't do. He likes to shake up the establishment. I would have thought he'd have loved to have been a pioneer, the first man to get himself a black manager. But he didn't. He blew the best chance he'll ever have to erase all the harm he's done.

I had talked to some of the Angels and they told me how everyone on the team went to Robinson, not to Winkles. How Frank really was the center of influence on the team, not Winkles. And how Winks just took it. It made me feel bad for Winks. I asked Frank about it and he said that was the way it was. He didn't badmouth Winks, but I could see he didn't think much of him as a manager. He said that on the one hand Winks had all these Joe College rules that turned the guys off, and on the other hand he tried to turn them on by being one of them. He said he wasn't behaving like a boss. Well, maybe it's not in him. Coaching college kids is one thing and managing major-leaguers another.

If Frank told me to bat right-handed, I'd think about it because I'd figure he knows something. But if Winks told me about batting, I'd ask him how the fuck he knew, he ain't even been to bat yet. It's tough, man. If you don't have a reputation, you've got to have something else going for you. He also doesn't have good ballplayers. If he was with us, he'd win because you can't lose with our players. In Anaheim, he's gonna lose. But there's still no way Robinson can win. In Orange County? Conservative country? A black manager? No way. Forget it, Frank. I told him that.

Monday, the 27th. We had fun flying home. Everyone was needling everyone else all the way back. Bando's behind a lot of it. He harasses one guy; then that guy gets on another guy and so forth. Bando has a good way of getting on a guy. So does Tenace. They get on you, but they don't get to you—if you know what I mean. They don't put the needle in too deep. Once in a while a needle goes too deep and that's when a fight starts, but not too often. It's good for the guys. We have a lot of stars, and stars' egos can get out of hand. The kidding cuts 'em back down to size. When a benchwarmer can kid a star, it's good; he becomes a part of the team. It inspires a lot of togetherness.

I'm on a hot streak. I've always been a streaky hitter. I once drove in ten runs in one game. I hit eight homers in six games. I hit over .600 for seven games. Now I've got another going for me. I went three-for-three tonight, all singles, but my batting average is up to .404. I scored a run and drove in two. We drove out a good pitcher, Joe Coleman, with six runs in the first inning and went on to whip Detroit, 12–2. Blue coasted to an easy win, but even with a ten-run lead, Dark went to the relievers the last two innings. This was the fifteenth straight game I've hit in. That may be the longest such streak of my career.

I'm making contact consistently. I don't strike out as much as I used to, but I still strike out. I don't worry about strike-outs. They pay off on homers, not strikeouts. If I hit 65 home runs, ain't no one gonna ask me how many times I struck out. I swing fast. I swing hard. With my swing, and my strength, I can really hit a ball. There is no thrill for a hitter like hitting one of those long 'taters out of sight. When I get me one of them dingers, I am the biggest man in town for that moment. The longest I ever hit—the biggest moments— were one estimated at around 520 feet in Minnesota that hit off the beer-barrel cap on a sign in right-center and one esti-

mated at around 550 feet I hit off a light tower on top
of the right-field stands in Detroit in the 1971 All-Star
game. They'll never know how far that last one might have
gone because it was still rising when it hit the tower. It felt
fantastic when I hit it. They still talk about it.

I don't strike out as much as I used to because I don't swing
at as many bad balls as I used to. I've learned my strike zone.
I've learned to be nice to the umpires. I seldom get on them
about calls. I try not to embarrass them or make them look
bad. It pays off because they make me look good. One umpire appreciates my manners so much that he reduces the
strike zone whenever I come to the plate. I don't believe he
does it deliberately, but he gives me the benefit of the doubt on
every close call. He has told me, "You'll get your pitch when
I'm behind the plate." I won't say who he is. The Commissioner could torture me and I won't tell. But I try not to lose
my temper with my umps.

I take every edge I can get. My pitch is any pitch I'm looking for. I don't guess. I call it calculated anticipation. I
figure out what a pitcher is gonna throw and I wait for it. I'm
a balanced batter. I'm not better on any one kind of pitch than
another. I have no pronounced weaknesses. I can tell because
no two pitchers pitch me the same. If he fools me, I'm gonna
miss the pitch. If he doesn't, I'm gonna hit it. But there's no
magic place he can put the ball I can't hit if I'm ready for it.
My only weakness is night games. I wear glasses because I
have bad eyesight. I don't see as well at night. If I played all
day games I'd rip this sport apart.

I'm left-handed, but I don't pull everything to right. I hit a
lot to the opposite field. I have enough strength that
if I take my big swing and get only a little piece of the ball
I can still hit it a long way. I've hit balls that were past me into
the stands. I've hit balls into the seats in left with half a swing.

I learn all I can about pitchers. I know what everyone has
and what he does. I don't write it down in a book. I keep it in
my brain. Some people are smart about some things, some
people about other things. I'm a smart hitter. I remember
what's happened out there between me and the pitcher. Lots

of people could be good hitters who aren't. They don't work at it. They don't think about it. They don't study their talent so they can make the most of it. They don't figure out the best bat for them. They don't figure out the best swing. They don't increase the speed in their swing or the strength in their arms. They don't use both hands on the bat. They don't learn the pitchers and learn to anticipate their pitches. They don't concentrate.

I hate public appearances. I hate going out in public. I hate airports. I hate airplanes. I've learned to deal with it, but I feel as though I'm in a cage, like an animal, looked at like I was some freak. But when I get on the field it's like I've been let out of my cage. I'm freed. I'm like an animal running through the woods. The running and catching and throwing is fine. I take pride in my performance in these things. But when I've got a bat in my hand, that's the best thing I do. No one can ask me for an autograph when I'm at the plate. No one's snatchin' at me. But everyone's payin' attention to me. It's me and the pitcher. He can try anything he wants. He can rub up the ball, move the fielders around, stare me down, make me wait, try anything. If I'm hot, I'm gonna hit that pitch.

When you hit a terrific shot, all the baseball players come to rest at that moment and watch you. Everyone is in awe. You charge people up. And when you're a good hitter, you do that every day. You're the center of attention, you have complete confidence and you have all your foes afraid of you. You're the dominating force from the minute you walk out of the dugout. For an athlete, there's no other feeling like that.

Confidence is half the fight. I've got a big ego, but there are times I lack confidence. It comes and it goes and it's hard to explain why. Maybe it's physical. Maybe your body's not quite right. An injury can throw you out of whack. If you've got troubles off the field it may show on the field.

Some guys, they get a hit or two in a game, they let down. They figure they're all right for another day. If I get one, I want two. If I get two, I want three. If I get a long one, I want a longer one. If I drive in five runs, I want to drive in ten. It's a big thing I've got going for myself. I'm never satisfied. The day I feel satisfied is the day I'll retire.

When I'm going good, the ball has eyes. You make contact, and the ball finds the holes in the defense. But when I'm going bad, I hit a line drive and it's right at someone. I get angry. My confidence fades. I'm looking for the curve and he throws me three or four fastballs and I say to myself, "the sonofabitch isn't going to throw me a curve." Then he does and I'm not expecting it and I lunge at it and miss it. My head gets all screwed up.

All right, my head's on straight right now. I'm in control. I'm confident. I've hit in fifteen straight. Maybe I'll hit in sixteen. Or twenty. Or thirty.

I could hit 60 or 65 homers some season. I should hit 30 or 35 every season. That's me. The big swing for the big bucks. Drive in the runs. That's what wins games. That's what they pay off on. I'm making contact now, but I'm not gonna cut down on my swing, so it cuts down my chances of keeping my streak alive. Tomorrow, the next day, the day after that, I'll be blanked. I'll come back to earth. I'll slump. It's bound to be. But I'm bound to bounce back, too.

They got Baby Ruth and Oh Henry! bars. I wonder what kinda candy bar they'll name after Reggie?

Wednesday, the 29*th.* My streak ended last night. Well, it had to end. I went 0-for-three against Woody Fryman and a real good, gutty relief pitcher, John Hiller. We lost, 3–1. Gary Sutherland, who doesn't hit home runs, hit two off the Cat. What can you say? Tonight I bounced back with a single and double and Holtzman stopped the Tigers, 3–1, so we won two out of three in the series.

One funny thing happened in this series. In the first game when we already were ahead, 12–1, and I already had three hits, they gave me an intentional walk with two out and no one on. The Detroit catcher Bill Freehan said to me while I was waiting out the walk, "Man, I don't understand Ralph Houk. You're killing us, but what's one more run? We can't win, why not let you get some more stats?"

I've been thinking about it and I guess it's a tribute to me, but I'd rather have the at-bat. I wonder how many intentional walks The Babe got with two out and none on? Maybe a lot. But it doesn't do anything for the game.

There were only 3000 or so fans in our mausoleum the last couple of nights. No matter how many reasons you figure out for the fans not supporting us, there really isn't any good reason why fans won't support a two-time World Champion better than they do us in Oakland. You never really get used to it. It's always a little disappointing when you see all those empty seats. We have to kick ourselves in the ass because the fans aren't there to turn us on. Hell, we'd draw four million fans in New York. I guess this city really doesn't deserve a big-league ball club, much less a big club.

Hey, I'd pay to see me play. Wouldn't you?

4 ☆ JUNE

Saturday, the 1st. *Time* magazine's cover story on me is out. Not many athletes have made that cover. It's a worldwide magazine, and I was very, very proud when I saw it. The story was something else. It wasn't bad, but it could have been better. The cover line referred to me as "The Muscle and Soul of the A's Dynasty." That's pretty heavy. I'm afraid some of the guys are going to resent it.

My main objection was that the story made it seem easy for me to be what I am. Well, it never has been easy, and it never will be. A lot of what I can do comes natural, but I've worked like hell to be able to do more, to learn to use what I have. I've put up with a lot of crap to get to the top—and I put up with a lot of crap now that I'm on top. It's not a game when you get where I am. It's a business. You gotta produce or they'll push you off to the side of the road. I'm not complaining. Most people have it a lot worse, I'm sure. But I just want to make it clear it's not ever easy.

The writer was basically honest and wrote the truth as he saw it. There's a lot of stuff in there about my ego and my need to be heard and be a leader and about my not being as black-minded as some of the other black players would like me to be. I guess all that's true enough. He mentioned about my having been in analysis. He wouldn't have known if I hadn't told him. I'm not ashamed of it. I think most people would benefit by talking to a psychiatrist and trying to think themselves through and trying to get their heads straight. I'm not nuts. I do ride a roller-coaster. My lows are too low, my highs too high. I've gotta get in balance. I started to go to my man about the time of my divorce, and it straightened me out a lot and got me back in balance. I don't mean I'm not still taking some rides on the roller-coaster. I'd be better off if I got to my man more often, but I just don't have the time. At least now I know where I'm at and what's with me. I know how to look at myself now and at the things I do. I can think things through. I can put myself in perspective most of the time.

The writer did get a lot out of me about my family. If it's there I guess it might as well be here. I was born in Wyncotte, Pennsylvania, but reared in Cheltenham, which is a sort of mainline suburb of Philadelphia, mostly white. We're black, but my father's people came from Latin America. My full name is Reginald Martinez Jackson and I have a lot of Spanish blood in me. Where I lived there wasn't much prejudice.

There were six kids in my family. I've got two older brothers, Joe and James, an older sister, Dolores, and two younger sisters, Beverly and Tina. My parents separated when I was four and got divorced later on. Joe and I and Beverly went with my old man and the other three went with my mother. Later, Jim came to live with Joe and me, while Beverly went with her mother. Joe is a career man in the Air Force. He's in Jersey right now, but he's been in Taiwan and he's going back. He's not married.

Jim is a tax lawyer. He was a real fuck-up for a long time, but he busted his ass the last couple of years in college and he graduated from Boston University. He married a brilliant girl, Maria, who got her doctorate from Harvard, and they've got a little girl named Imara. He's been working for the IRS in Boston, but I think he's going to go to work for my real estate company in Arizona.

Dolores was married, but got divorced. She has two girls—Wanda and Wynoka. They live in Baltimore, where my mom lives. Beverly and her husband, Maurice, and her two kids, Carl and Greg, live in Baltimore, too. They own a furniture store there. Tina, the youngest, isn't married. She's moving back to Baltimore. She graduated from Morgan State with majors in Education and Spanish, but she works as a dental assistant.

Dad's a tailor. When I was growing up he had a dry-cleaning delivery route. He left for work early. I got up and got dressed and got to school myself. I never ate breakfast weekdays because there wasn't time or that much to eat. When dad got home—eight, nine, ten, eleven at night—that's when we ate supper. He did anything and everything he could to make money for us even though he sometimes got hassled for it. It wasn't always legal, but it was what he had to do to get by, to get his kids fed and clothed and grown up. He always managed to throw something on the table. But if I asked him for a quarter to go to the movies he always asked me what I'd done to earn it. If I wanted pocket money I had to bust my ass on the back of his truck for it. If he sent me to the store for some ice cream, he expected me to get it. He didn't want to know if it was raining or snowing or I had to hitch a ride or walk; he wanted me to bring back what I'd been sent for. He had a phrase: He didn't want to hear any "ar-ray-boo"—any bullshit, in other words. I believe in that. If you've got something to do, do it. Don't make excuses why you can't do it. And do it right.

My dad's a good old dude and I got a lot of respect for him. He's a fighter. He was a fighter as a young man—a boxer. My brother Jim was nicknamed Slug because since dad was a boxer someone stuck the name on Jim. My dad's crippled. He got crippled in the Army. But he could fight crippled and he could play ball crippled. He was busy hustling for a buck while I was growing up, and he didn't have a lot of time for me.

My brother Joe really raised me. He's tough, too. He used to beat the shit out of me if I didn't do my chores at home. I had to wash the dishes and clean the house and rake the leaves. I'm grateful to him. He's responsible for me being the way I am. I keep a clean house. I can afford help, but if someone

doesn't do it for me, I do it. It's got to be done. And right.
I'm a perfectionist. I got that from Joe.

Later Jim would haul ass on me too, if I didn't do right. He
came to live with us my senior year, when my dad was away.

I was a wild kid: big and strong and tough. And when my
dad wasn't home with me, it made me bitter. It left us alone,
but we got by. People who have to hustle to get by have no
respect for convention. Me and my buddies would drive our
'55 Chevys into church parking lots and drink beer and raise
hell with the straight suckers who came out. We'd crash par-
ties, beat up on rich kids. We'd take their coats, 'cause it was
cold and we didn't have decent coats. We'd wear 'em to school
the next day and those rich kids didn't dare say nothing to us
because they knew we'd kick the shit out of them. It wasn't
right, but that's the way it was.

One day some kid stole my lunch. Lunch? It was a box of
pretzels. A lousy box of pretzels. I told the teacher that if I
didn't get it back I was gonna bust someone.

One of the guys was smiling because he saw she wasn't going
to do nothing. So I grabbed him and shoved him up against a
wall and I said, "Boy, don't you know I might kill you?"

And he got nervous and he said, "Man, don't you do that.
Why you want to do that?"

" 'Cause I'm crazy." I wasn't, but they thought I was—which
was what I wanted because it made them scared of me.

The teacher was scared. I remember the whole scene. My
girl friend was in back; she was a Jewish girl, and she was crying. They used to tease her about me.

In her home-ec class one time the teacher told her, "I heard
Reggie went on another tantrum today." My girl told me and
I went to the class and told the teacher off. I was suspended
from school three times. But I got back because I could play
football and they liked winning football games.

I was a hell of a football player. I liked that contact. One
time I hit the line and a defensive lineman punched me in the
mouth and broke my tooth. I asked the quarterback to call my
play again and I ran right over him.

Football was my way out. I had a lot of scholarship offers. I took the one at Arizona State because they had a big baseball program there, too, and I wanted to play baseball as well as football. I was pointed at pro ball, but it became baseball instead of football. I hurt my leg and they moved me from the offensive backfield to the defensive backfield in football. The offense has the glamour, not the defense, and I'm a glamour guy. I quit school after my sophomore season when I got the big bonus offer from Finley. But going to school was good for me. It got me away from my family and my hometown and out on my own. Tempe, my college town, became my hometown. I fell in love with the place and I'm liked there. I'm known as a ballplayer there, but liked as a person.

I've learned a lot of lessons in my life and I've grown up. I'm no longer the boy who steals from rich kids. Maybe because I'm rich and don't have to steal to get by. If I had to, I guess I could still do it. But I haven't stolen since I went into a store with my father and lifted a candy bar. He found out about it and made me go back and tell the cashier I took it. I was so ashamed, I never have stolen anything again. Getting caught is what hurts the most I guess.

My dad having to go hurt me. I mean I missed him. I felt alone. I was lonely. I was sad all the time until he got out and got back. It's a bad memory for me. Maybe it's what they had to do, but they should have seen it's what he had to do, too.

My dad still works as a tailor. Because of me he's the biggest man in his part of the world. He's practically the mayor of south Philadelphia because he's Reggie Jackson's old man. He's thrilled when guys like Henry Aaron come to town and give him a call. He loves baseball and he loves being a big man and he eats up all the attention he gets because of me. He can't get enough of it. He gets mad when I don't call him up or fly him out to this big game or that big game. I do a lot of it, but it seems like I can never do enough of it to suit him. He figures I owe it to him. I know I do. I owe him everything. I give him everything I can. He has his own tailor shop. He wants to work. He doesn't want to retire. He doesn't want to sit around doing nothing. But it's nice for him knowing he doesn't have to work.

My mom works but she doesn't have to. I didn't say the name "Mom" until I was thirteen or fourteen. I didn't even get to know her until I was eighteen or nineteen. But I don't hate her for it. She coulda kept closer touch, but she was a long ways away and she had hard times. She won't have hard times ever again. I bought her a house. She lives downstairs and rents the upstairs. I help out with money now and then. I feel like I know her now, both as a mother and as a friend. I see her and the others who are in Baltimore every time we play that town, and I fly her around some too.

I'm out of touch with Joe. He did so much for me, but he's been so far from me the last eight, ten years I don't really know him anymore. And he doesn't know me. At times he treats me like I'm a baseball player, not his brother. Everyone in the family does, which really bugs me. They're sort of in awe of me. They're afraid of wronging me, like I'm the only one who's got real money and I'm their insurance policy. Well, I want to be that, but I want to be one of them, too.

When I'm on the field, I'm a baseball player. When I'm off it, I'm just another guy, a person just like any other person. I have my strengths and I have my weaknesses. Jim—I call him Slug—is about the only one who knows me. He's about the only one I can communicate with, have a conversation with. We speak the same dialogue. But even he keeps on me to keep up a big front because I'm big in baseball and have a responsibility to my name and the game. I don't want to hear that. I just want to be me. Down deep I know he's right, but at times I resent him reminding me of it.

Dolores is a doll and I love her dearly. We get along about the best, I think, though I don't know her as well as I wish I did. I know Beverly better because we were together more as kids and I feel she really loves me, she digs me, and it's a great feeling. Tina is the youngest and I would like to know her better than I do. It's harder for her to see me as a brother than it is as a ballplayer. Sometimes I help her financially and I wonder if it hurts more than it helps. Maybe we should find our own way. But I have it, I want her to have it if she needs it.

The thing about the money is I make a lot; but taxes take a lot and I send my family some and I have a lot invested and I don't have a lot laying around. I want to have something left when I'm through playing because I can't play forever, and I don't know what my business will be worth to me later. I feel real love for my family and I want to do things for them and take them places and be with them, but there's only so much money and only so much of me.

I'm sure my mom was grateful for the house I got for her, but the first thing she did was send me a list of things she wanted to do to the house, costing eight or ten grand. I have a couple of costly houses. I think they resent it. I have a fancy car. Sometimes I feel they resent that also. It's not the money. It's the wanting from me instead of the wanting to be with me that bothers me.

I found out Dolores's two kids didn't have a TV, so I bought them a color set. They see me coming, they say, "Here come Uncle Reggie, Uncle Reggie." They love their Uncle Reggie and I love them. I love all my brother's and sisters' kids. I'm hooked on them and they could rape me financially and I wouldn't mind a bit, because they're kids and they got something better coming to them out of life than I had. I want to give something more than money to my brothers and sisters, to my father and my mother, too. I want to give them *me*. Not the way they think I am, but the way I am.

When I married a Mexican girl, my mother didn't come to the wedding. When I date a white girl, my family always wants to know what I do that for—why I don't spread the riches around my fellow blacks. I see people for what they are inside, not the color outside. My family doesn't always. My business partner's white, so they're always worried that he must be screwing me. He's not, but they don't want to believe it.

I don't want to worry about what my family thinks when they read something I say about them. I'll only say what's in my heart, I'll speak the truth as I see it, and that should be enough for anyone. I want to be able to talk to them honestly, and I

want them to be able to talk to me honestly. I want to be close
to them because they have done more for me than I could ever
do for them—and I love them each and every one dearly.
There is blood between us. We are family and I feel a lot for
family.

I will never put them down. I only wish they wouldn't put
me on a pedestal. If I don't call or send for them or send
them something, they say I'm stuck-up. They say I'm a
bighead ballplayer who has let success spoil me. Well, lots of
sons and brothers are bad about calling or doing for family and
they're not bighead ballplayers. And as far as my family is
concerned, they should just think of me as a son and a brother
who doesn't always do what he should do—not as a bighead
ballplayer. But when your face is on the front of *Time*
magazine and your guts are spilled out all over the inside, it's
hard for people to accept you for yourself.

Monday, the 3rd. Milwaukee came to town and that made me
happy because George Scott comes with them. He hits 'em out
of sight. And he is an out-of-sight guy. He is a funny fellow,
and I laugh a lot when I'm with him. I was with him on and
off for a couple of days between games. One day he was looking through my closet and he took a liking to a $150 coat I had
there so I gave it to him. It made me feel good to be able to
give him something and it made him feel good to be able to tell
people I'd given it to him.

Saturday I was chatting with Clyde Wright and he was telling
me his troubles. I was so sympathetic, Clyde asked me if I was
trying to butter up pitchers. I said I sure was. The next day I
hit two home runs off him and I think he's still trying to figure
out if I conned him into serving up soft touches.

We swept three straight from Milwaukee. Rudi hit a three-
run homer in the first one to win it. Deron Johnson, who is
not hitting, hit a homer and double to win the second one. My
homers helped us to the third one. And Rudi hit another
three-run homer in this one. Joe has got to be the most
underrated player in baseball.

We had an off-day today to travel to Detroit to start a road trip. I spent a lot of the day talking to John Summers. He is young, but wise beyond his years. He told me a lot of guys were wising off about me behind my back, jealous of the publicity I'm getting, looking for ways to cut me down to their level, I guess. He said I should shut up and back off a bit. He said they take me for granted and expect me to put money in their pockets and don't think they owe me any thanks for it. It's true, I know. I'm a fellow who needs a pat on the back once in a while and never gets it. It's tough when some of the other fellows are feeding on you, taking from you, pulling out your shirttail and riding on it and never giving anything back. I'm not talking about the Bandos or the Rudis or the Cats.

Wednesday, the 5th. I spent yesterday with Archie Clark, the pro basketball player who is now with the Washington team. We talked about being black athletes in a white man's world and how whites resent the fact that most of the best athletes today are black. I've known Archie about five years, but I haven't really gotten into him before. He told me how he was running out of time and was worried about his future because the big paychecks weren't going to be coming in much longer. He was happy his bar was bringing in extra money because he was putting a lot of money out to pay off for two divorces. He said he is 33, which surprised me. I just never thought about it. I'm 28. One day I'll turn around and I'll be 33. It sneaks up on you. You got to prepare yourself for it.

We went over to visit with two other basketball players we know, Charlie Scott and Lucius Allen, who were at a hotel downtown. We talked some more about money. Some of those basketball players make more money than athletes in other sports. The war between the ABA and NBA brought that about. Clubs in both leagues bid for players, putting the salary levels way up. I'm making $135,000, but Charlie Scott is making twice that much. I'm more prominent in my game than he is in his, but mine doesn't pay as much as his. He has a contract that will make him more than a million dollars over a period of years. Allen is making a lot of money, too. We all are.

But let's face it, the owners wouldn't pay it if they couldn't afford it. We haven't got guns at their heads. The owners are making money. And I don't know an owner who brings in a buck at the box office. The ballplayers bring in the bread and they're entitled to a piece of the pie. They say a lot of teams are losing money. But with tax write-offs and such I don't think many owners are. They always seem to be able to sell their teams for more money than they put into them.

I have been the designated hitter for a couple of weeks, but now I've returned to right field. However, my leg still aches and it worries me. I spoke to Alvin about it and to Finley on the phone, and they said it was all right to return to right field, but it would not be all right if I took any foolish chances of reinjuring myself. They wanted me to play if I could, so I said I would—and paid a price. We had a twi-night doubleheader last night, and we won one and lost one. In one of them I hit a ball between the outfielders, and as I was going into second I saw I could stretch it to a triple. But I felt a little pain and decided not to run any risks and pulled up at second. Deron Johnson then got a short single that would have scored me if I'd been on third. The third-base coach was waving me around anyway, but my leg was aching so I stopped at third. I didn't score.

Today I talked on the telephone to some people in Oakland who told me that Monte Moore had ridiculed me on his broadcast for not hustling. And John Summers told me some of the other players resented my not busting my ass on the thing. What am I gonna do? Tell them The Man told me to take it easy? Forget it. Few see beneath the surface of things. Few even bother to look. I should be on the bench, but no one wants to know that.

I was down and I wanted to be with people who didn't want anything from me, so today I got together with Archie and Charlie and Lucius again. A chick called them, and when she was told I was there it turned out we knew each other and she wanted to talk to me. She was Billy North's ex-girl friend, or so I thought. She said she'd heard Billy and I weren't getting along and she wanted to know what was happening. I told her the way it was with Billy and me, me getting on him for loafing and him getting on me ever since. We had a little chat, nothing special.

That evening after I got to the ballpark, I had stripped off my civvies and was sitting by my locker without any clothes on, getting ready to get into my uniform.

In walked Billy and he began to blast me. "You're a fucking jerk, you know that?"

I was surprised by it. He'd been baiting me, but this was heavy talk. "Hey, what's going on?" I asked. I wasn't angry. I figured he was having fun.

"You're a fucking asshole is what you are! You're no fucking good! If you're a superstar, I never saw one."

I started to lose my temper, but I couldn't figure out why the sudden assault. I said to myself, "Hey, hold on, find out what's happening here." And I asked him, "What's eating you?"

He said I was. I told him to just go away and leave me the hell alone. He said he wasn't going anywhere and he wasn't going to get off my back. So I went at him. I don't know why. I lost my temper, but I wasn't real angry or anything. It just seemed silly—him being mad at me when nothing new that I knew of had happened. I grabbed him and he grabbed me and we wrestled down to the ground and some of the guys grabbed us and pulled us apart.

We stood there and he shouted, "You know damn well what this is about! You're trying to steal my girl from me is what this is about! You trying to get back at me or something?"

And then I saw it. The gal I'd talked to on the telephone had later talked to him. While she hadn't had anything to tell him, she'd told him something that had made him mad. I said, "Hey man, I don't know what the hell you're talking about. I talked to a girl on the telephone, that's all. I didn't ask her for a date. I didn't ask her for anything. I don't want anything from her. I don't want your girl. I don't want anything from you."

And he sneered, "You don't want my girl because you're a fucking faggot is what you are!"

"Wow, man, this is too much," and I went at him again, and down we went again. It's hard as hell to fight without any clothes on. It feels funny. You feel defenseless. I had lost control and I couldn't fight right, anyway. I didn't punch at him, I just kinda lunged at him. I didn't have any shoes on and I slipped and fell against one of the metal lockers. The guys went back to breaking us up again. There was a lot of banging into lockers before we were apart again.

That was it. I didn't think any damage was done, but my shoulder was bruised and Ray Fosse, who'd been one of the peacemakers, said he'd hurt his shoulder, too, or his back or something. Bando got between us and told us to take our troubles to a cold shower and cool off. I went into the whirl-pool instead to soak my shoulder, which was starting to hurt like hell. Then I put some ice on it and lay down and got a rubdown. I didn't want to play, but I figured I'd better. So did North, who'd hurt his arm.

As fights go it was a farce, but Watson Spoelstra, the sportswriter from Detroit, had been in the clubhouse. So I knew he'd report what he saw and it would be spread all over the newspapers the next day. It was just a misunderstanding between men. It didn't amount to much, but the press and the public were bound to make more of it than there had been. So both Billy and I played. But my shoulder got so sore I had to leave after five innings. I was hitless, but we got nine hits and nine runs and won, 9–1. I'm sure the papers will report that after the angry A's beat up on each other in the clubhouse they got together and went out and beat up on the other team on the field.

Right after I got to the dressing room, John Summers got to me and said, "Hey, man, this isn't like you, this isn't your style, you got to keep your cool. If Billy's bad for you, steer clear of him."

I felt lousy that I'd lost my temper. He'd asked for it, but it was my fault for giving in to him. That kind of stuff is for kids. It's the A's way, but it's the wrong way. The only good thing about it was that I knew we had the sort of team to shrug off such things.

Afterwards, Dark asked me about it. He hadn't been in on it. He should've been. A manager should somehow be where the action is. He has to be alert to such activity. But Alvin is aloof from the inner workings of our team. He was kind enough not to make a big deal out of it. I told him we'd had an argument and had scuffled and I was sorry. I said it didn't matter whose fault it was, it shouldn't have happened. I said I knew it was what people expected of the A's and I was embarrassed to have heaped fuel on the fire. I'm 28 years old, I've been in the league seven or eight years, and I should be beyond behaving like a little boy. Dark said to forget it and he'd talk to Billy and try to get him to forget it. I doubt that anyone will ever let us forget it. They remember things like this long after your career is completed. It's not what I want to be remembered for.

Friday, the 7th. Like I figured, the fight was all over yesterday's papers and it's still smeared over today's papers here in Milwaukee where we have a series to play. Also like I figured, a lot was made of The Fighting A's fighting among themselves and then beating the crap out of the other guys. Fortunately, we're so used to turmoil it doesn't hurt us. But unfortunately, Finley figured it was his place to fan the fire.

Charlie came in from Chicago and he called me and Billy into a meeting with Dark in the trainer's room before tonight's game. The door was wide open and he spoke so all the players could hear all that he said. He was on stage and he wanted the spotlight. And his plan was to put the superstar in his place. He didn't ask anyone what happened or why it had happened. He didn't try to find out who was at fault. He wasn't about to blame Billy. And so he zeroed in on Reggie.

Charlie ranted and raved dramatically how it didn't matter how big a star a player was or how much money he made, we were a unit and all the players were going to be treated alike and pull together or he'd fix them. He hollered that he wasn't going to let any egotistical superstar cause trouble no matter how much publicity he brought the team.

I was so shocked I didn't say anything and neither did Billy or Alvin. After awhile, Charlie sent them away and turned on me directly. He said I had been a troublemaker from the time I had joined the team, that I'd argued not only with him but with my managers and my teammates. He said he'd traded one player because of a fight I'd had with him—meaning Mike Epstein—but he was not about to trade this time because North's his best player. Best player, crap! As he was talking about him, Billy got better and better. Charlie hoisted him up on a pedestal and knocked me down on the ground. He said I hadn't been the ballplayer I should have been and hadn't become the man I should have become.

I felt like punching him in his damn mouth! I don't know why I didn't. I had done wrong, but I hadn't been the only one. And I hadn't done anything to deserve *this*. I wanted to walk out on him; I don't know why I didn't. The owner is the boss and the ballplayer is his property—but I took crap from him I wouldn't take from any other man. I was just stunned by the whole situation. And I think I instinctively didn't want to add to the turmoil on the team. Before I knew it he had walked out into the clubhouse meeting and was telling all the players what they'd already heard. He said there were some horses' asses on the team and anyone who didn't want to play, he'd find some other place for them. Here we were winning and he was going out of his way to make a mountain out of a molehill.

He strutted out of there like he'd performed some sort of public service. I sat down by my locker and a lot of the guys came to me to tell me not to take it to heart, that it was typical of Finley. I appreciated those who did this. I wish there had been more of them. I went out tonight and got two hits, but we lost. Who gives a damn? Right now, I couldn't care less. The more I think about it, the madder I get. I've done my best for this ball club. I've been a good ballplayer. And I'm a man. I'm not perfect; but who is? There was no need to deliberately humiliate me in front of my teammates. Finley has treated a lot of people badly, but this is the first time in a long time for me. I feel less than a man for taking it from him. I feel really rotten.

Sunday, the 9th. The day after Finley took me apart, I spent the day with Lucius Allen and Kareem Abdul-Jabbar. They made me feel a little better. They made me feel like I wasn't alone out there in that jungle. Kareem pointed out how people expect a superstar to perform like a superman night after night and how his own teammates get jealous of the attention he gets. How you have to put yourself above it and learn to live with it. He said it was the price you pay for being a superstar. I see the sense of that. My problem is I haven't been willing to pay that price. I don't want to set myself above the others. I want to be one of the guys. Kareem said some day I'll see I can't be.

Lucius said I shouldn't expect my teammates to side with me. I was in a position of power and most of them weren't, and I couldn't expect them to risk their shaky positions to support me. He said I was the star and I had to be behind them when they needed it—but couldn't expect them to be behind me. He pointed out that I had to pat them on the back, but that they wouldn't think to pat me. One who was willing was John Summers. He came to me Saturday and said he was with me, he was staying on my case.

I didn't play that night. My shoulder hurt and I said the hell with it. I played today and got two hits and we won, 5–4, but we almost blew a four-run lead before it was over. We haven't played a good game since Finley decided it was time for him to talk to his boys. I didn't play a good game, despite the two hits. I got picked off first, for one thing. I was there physically, but not mentally. My mind was on Finley. For the first time in years I had let him get to me.

I figure he's jealous of me. He has more money than I'll make in my lifetime. He's succeeded in business the way I never will. But he resents it when anyone steals the spotlight from him. I'm sure he hated it when I was on the cover of *Time* and he wasn't. I'm sure he resents my prominence. Well, there's nothing I can do about that.

But I figured there was something I could do about him making me feel like less than a man. I knew I had to stand up to him before I could forget the incident and go back to baseball. So tonight I telephoned Finley. I said I wanted to talk to him about the talk he'd put out the other night.

He said, very sarcastically, "What do you have to say, Mr. Jackson?"

"I don't know why you don't like me," I said, "but I know you don't. I don't know if it dates back to my first holdouts. I know a lot of people feel that you don't like anyone who takes the spotlight away from you. Whatever the reason, I am not going to be treated the way you treated me the other day.

"You don't have to like me, but you do have to treat me like a man. You did not treat me like a man the other day. You did not try to find out what had happened or why it had happened or who was to blame. You put all the blame on me and you went out of your way to humiliate me in front of my team-mates.

"I have been trying to figure out why I didn't punch you right in the mouth and I have decided it was because I have respect for my teammates and didn't want to cause any more trouble than you had already caused. I didn't want to sink to your level. But most of what you said simply wasn't true and I am not going to stand still and let you heap shit all over me ever again."

"I don't have to listen to this!" he said.

"Well, I listened to you and I think you owe it to me to listen to me. You said if any player didn't want to play here, you'd find some other place for him to play. Well I'm telling you right now, I don't want to play here anymore. I know my teammates have made me the ballplayer I am and I don't want to leave them. But as much as I love them, that's how much I hate you. I don't want to play for you anymore, so I can't play with them anymore.

"And when you find me a place to play, you make sure it's a place I want to play because if I don't want to go there, I won't go. I'm a player other people want playing for them—even if you don't want me. I'm going to use that power. You're not going to tell me what to do, because if I don't want to do it, I won't do it. And it's gonna make you look bad. You said there were some bad guys on this ball club, but the worst one is you. If there's a horse's ass on this team, it's Charlie Finley!"

With that, Finley, who had been huffing and puffing and saying he didn't have to listen and threatening to hang up, finally said he wasn't going to listen to any more and did hang up. Well, it was done and I felt good for having done it. Maybe I had sunk to his level, but I hadn't dragged him down in a crowd. I'd called from the clubhouse, but only the trainer and a clubhouse custodian were there as witnesses.

I wasn't scared at what I'd done. I know now my power as an important player is real. The game can get along without me. The game can get along without Finley, too. Better players than me have come and gone—and so have better owners than Finley. But as long as I'm playing, I'm important to the people that pay salaries and want to pull in crowds and win pennants and make money. I'm more important than a manager. If it came to a test between me and Dark, for example, I'd win, because I can win more games for a team than a manager can. Maybe it's unfair, but that's the way it is. And I'm still a man. I have a right to be treated decently and to holler when I'm hurt.

I know what will happen now—nothing. Charlie won't trade me because I asked to be traded. Maybe next winter or next year, but not now. He needs me now to help him win and he wants to win because it makes him look good. He won't even tell anyone about this because it would make him look bad. If I was an ordinary player I'd be benched or suspended or fined or traded or released, but I'm not an ordinary player. Charlie will let it go because he figures no one else knows about this but me and him. He'll pretend it never happened. He'll talk to me when it's time to talk to me as if I never told him off. But I don't think he'll ever tell me off again—not until he's ready to turn me loose, not until he figures he can get by without me. We'll go back to where we were, kidding with one another, in a sort of armed truce. Now that I'm even with him, I don't hate him so much anymore.

Monday, the 10*th.* On the plane, on the flight to Boston, Dark came to me and asked me to dinner, but I said I had a date. Today, I did get together with Dark. It turned out Finley had telephoned him and asked Alvin to talk me out of wanting to be traded and to get me to feeling good about Finley again. It was a complete about-face, but that's Finley for you, Jekyll and Hyde. All right, I guess I'd made my point and should be grateful he was giving in, but it's just a pain in the ass to have to deal with.

Dark said we all have to expect Finley to meddle in everything, but he's the boss and it's his right and the best way to handle it is to not let it get to us. He said he hadn't spoken up for me during Finley's tirade because he was so embarrassed he couldn't look the man in the eye, much less talk back to him, and what he said wouldn't have affected Finley anyway. That wasn't the point. A manager has to stand up for his player if his player is in the right. But Dark's off by himself somewhere. I did agree with Alvin that I can't afford to let Finley affect my play, but it's easier said than done. Dark also told me Finley had reamed him out back in spring training for giving me the day off to play golf with the Vice President.

Tonight was a national-television game and Dick Williams was the guest commentator for the game between his two former teams. I talked to him before the game. I told him about the fuss with Finley and he said, "Well, Reggie, the more you have to deal with him, the more you'll see why I had to leave the man, even if I didn't want to leave the team." I said I could see it. I told him it had taken more guts to walk out on a championship team than most men have and I admire him for it.

He said he was happy with his life and wasn't hurting but he would like to be back in baseball. He said everyone was waiting to see what he'd say about the Red Sox or the A's and Finley, but he wasn't going to say anything because there wasn't anything to be gained by it.

On the way out of the clubhouse, we ran into the announcers, Curt Gowdy and Tony Kubek. In talking to Gowdy I told him about this thing on my mind about Finley. He knew about it. Everyone did. About Finley's part, not my part. Gowdy said that the higher you got on the ladder, the more people were going to try to knock you off—that it happened in his business and was bound to in mine. He said that the only thing you can do is be honest with yourself and do your job as best you can. I feel as if he's been around and knows what he's talking about and I thanked him.

By the batting cage, all the media wanted to know about me and Finley. I talked to them about it, but I didn't tell them about my call to Charlie. Dark came to me and told me I had a call from Charlie. I told him I wouldn't take it. I told him I had a game to play and I wasn't going to permit him to take me out of it with any more of his talk. Dark said he'd been asked to ask me special. "Hey, man," I said, "I just don't want to talk to him unless he's going to tell me I'm traded or fired or something like that." Alvin told me Finley said he couldn't afford to trade me, but he did want to make peace with me. He said Finley was a different man today than he had been the other day and, if he was holding out his hand, I should shake it. We all had to work at keeping him happy for the sake of the team.

Alvin was almost begging, so I gave in and went in and took the telephone and talked to Finley. I'd made him wait and he'd waited. He said we should let bygones be bygones. He said I should go out and play ball the way I could and to hit a homer for him and one for myself. I said I'd do my best and thanked him for calling and hung up. I think Finley respected me for respecting myself and standing up to him, which is fine except he keeps putting people to the test. You never know what to expect from him except the unexpected.

I doubled, but I didn't hit a homer. I haven't hit a homer since I hit two in one game six or seven games ago. And I don't feel like I'm going to hit one for a while. My shoulder is hurting from my bout with Billy, and I'm not swinging strong. Anyway, Luis Tiant was pitching and it's hard to hit homers off of him.

The last time I hit off of him, he had been needling me, "I gonna get ya." He struck me out. He hollered, "I got you that time, big guy."

It broke me up. I hit a home run and as I ran around the bases I pointed at him and laughed and hollered, "I got ya a big one."

And he said, "Is OK, is good, big guy, you go ding-dong off

me all you want as long as I win the game. You laugh now, I laugh last."

He was right, too. He won that one and he won this one, 4–1, beating Blue.

He wins because he's smart. He's supposed to be 33, but he may be 43. He's been around and he got to the big leagues late. And by the time he got here he knew what he was doing. He has about 33 different pitches and about 33 different motions, and you never know what he's going to throw you or where it's going to come from. He starts and stops, starts and stops, gives you a little of this, a little of that. Hell, sometimes he turns his back on you. He looks out over left field, but before you know it he's wheeled one in knee-high on the outside corner. He's hard to hit and the hardest to steal on.

He's one of the three or four best pitchers in the league. He can't overpower you, but he can outmaneuver you. He has fun with you. But it's no fun to try to hit him. He's one of the few who can make a fool out of you. He embarrasses you. I like to face the best pitchers. I like the challenge. But I don't like to face him because he can make you look so bad. I like to watch him pitch to other hitters.

Wednesday, the 12*th*. The *Sports Illustrated* cover story came out. Coming out right after the *Time* cover story, it's stirring up a lot of talk. The story is titled "Everyone Is Helpless and in Awe," which is a little heavy. John Summers told me one of the players had the magazine and asked him, "Who's the asshole on the cover?" I won't say who, but it's a guy I've befriended and felt close to, and here he's sniping at me behind my back.

I'm beginning to wonder if it's worth it. I mean I don't need it now, these stories. I don't need my face on the cover of magazines. I've been there. I know it's supposed to be part of my job. I cooperate with the press. I talk straight to the guys. I give 'em almost all the time they want. And it's fun to be famous. But it stops being fun when it starts to hurt me. If it cuts me off from my teammates, it's no good to me.

I've been burned, but I haven't gone into a shell. I've had writers talk to me one way and write another way. I've told members of the media things in confidence and had the trust broken. I've been misquoted. They've said I said things I never said. And it haunts you because the wrong quotes keep turning up in other stories. It's something you just have to learn to live with, I guess.

Most of the writers have been good to me. They've built me up and treated me fair and tried to quote me accurately. But the writers don't have room to put in everything I say. When they take comments out of context, it sounds like something else than what I tried to say. If they can't go into depth about something, maybe they shouldn't go there at all.

I was told that Leonard Koppett of the *New York Times*, who is now working out of the Bay Area, called me "the best reporter" among athletes. By that he meant that I saw where the story was in something and was able to give the writers stuff they could use. That's a compliment and I appreciate it. The writer who's working with me on this book says I shouldn't stop talking freely to writers even if I'm burned once in a while, because it's through the writers and broadcasters that the public gets to know me. And that I have a beautiful image now for being a good guy, honest and outspoken, which I can live with long after I'm no longer playing. I can see the sense in that. The only thing is that I don't like stories that show me as something other than I am. And make me misunderstood.

I'm not perfect. I'm not looking for puff pieces. I'm a little thin-skinned. I suppose most people are, more than they realize. Most people don't have to live with their lives being laid out in public. But I can live with criticism. As stories go, this one in *Sports Illustrated* was a good one, better than the one in *Time*. They used a term—"superduperstar"—I didn't like, but there was some strong stuff in the story.

Richie Allen says in there he wonders how I can do so much talking when I never hit .300. It hurts, but it's true, I never hit .300. Stan Bahnsen says that he thinks I'm a helluva player but he doesn't like me as a person. If that's the way he feels, that's real, and it's fine. But I expected to see some stuff in there about people like Frank Robinson who helped me along the way and about my feelings about my teammates and the help I get from them.   That wasn't in there because it wasn't controversial.   It isn't fair to me because it makes me look like an ungrateful guy.

The other night I talked to Darold Knowles.   I said I didn't feel like one of the guys on the team.

"Well, Buck," he said, "you're the MVP, you're on the cover of every magazine, you're out of our class."

I said, "I'm not out of the Cat's class, or Bando's."

"They're not on the covers of those magazines."

I asked him why the guys all went their own ways after games and never asked me along.

"The married guys go home," he answered. "The single guys go out looking for girls.   You've always got a girl.   You've got people to see in every town.   You've got a lot of business to take care of at home.   The guys don't want to bother you."

"The guys don't mind coming to me with their troubles, but there's only a few guys I can go to with my troubles."

He said, "They don't think you've got troubles.   They think you've got all the answers."

"I try to pick the guys up when they're down.   But no one tries to pick me up when I'm down.   I need my batteries recharged sometimes, too."

"Well," he replied, "you're just going to have to go to the guys and let them know this because they don't know it now."

I can talk trouble to John Summers.   He's young, but he sees through things.   But then John's got his troubles, too, and he can't see through his the way he can see through mine.   He pinch-hit and struck out last night and he asked me to wait for him after the game because he wanted to talk to me.   He said he can hit in this league, but he can't prove it if he sits on the bench all week and gets one swing a week as a pinch-hitter. He's afraid he's going to go down.   He asked me to talk to Dark and Finley and ask for him to get his chance to prove himself.   I admitted I didn't want to because of the way it was between me and Finley right now.   He said he talked to his wife and they decided he should have it out with them.

Today he talked to them.   He said Finley told him on the phone Dark wanted to send him down.   He said Dark told him

Finley wanted to send him down. He knew one was lying, but he didn't know which one. He said he told Dark he could do a better job for him than a lot of the players on the team. Alvin said maybe he could, and he'd give him every chance to prove it before he was sent down, but if The Man wanted to send him down, there wasn't anything he could do about it. Later, Alvin must have gotten a phone call from Finley, because he sent for Summers and told him he was going to go down the end of the week. Summers was sick about it and so was I.

That night there was a situation where John could be used and he went up to Alvin and asked to be used. Alvin didn't answer him and didn't use him. Afterwards, Summers said he had lost all respect for Alvin. Summers said he felt like he might as well quit the game and go home. I talked him out of it. I told him a guy is going to get the shaft in this game until he proves himself. He should go where he had to go and prove himself when he got the chance and when he got the power he wouldn't get the shaft anymore.

I had mixed feelings about it. I felt sorry for the fellow. He is a fan and a friend. He's helped me and I wanted to help him. But going to The Man wouldn't get me anywhere. The funny thing is The Man knows what he's doing in these cases. It's the way Finley does things that fucks us up, not the things he does. He does know talent, and when he makes moves with players, they may not look right at first but they usually work out right in the end. He usually comes up with somebody better. I know John is good people, but I don't know how good a player he is. I do know this is a business, and you aren't going to turn a profit if you make moves based on sentiment. It's just that it's a very hard business to be in sometimes. Most ballplayers don't make it big and are kicked around from city to city. There's no security or stability in their lives or in their families' lives. After a lot of years, they're left with little to show for all they've put into it. My troubles are nothing compared to most. It's just that when they're yours, they hurt the most.

Before Tuesday night's game, Billy North came to me to tell me my troubles were over as far as he was concerned. He said he was sorry when The Man got into it. He said The Man was way out of line. He also told me a lot of the players were rapping me behind my back, and he felt bad because he'd brought a lot of this on. He thought it would be better for me if they saw we were friends again. He suggested we forget our differences and play ball.

I said, "Hey, right on, let's play ball." I appreciated him coming to me.

That night we lost, 10–9, despite an outasight five-run rally in the ninth. Tonight we lost, 5–3. Deron Johnson hit homers in both games. I'm not hitting homers. I've lost the RBI lead to Jeff Burroughs. I'm in that slump I knew was on its way.

Sunday, the 16*th*. We had an off-day Thursday. I was really down, so I went and picked up this girl I'm dating, Mary. We spent the day together and I poured out my heart to her, which is when a woman can mean something to a man.

Friday, the Yankee series started and I went to Dark because my shoulder was sore as hell and I asked for a couple of days off so I could heal up. He said he'd appreciate it if I could play because just my presence in the lineup meant a lot to the team. I said that was good to hear, but I really could use the rest.

He said, "Well, I'd like you to play."

I finally gave in. "All right, all right, I'll play!"

Every game counts, but the players should count for something too. I've busted my ass for the team and now it can do something for me by giving me a couple of games off so I can get back in shape. They'll risk the rest of the season for a couple of games in June. They couldn't care less for the player. Well, fuck it. It just saps all the enthusiasm out of you.

We lost, 5–1, to a pitcher by the name of Tidrow on Friday night. I couldn't swing the bat right and didn't get a hit. Bill Sudakis hit Holtzman for a home run and a double, driving in three runs. We won, 9–1, Saturday afternoon because Bando hit a three-run homer and Rudi ripped a grand slam in support of Blue. I got a dinky little single. But we lost, 5–3, today and

I went without a hit again. On top of everything, I crashed into North making a catch. A ball was hit into right-center. We both dove at it at the same time. I caught the ball in my glove as he banged into my back. The ball jarred loose. His head hit my back and my knee hit his head and my foot hit his neck as I fell backwards on him. I got up right away, but he didn't. He was knocked unconscious for a few seconds. He left the game and I stayed in. But I was shook and I butchered a ball in the ninth that helped them win. The hell of it is the coincidence. It was just an accident, but everyone sure as hell is going to tie it into our fight, as if we were ready to run right over each other and didn't care about one another. No one knows we made up.

Since our fight, the A's have lost seven out of ten games. We had a big lead built up over Kansas City and Texas, but now it is getting away from us. I was leading the league in batting average, home runs and runs-batted-in, but I have lost 35 points from my average, I have not hit a home run, and I have driven in just two runs. Rod Carew is leading the league in average, Richie Allen and Willie Horton are leading in homers, and Jeff Burroughs is leading in RBIs. It gets away from you fast.

I have been hurting like hell and haven't had the time off to heal. Ray Fosse claims he ruptured a disc in his back breaking Billy and me up. He had an operation about a week back and he will be on the disabled list awhile, which catches us short of catchers. Gene Tenace was returned to catching, but he prefers first. He says he has a pinched nerve in his neck, so Larry Haney is handling the big mitt. I don't think the fight was responsible for all this, but people will believe what they want to believe. What I believe is we have been going bad since Finley popped off.

Thursday, the 20th. Just like I figured, the writers hinted bad blood was behind the collision. I had breakfast with Billy and he was still groggy. He didn't play Monday night and I shouldn't have played either. I'd gone to a doctor before Sunday's game to get a shot of cortisone to ease the pain in my shoulder, but after the collision it hurt worse than ever. I went back to the doctor and got three shots Monday, but it didn't take all the pain away. I told Dark there was no way I could play and he said OK. But late in the game, when it was tied, I was in the clubhouse listening in on the radio when the trainer, Romo, comes in and says Dark wants to know if I could pinch-hit. It pissed me off.

I said, "Hey, Joe, you know I've taken cortisone shots and am hurting. If I have to play, I will. I'm a pro. I'll tear the motherfucker off the hinges if it will help us. But you're a trainer, you shouldn't even be asking me."

He said, "I'm not asking, Alvin is."

"You go out and tell him I don't feel up to it," I said, "but if he asks me, I'll do it."

So he went out and then he came back and he said Alvin's asking you. I went out and he sent me up with a man on first and I couldn't swing the bat and I made out. I went back to the clubhouse steaming. All they care about is what they can get out of you.

We won in the ninth on a wild pickoff throw by their catcher, Carlton Fisk.

Tuesday night, Alvin left me alone. I didn't play. We got ten hits off Rogelio Moret, but lost, 6–1. Last night I was back on the bench, but was brought in to pinch-hit again. There's just no way they're going to give me two games off. With a man on in the ninth, Tiant threw me a hooker and I hammered it on a line 400 feet to the center-field fence, where it was caught. Don't ask me how I hit it that hard or that far because I don't know. It was an accident.

The guys figured Dark blew this one by batting me before there was a man in scoring position. My long fly would have brought in a runner from third. It was a terrific pitcher's duel between Blue and Tiant, and Tiant took it, 2–1, in eleven innings. Blue was beautiful, but Alvin lifted him with one on and one out in the eleventh for no reason that's worth anything. He brought in Fingers, who walked the first man he faced. Dark lifted him and brought in Lindblad, who walked the first man *he* faced. That loaded the bases and Bob Montgomery hit a fly ball that brought in the winning run and we were beat. It was unbelievable.

I didn't think about it too much because I don't second-guess a lot. The manager makes the moves and I've learned to live with them. When Williams was managing us he made so few mistakes the players stopped thinking about his moves. But a lot of the guys are taking apart every move made by Alvin.

Coming into the clubhouse, Bando kicked a trash-basket across the room, which quieted everyone up in a hurry. He hollered, "That motherfucker couldn't manage a fucking meat market!"

Fingers was the first to agree, saying, "He couldn't manage a marbles tournament."

The funny thing was, Dark had walked into the room when Bando did, but Bando hadn't seen him. Dark usually goes his own way to his room at the other end of the clubhouse, but this time he had followed us into our clubhouse. He said later he wanted to sympathize with the guys and with Blue for losing such a tough game. But Blue and the guys figured he'd lost it for them and they didn't want his sympathy. Glen Dickey, a writer for the *San Francisco Chronicle,* was there. The players call him "Poison Pen" because they figure he'll write anything to make a story. We all saw right away he would write this thing and stir up trouble.

Bando saw what the situation was and he sort of bowed his head and walked to his locker and sat down with his eyes on the ground, not looking at anyone. And Dark walked up and down looking at Sal. You could see he was trying to figure out whether or not to talk to him. For the first time Dark was pissed off. Finally he went over to him and asked him to talk it over in the manager's office. Sal went with him and they talked it out and shook hands on it.

It would be forgotten except that it will be in the papers and the people won't ever let us forget it. Sal said he was sorry. You have to understand about Bando. He's a fiery guy with a trigger temper. He speaks his mind. And he speaks the truth. If he says Dark has done a bad job of managing, that's the way it was. But he wouldn't have said it if he'd known Dark was there. He'd say it to Alvin's face and he'd say it to his teammates, but he would never say it to Alvin in front of the team and a writer because he is not the sort of guy to go out of his way to embarrass anyone. He is a competitor, who hates to lose. He was bleeding because we'd lost one we should have won.

Bando really feels bad about it, but it was good in one way because Alvin showed us a lot of class the way he handled it. He didn't jump all over Sal or suspend him or fine him or even reprimand him. He talked to him, man to man, and let it go. He said something about Christ teaching us to love, which is Alvin's way, quoting from the Bible. Finley phoned him today, of course, after it was spread all over the newspapers, but Dark didn't take any action, anyway. And Charlie didn't show up to make a speech to Bando, so maybe my little talk with The Man made him cautious this time.

I spoke to Sal last night and told him I understood his outburst and I was in his corner. He thanked me. Then I went to Alvin and I said, "Skip, forget it, tomorrow's another day. We'll all be here and life will go on as always." He had been sitting there, staring at the floor, really down, and he looked up and sort of smiled and said he appreciated it. I could see it gave him a little lift. I felt sorry for him.

The thing is, you shouldn't have to feel sorry for a manager. It might be better to hate him. He should be strong. It's as if someone has taken away Dark's inner strength. He should have been angry about losing, not coming into the clubhouse to hold our hands. We're pros, we don't need anyone to come in to try to cheer us up. Alvin doesn't know what to do. And he always winds up doing the wrong thing. And all we have to do is keep our cool, but it seems to be the thing we do worst.

Friday, the 21*st.* I'm moving into my new place now. It's a condominium that is costing me 85 grand. It's in a section called Hiller Highlands, a series of hills overlooking the Bay. I'm on a street named, of all things, Yankee Hill. From the living room balcony I can see from San Jose to Sausalito—about 40 miles—on a clear day. I'm surrounded by other condominiums in this complex, yet each one is sort of secluded. I can have a lot of privacy. No one knows or cares who comes or goes. All the other owners are white, but I don't care about that. Most are old, but I don't care about that, either.

It's a beautiful area, a beautiful layout and a beautiful house. It's a big house, about 2700 square feet. The bedrooms are downstairs, the kitchen and living areas upstairs. There's room to stretch out. And room for company. My brother Slug, his wife Maria and their daughter Imara are coming to spend the summer with me here. He's going to do some work for the tax people in San Francisco. My sister Beverly and her husband Maurice are going to get me furniture from their store in Baltimore. I have a lot of plants around. I love plants. It's gonna be nice having a place of my own here like I do in Arizona.

Sunday, the 23rd. The Kansas City Royals came to town closing in on us. They left falling back after losing three of four to us. They came to town shooting off their mouths about beating us. We beat them and shut them up. Before the first game of the series Thursday, there was a story in the *Oakland Tribune* quoting Cookie Rojas and Amos Otis to the effect that all the feuding and fussing on the A's is getting to the team, that we're not the team we were, that we don't want to win that much anymore and that they've become a better team and were going to win the division this year.

I cut out the article and taped it to the batting cage and pointed it out to the other players at practice that night. The guys laughed it off, but it made 'em mean. The Royals are fools. They should let sleeping giants lie, but instead they woke us up. They are not as good a team as we are. They know it and we know it. If we are fucking up they should shut up and sneak up on us. Maybe that way they'd whip us. Just shut up and leave us be. Don't be fools.

When the series started we were only four games over .500. We have won three divisional titles in a row and we know we will win a fourth. We can't get worked up about it. We win a few and build up a big lead and we let down a little. We are overconfident and there is a little danger of complacency, but we are professionals and we will play the way we can when we

have to stay on top.   The Royals have never won a pennant.
They've never even made the playoffs.   And here they were
popping off about being better than we are.   Hey, man, if you
are, show it, don't talk about it.   They've got some good ballplayers.   Otis can hit.   Mayberry can hit.   Busby throws bul-
lets.   But they're not enough.   They're becoming a good team,
but they're not a good team yet.   They're up with us now, but
they'll be far back at the finish.   They finished second last season, but I don't think they'll finish second this season.   I think
Texas will, because Billy Martin has as many good players on
his team and he has them pulling together and playing as a
team.

The Royals are not together as a team.   They have an
owner—Ewing Kauffman—who is meddling like most owners,
and their team isn't used to it.   He just fired the general manager, Cedric Tallis, who traded them into a team.   I guess he
was running the team, and the owner wanted to run it.   Well,
he'll run it right into the ground if he's not careful.   Everyone
can't get away with what Finley gets away with, because they
don't have the players Finley has on his side.

Before the first game of the series the Royals were kidding
me and North about being Muhammad Ali and Joe Frazier.
We let the Cat loose on them and he shut them out, 4–0.   I
didn't get a hit but I was happy for him because he has not
been pitching that well.   He had lost three straight, but when
it's time to win one he's the one who can win it for you.   Friday
night they had us on the hook, but we got four runs in the last
of the eighth to beat 'em, 5–4.   Saturday's game was tied, 2–2,
into the last of the ninth, Holtzman against Paul Splittorff.
Bando doubled and I singled him to third.   Rudi was walked.
Garber, a reliever, threw a wild pitch and they lost again.   We
didn't beat them as much as they beat themselves.   They sal-
vaged one Sunday, 4–1, but they were beat back by then.   We
played pretty well.   I played right field, but didn't hit much.
Dick Green played second base.   Having him back helps a
hell of a lot.

Hunter and Holtzman gave us top pitching in this series,
which is what we expect from them when a series means some-

thing. Holtzman is a special sort of person and pitcher. He came here from the Cubs where they didn't know how to win, and he fit in fine with a team that knows the way. He's very reserved. He's a very unemotional man. He's the same when he's losing as when he's winning. He accepts life the way it is and he doesn't let it get to him. He hates Finley and he isn't turned on by baseball. He's in it for the money and he makes no bones about it. It's a business to him and when he thinks he has enough money and can get out of the business he'll go and he'll never look back.

He'll go to the wall for you, but he won't try to run through it. He doesn't give that little extra that might make him great because he doesn't care about being great. He'll win 20 games a season or close to it and that's all he wants. He'll win the big games in the playoffs and World Series for you almost as surely as Catfish will because Kenny is cool and confident and he has talent and knows how to use it and isn't affected by it being a big game.

He throws about 80 fastballs out of a hundred. He doesn't have a lot of heat, but he doesn't have to because he sets the batters up so well. He'll throw ten, fifteen change-ups a game. Six or seven curves. He puts everything exactly where he wants it. He won't give a hitter much to hit. He's smooth. He doesn't seem to be working as hard at it as Hunter or Blue. Well, he isn't.

He gives me a funny feeling. You know sometimes there's a situation where I have to get myself in scoring position for us to win. I figure I'll do anything to get to second. I'll stretch a single into a double. I'll steal. I'll drive my car on the field. Hire a cab. Anything. You got to get there so you get there. If I don't—and there's a lot of times I don't—I'm mad at myself. Some guys don't care. They say, "Well, I tried," and let it go at that. Kenny is like that. And yet he wins. Maybe he could win more. I like him as a person, but he bugs me as a player.

There are guys who would do anything to do well and it doesn't always work for them. Deron Johnson is in his mid-thirties. He's played pro ball about fifteen years. He's played for six or seven teams. He's been bounced around. But he's always given a day's work for a day's pay. He has swung a big bat and has had his big years. He hit something like 20 homers and drove in something like 80 runs for us as designated hitter last season and he helped us a lot. But he didn't do much after August. He jammed his thumb, couldn't grip a bat right and didn't hit after that. He had a bad playoff and a bad World Series. Over the winter he had an operation on his thumb, but it didn't help.

He had a stretch there where he hit some homers so they hung onto him. But today he was sent in a waiver deal to Milwaukee. There is not a man on this team that does not feel bad about it. Going bad did not turn him bad. He had become family. It hurts. When a teammate who has been with you a long time is traded it's like having a brother sold from the family. But it's baseball, the hard reality of our life. He was making 85 or 90 grand a year and he wasn't giving us anything back. Finley got 20 or 25 grand back on him, saved the rest of his salary and they threw in a pitcher who was put in the minors. It was business and I can't blame The Man. My time will come, too.

Wednesday, the 26th. I looked forward to the Angels arriving in town because we need to gain some ground and they sure as hell aren't going to stop us. They're not going good. I feel sorry for Winkles and Robinson. I wanted to rap with them. I knew they weren't getting along and Winks's job was in jeopardy and Robby wanted it.

I didn't play much. I started the first game, but my back hurt so bad I had to get out of there. I went to the hospital and was told I had pulled a muscle. The doctor gave me a couple of shots to kill the pain and he told me I could play, but I figured, fuck it. I told Dark I wasn't going to play for a couple of games and he said it was all right if it made me all right. The A's can win from the Angels without me.

We won three in a row. Bando hit a grand slam and drove in five runs and the A's routed the Angels, 11–3, in the opener.

Blue breezed. Hunter won his tenth the next night, 6–1.
And Dave Hamilton pitched his first shutout of the season to
win the last day, 5–0. We didn't draw Ryan.

I got to Winks before the first game. Because of my bad legs
I do extra exercises on the field after the other guys have gone.
I was the only one out there when the Angels left and Winks
came walking across the field about an hour before the game.
I asked him what was happening. He said nothing good.
He said Dick Miller and some of the other southern California
writers had already fired him in the newspapers. He said the
players resented his rules and weren't respecting him.

I felt funny talking to him. He'd also been like a father to
me. Now the roles were reversed. But I had to say something
to him that might help him because I could see he needed
something. He was way down. He'd come out of college
without realizing the pressure of the pros and now the major
leagues had been beating on him. He seemed beat up.

I said, "Look, when they hired you out of college they knew
where you were coming from. If they won't give you a chance
to make the changes you have to make, that's not your fault.
If your rules aren't working, make different rules. Adjust.
No one knows more baseball than you do. Run the games
right and if you don't win, don't worry about it. You can't feel
you've failed.

"Look at the talent on your team. Go down the lineup,
first, second, third and so forth. Compare your club to ours.
Do you have one single regular who would be a regular with
us? No way. Robby's getting old and after you get him out,
who does the other team have to worry about? Ryan could
pitch for anyone, but Singer's hurt and after you face Ryan,
who does the other team have to worry about? You've got kids
who may get there, but they've got a long way to go. How the
hell can you expect to beat the Jolly Green Giant?"

He said you want to win so bad you think you can. He said
he'd been honest with everyone and what hurt was no one was
being honest with him. He said no one, not the owners, not
the general manager, not anyone, told him what his position

was. He said he only knew what the writers said. He told me he wasn't communicating with Frank. He said Frank seemed to have taken the team away from him.

I said, "I'm in a funny position because I probably like the two of you as well as I like anyone. I think Robby respects you as a manager and I know you respect him as a player. What happened is that other people probably got between you. You just have to try to get together and settle it."

He said he thought it was too late. I thought that was sad, and I told him so.

For three days all the talk was Winks was going to get fired. The talk kept getting worse and worse. Sometimes I think if you talk about something enough you may make it happen. Winks might not be on the ropes if the rumors hadn't put him there. The rumors were so strong by the end of the series that after the last game I went to the Angels' dressing room to talk to Winks again in his office.

I said, "Skip, now's the time to protect yourself. Whatever's gonna happen is gonna happen, but you can be prepared. Get out of the open and out of the line of fire. Quit talking about being fired and wait to see if it happens. Surround yourself with people who will give to you instead of taking from you. Stay close to your family and friends, your loved ones. Don't be afraid to lean on those you can count on." I told him he could count on me no matter what happened, and I would always be there for him when he wanted me. He thanked me. He was grateful for my friendship.

I saw him again at the airport. He said he heard they had called a meeting to fire him. I said I was sorry, that if he wasn't fired now he would be sooner or later so why worry about it? In sports a manager or a coach being canned isn't an embarrassment or anything like that. I said he was a good man, so there would always be good jobs for him to go to. If it happened, the thing to do was accept it and not behave badly about it. He said he was going to have to be honest, he was going to have to tell the truth about the way he'd been treated. I guess he'll just have to decide for himself how to handle it. I wished him well and went on my way.

I didn't really get to talk to Robby until we got to the airport after the last game to fly our separate ways. There was a little time there. I said I felt sorry for the spot Winks was in. Robby asked me why I felt for the man. Robby said, hell, that was baseball. I said I liked Winks and hated to see him lose his job. Robby shrugged and said he liked Winks too. But he hadn't done his job so he had to go. They hadn't been talking to each other. He didn't know why, but they'd gotten out of touch. The ballplayers had begun to come to him and he wasn't going to turn them away even if the manager resented it.

I asked him who would take over. He said they wanted Dick Williams. I said there was no way Williams would go with them. Williams was a winner and there was no way he was going to go with a loser. Robby wasn't so sure. He figured if the numbers were right, Williams would go anywhere. I said I didn't think there was enough money to make Williams go where he shouldn't go, and if he did he'd be making a mistake. Robby said Drysdale wanted the job. I couldn't believe that; Don wasn't breaking his back broadcasting and he was leading too good a life to turn into a manager of a bad team at this time. Robby thought Drysdale wanted it but wouldn't get it.

I asked Robby if he wanted it, and he said he did. Gene Autry's a fine owner. He's never created problems for the players. Harry Dalton is maybe the best general manager there is. But, I said, they can't give you the job because they got the team in Orange County and that's John Birch country and there's too many who hate niggers there and you're a nigger. Frank sort of shrugged. I said if I had a team in Orange County, I wouldn't bring a black man in to manage.

I said if I had a team most places, I'd want Frank Robinson to be my manager. Frank Robinson has done more for me than anyone. Frank Robinson has done more for baseball players and for baseball than baseball has ever done for him. And if they don't get around to making him a manager somewhere soon, it is going to be baseball's loss—not Frank Robinson's loss. If he was white he would have been offered managers' jobs long ago. I told him he sure as hell shouldn't take the first lousy job offered him. He said he felt he could make it a good job, that he saw how Billy Martin had turned the Texas team into his team and made a winner out of a loser. Robby felt he could do the same with the Angels.

You speak to Winkles, you wonder why anyone wants the job. I want to own a team, not manage one. Managing has to be the worst job in the world.

Thursday, the 27th. Winks was fired today. I don't want to talk about it.

Friday, the 28th. Winks was fired and Williams was hired. And Finley let him go. I guess Finley figured he'd punished Dick enough. I didn't think Dick would take the job. I was surprised. But nothing should surprise me in sports. There's no way he can win with that team, not even Williams. Maybe next year. Or the year after. But not this year. He'll have to make it his team first. He'll have to make a lot of changes. I never yet knew a manager who could hit a home run for you, but a manager can get a player who is capable of hitting a home run and show him how.

I feel let down. I think what I really feel is jealousy. I want him with us. I don't want him over there managing them against us. And that's where he'll be the first of the month. Well, Williams is a manager, wherever he is. He's baseball. He's a smart baseball man. And a strong personality. He's flashy, flamboyant, a hot dog. He's what a team and a town needs that has to be turned around.

I hope Robby isn't too bitter. And Winks holds up. He told it the way it was, that he hadn't been told anything, that he'd been made to suffer, that he'd been treated terribly. I hope it doesn't hurt him. No one is bigger than the bosses. Or the game. The game goes on.

Sunday, the 30th. We lost three out of four in Kansas City. I'm as responsible as anyone. I got one stinking hit the whole series. I'm hurting and still a long way from right. I've lost my timing and I'm in trouble at the plate. I know it's there and I know it'll come back, but I don't know when. I don't believe in changing a lot of things. I know what has worked for me in the past will work for me in the future.

I could use some breaks. I usually get some from the umpires. I treat them decent so they treat me decent. The close pitch to me usually is called a ball. But right now I can't even get the calls.

In the first game in Kansas City, Marty Pattin was pitching with three balls and one strike on me. He threw one eye-high and six inches outside, and I was ready to take my walk when the umpire said it was a strike. I took my time, reached down to get some dirt and said real soft, "The ball was a little high and wide, wasn't it?" He didn't say anything then, but the next time I came up, he said, "Reggie, that pitch was high. I called it wrong and I'm sorry." Well, what could I say? I said OK. Sometimes you speak before you think and the ump had just called it too fast.

I ran into him outside the stadium that night and he thanked me for not having made a big show of bawling him out in front of the crowd. I said we all make mistakes and I'm not looking to try to make anyone look bad. Maybe the next time I'm running to first I'll get the close call. Maybe not. But at least I know I treated some good guys right who have a bad job to do.

We lost that game by one run. We won the second one big. Campy went on a tear and Abbott breezed. But then Busby beat Blue, 2–0, before almost 40,000—the largest crowd they've ever had in the Kansas City ballpark. And then we blew a lead and lost a lousy game, 8–7, in the ninth when Dark started to run in a lot of relievers and Knowles got run right out of the ballpark. It doesn't seem to be Darold's year and we're right back in trouble, with KC and Texas within a game or two of us. The only one we should have lost was the Busby–Blue matchup. Busby gave up five hits and Blue four, but Busby didn't give up any runs and Blue gave up two.

Busby is the best pitcher to break into this league since Blue; the best young guy in the league right now. He has a good fastball, a good slider, a good change-up and a real good curveball. He's got four top pitches and he can get all of them over all of the time. He's good-sized, has stamina and is a good competitor. He's confident. He'll challenge you, which few pitchers will do. He's a lot like Hunter. He's not afraid to pitch to your strength. He'll give you balls to hit, but you'll have to hit them to beat him. He may give you what you like to hit, but not when you're ready to hit it. For a young pitcher he has a lot of poise. I really respect him.

So we go to Anaheim. Winks won't be there, but Williams will be. They gave Dick a couple of days to straighten out his affairs, so he'll make his debut against his old team in his new town. I'll have to talk to Finley about how he arranges to get us in such dramatic situations.

5 ☆ CONVERSATION WITH CHARLIE

Monday, July 15th. I keep getting these calls from Finley. I thought you might want to hear what a conversation with Charlie was like. So I taped one. You'll have to imagine how Charlie talks—deep voice, very slow, very theatrical. I talk real nice, of course:

C: Reggie, this is Charlie.
R: I guessed that right off. Charlie, this is Reggie.
C: All right, Reggie. Howareya feeling?
R: Fine, Mr. Finley, fine. And you?
C: Just fine, Reggie. Just fine. That was a fine doubleheader you boys played yesterday.
R: Especially since we won both games.
C: I thought Alvin made some good moves.
R: How'd you know that?
C: Listen, if I don't see the game, I'm listening. I don't miss a single game.
R: You listened to the game yesterday?
C: I listened to both games.
R: Yeah?
C: I listened to both games. I always listen to the games, Reggie.

R: Yeah?

C: What's strange about that? You know that.

R: I didn't know you listened to every one.

C: I listen to every game that's humanly possible. All I do is call the radio station.

R: Can you afford it?

C: I have a WATS line. [You can make all the calls you want for one base price.] When the time comes that I don't have the money, I know where I can get it.

R: From where?

C: Well, I think I know a millionaire that lives out there by the name of Reggie Jackson.

R: Yeah, I'd do what I could for you.

C: Well, I'm sure you would. Sure you would! What the hell, you know turnabout is fair play.

R: That's right.

C: I've loaned you money at times.

R: That's right. Hey, the guys were real happy about your getting us the change in flights we wanted.

C: Well, it's just a pleasure to be of service.

R: They were happy, and I thought I would relay that message to you.

C: Nice to hear some nice things once in a while instead of all this bitching.

R: Well, they said they were happy. Anyway, you know the guys that are going to the All-Star Game, they were wondering if they could maybe take their wives. [Long pause] You stopped talking.

C: You're not kidding.

R: What happened?

C: I'm not sending the players' wives to the All-Star Game, no.

R: Well, you have every other year.

C: I don't know about that.

R: You know, the guys thought it would be nice.

C: Oh, yeah, sure. Real nice. Real nice. I said I'd take them to the World Series.

R: This year?

C: What?

R: In nineteen seventy-four?

C: Yes, sir.

R: How about this All-Star Game?

C: I'm not sending any wives to the All-Star Game, no. I can't afford it.

R: You did last year.

C: I don't know that I did.

R: You did in Atlanta. They all went to Atlanta.

C: You don't know that I did.

R: Yeah, you did.

C: No, I don't think so.

R: Yes, you did. See, you forgot already.

C: Well, maybe I did. I don't know.

R: Okay, I'll tell them it's not possible this year.

C: Why not?

R: Because you said no.

C: Even if I said yes, you couldn't take anybody. You're not married.

R: I could always take a girl friend or something, you know.

C: Oh, I see. Girl friends come next.

R: Well, you know. I mean, I gotta have a girl friend, don't I?

C: No objections to that.

R: Okay.

C: It's your prerogative.

R: What else is new?

C: I think things are looking up.

R: Are they?

C: I think things are looking up. I think that.

R: I guess things are looking up.

C: You know, if everybody just does their job, I can't see us doing anything but repeating.

R: Same here. Hey, maybe it would be nice to kick the Dodgers' asses in a World Series. They talk too much.

C: I'd like to play those Dodgers, you know.

R: Me too.

C: I would just really love to play those Dodgers, because I think that by beating them it would help our attendance.

R: Yeah, me, too.

C: Because I just got a sneaking hunch that Californians think the only baseball team that's in California is the Dodgers. What do you think?

R: Well, you might be right there. I don't really know. You think we're going to stay in Oakland, or what?

C: They say it's one of the greatest towns in America. Weather's fine. Beautiful stadium.

R: If we win, man, shit we ain't gonna be able to go nowhere.

C: Huh?

R: If we win, we ain't gonna be able to move. I just bought a house out here, too.

C: Oh, did you?

R: Yeah. I might have to put a "for sale" sign on it.

C: Where'd you buy your house?

R: Berkeley Hills.

C: What kind of house is it?

R: A condominium.

C: Boy, you gotta be careful buying those things.

R: Why is that?

C: How old is the building?

R: A year.

C: Every time you turn around, after awhile, there is something you gotta chip in for.

R: I've had pretty good luck with mine in Arizona. And this one here has been fine so far. Of course, I've only been in it a few weeks.

C: How many rooms you got?

R: It's twenty-seven hundred square feet. It's pretty big.

C: That don't tell me anything. How many rooms?

R: I got four bedrooms.

C: Four bedrooms!

R: Four bedrooms.

C: Four bedrooms!

R: Three bedrooms. I'm gonna make an office out of the other one.

C: I see.

R: A utility room. An extra room for luggage.

C: How do you like your new suitcase?

R: I ain't got it.

C: Where is it?

R: I loaned it to John Summers.

C: Well, all you gotta do is call John Summers and tell him to ship it back.

R: Yeah, well, you sent him back to the minor leagues, you know. He needs one, you know. He's too far away to send it. I'll get it back when he brings it back in September, when you call up the minor-leaguers.

C: September?

R: September, yeah.

C: Is that a promise?

R: Yeah, that's when he's gonna bring it back.

C: All right, I'll let you have a new one if you promise to give the other one back.

R: Oh, yeah, I promise to give the other one back.

C: All right. You gonna send me a note in writing?

R: Yeah. I owe you. We settled it on the phone.

C: That's no good.

R: No good?

C: I want something with your signature: "I hereby promise to return the other suitcase no later than September one as a result of receiving one of the new superduper suitcases."

R: Okay. I like that "superduper" word there.

C: I figured you'd pick that one up. That's the first time I ever heard it.

R: What are we getting from the Angels? They get Williams, we get Winkles? We get Winkles for Williams?

C: No, we got Winkles because you're hard to handle.

R: Is that right?

C: Winkles said he could handle you like a baby.

R: That's the first bad deal you ever made.

C: Are you serious? [Long pause as he speaks to someone on his end of the phone.] Who? Frank Lane? Tell Mr. Lane I'm talking to Mr. Reggie Jackson and I'll call him back as soon as I'm off the line.

R: Who's he work with now, Frank Lane?

C: He's a superduper scout for the Texas Strangers.

R: The Texas Strangers, huh?

C: The Texas Strangers!

R: They're startin' to find themselves now.

C: Well, I'll tell you, they got a pretty good manager down there.

R: You shoulda got Billy Martin.

C: Well, I gotta look out for Reggie.

R: Yeah, me and him mighta went at it, huh?

C: You said it.

R: It would either be me or you. I'd get into it with him or you would. One of us would get into it with him.

C: Well, I'll tell you, he doesn't scare me at all.

R: No?

C: No, sir!

R: There aren't too many that do scare you, are there, Charlie?

C: Well, you're the same way, aren't you, Reggie?

R: That's right.

C: Yes, sir. Yes, sir. You know, some people when they see trouble brewin', they run. . . .

R: You and I see trouble brewin', we jump right in the pot, right?

C: That's right. We jump in to face it. It's the difference between sittin' on the bench and playin' in the ball game.

R: That's right.

C: Really, it is!

R: I believe you.

C: Hey, you know I like to stand up and fight for what's right. But I try to make sure I'm right before I stand up. You know?

R: Yeah, I know. Well, I better let you get back to work.

C: Has your mother come out?

R: Yeah, she's here.

C: Can I say hello to her?

R: She says she don't want to speak to you.

C: I understand.

R: No. Just a minute, I'll get her.

C: Okay.

(Taping discontinued while owner and mother chat. It resumes when they finish.)

R: Okay?

C: Okay. Everything else all right?

R: Everything's perfect.

C: How many guys have we got goin' to the All-Star Game?

R: Shit, I don't know.

C: Hey, don't say that in front of your mother.

R: Oh, okay.

C: What's the matter with you?

R: I'm sorry.

C: Your mother's voice sounds so much younger.

R: Younger than mine?

C: No. No. So much younger than the last time I talked to her.

R: Oh. Well, she's probably happier now, right?

C: Right. I made you happier, she's happier.

R: If you say so.

C: Well, how many guys we got going to the All-Star Game?

R: Let's see, there'll be myself, Campy, Rudi, Bando and Hunter. That's five for sure, that I know of. And maybe Fingers, but I don't know about him.

C: Bando without a doubt. I mean he's the largest vote-getter of everybody.

R: Oh, is he?

C: And Campy. Campy's even getting more votes than you, isn't he?

R: Nice try. It was a nice try.

C: No. What's the count? I've been watching.

R: I'm the leading vote-getter. Last week, I became the first vote-getter ever to go over two million votes.

C: Oh, really?

R: Yeah.

C: Oh, I didn't know that. Uh, my son here says that's right. You're the first one ever to go over two million?

R: Yeah.

C: What's Campy got?

R: About a million two or three. They say I have a chance to lead all the major leagues.

C: I hope so. Where the hell did I get Campy having more votes than you?

R: Well, I been stuffin' the ballot box.

C: I know what the hell I was thinking about. He's leading the shortstops.

R: Yeah, that's right. You'll be okay.

C: Eventually.

R: Yeah.

C: I wasn't trying to be facetious. I just got confused there for a second. Where's Bando stand?

R: He's number two at third base, behind Brooks Robinson.

C: Well, he oughta go.

R: Well, Williams, you know, he's back in baseball so he's back managing the team and he can select everyone but his starters. I don't know how he feels about the A's right now.

C: But you think Rudi will go?

R: Well, he's fourth in the outfield voting now.

C: I'm afraid he might not go.

R: They'll pick him. They think a hell of a lot of him.

C: What about Blue?

R: He's pitching damn good, but he's nine-and-ten and they usually won't take a guy with a losing record.

C: But they'll take Hunter?

R: He'll definitely go. And Fingers probably.

C: How do they work out the transportation for that game, Reggie?

R: I think that you pay for it. I don't know. Don't you?

C: I think they do.

R: The league pays for it?

C: Someone asked me that the other day, and I said it was something I never looked into.

R: Well, if you don't know about it then the league must take care of it out of the proceeds from the game.

C: Somebody pays for it.

R: Right.

C: You guys don't pay.

R: Right.   The players don't pay.

C: When you gonna get back from the game?   The next day?
    You'll be back in time to work out on Wednesday, won't
    you?

R: Yeah.

C: Yeah, you'll be back in time to work out on Wednesday.

R: Yeah.   At least in time to listen to the workout if they put it
    on radio.

C: You gotta work on throwin' that ball, you know.

R: Yeah, throwin' that ball.

C: Throwin' it hard.

R: Throwin' it hard.

C: Throwin' it hard.   Not underhand.

R: Throwin' it hard.   Not underhand like I did on the play to
    second in yesterday's game.   I can imagine how Monte
    Moore explained that on the radio yesterday.   Did you
    talk to Alvin about it?   If you talked to Alvin about it, that
    would be good.   If you heard it from Monte, that would
    be bad.

C: Well, I listened to the ball game.

R: Yeah, but I think there are a lot of things said in the radio
    booth.   Those guys don't know what the hell they're talkin'
    about.

C: Oh, I wouldn't worry about what they say, Reggie.

R: It depends.

C: Don't worry about what they say.   Anyway, I talk to my
    manager every day.

R: Right.

C: It's my business to do that.

R: If you do that, then I'm in good.

C: He told me that in your conversation with him yesterday
    you agreed that you threw the ball to the wrong base.

R: Right.   Underhand and to the wrong base.

C: So what?   That's nothing.

R: Right.

C: Nobody's infallible.

R: If that's the only mistake I ever make I'll be fine.

C: You can stand ten feet high if that's the only mistake you ever make.

R: That's right.

C: You know what I have always done? And you can check with Monte. You can check with any announcer that I've ever had. You know what I tell my announcers?

R: What's that?

C: Call the play, describe the play as it actually happens, give the fan the right description of what happened. I don't try to tell my broadcasters what to do unless I think they're out of line. Like I heard one yesterday continuously saying how bad New York was and how the players disliked New York, you know?

R: Yeah.

C: And all of this gets back to California. I didn't like that, and I let them know about it this morning. And I heard them talking about all the problems they're having in Baltimore right now—the policemen are on strike, the garbagemen are on strike, and all that stuff, you know?

R: How come that bothers you?

C: Well, I don't think things like that should be stirred up. We've got plenty of unions back home.

R: Oh, well, okay.

C: When you have unions back home and, uh, a hell of a lot of union people, I don't want my announcers to offend any union members. That's none of the announcers' damn business.

R: Right. And you don't tell them how to broadcast.

C: Right.

R: Right.

C: Well, let me give some thought to that All-Star business.

R: Okay.

C: You caught me off guard.

R: That's the best way to catch you.

C: Maybe we did send the wives last year. I'll tell you what I wish you'd do.

R: What's that?

C: Get back to me tomorrow morning, if you think about it.
R: I'll do that.
C: I'll talk to you about it then.
R: Okay.
C: Thank you, Reggie.
R: Thank you, Charlie.
C: Goodbye, Reggie.
R: Goodbye, Charlie.

6 ☆ JULY

Tuesday, the 2nd. It was ironic that Dick Williams came back to baseball against his old team in his new town, but that's the way it worked out. It seemed strange to see him in an Angel uniform. He belongs in an A's uniform. He *is* the A's. Whatever we are, which is the best, is because of him. But Finley fucked that up and now Dick is over in the other dugout with a fucked-up club. I went to Williams before the game and wished him well. A lot of us wished him well. We all respect him. More than we respect Dark.

All during the game last night, Hunter was hollering at Alvin from the bullpen: "Hey, genius, Knowles is ready. . . . Hey, genius, what the fuck you want to bring Fingers in for? . . . Hey, genius, when you going to take him out?" Hunter hates Dark. And Alvin just takes it.

In the dressing room Vida hollers loud enough for the man to hear, "I still say the motherfucker couldn't manage a fucking meat market." And Alvin just takes that too.

The only coach Alvin talks to is Wes Stock, the pitching coach. He doesn't talk to Vern Hoscheit, even though Vern kept the little black book Williams put together on how to pitch to different hitters. And Dark doesn't talk to Jerry Adair, who has moved the infielders around to be sure they're where they should be in different situations. Or Irv Noren, who has moved the outfielders around. They don't do much of it any more because Alvin doesn't want them to. Alvin says he'll do it, but he doesn't do a damned thing. The coaches don't have anything to do. We win without help.

When he can, Williams will probably take some of these coaches back with him. But now he's on the other side and we want to beat him. We beat him last night and we beat him tonight. We beat Nolan Ryan last night. Sometimes he can be hard to hit and sometimes he can be easy to beat. On his best night, you can't see his pitches, much less hit them. No one ever threw balls as fast as he throws them. I haven't seen everyone, but I know in my bones that's so.

He's the only pitcher who scares me. If he ever hits me, he may kill me. I stay loose up there facing him. No one else, just him. Everyone does. He's a killer. A baby-faced killer. He acts like a good guy, a gentlemanly, modest man who wouldn't hurt a fly, but he wants to win.

He says he doesn't try for strikeouts, but that's all he tries for. He could throw half as hard and win twice as much, but he throws as hard as he can on every pitch, harder than he can control, so he loses a lot he should win. He's strictly heat. He can bend them, but he can't control his curve. He wouldn't know a change-up if it followed him around for a week. He just burns you with heat. Most games, he gets by. Other games, he gets beat by bad support. Or beats himself. Last night he walked three and hit a batter to help us score two runs. He led, 3–2, when he lost on three runs in the eighth. Hits, walks and wild pitches.

Tonight, Mangual drove in four runs with a home run and a double and we won a wild one, 7–5. So Williams has lost his first two and he'll lose a lot more, too, before he straightens out that team.

After Dark pinch-ran Washington for Rudi, Joe said, "John McGraw must be turning over in his grave."

Thursday, the 4th. Last night we won a game we should have lost, which is something Williams will have to get used to. It was one of those games when pitchers without much reputation perform like pros. Glenn Abbott of our club is a six-six kid who throws like a big, young Catfish Hunter. He had the Angels shut out until Lee Stanton's two-run double over my head put them ahead, 2–1, with two out in the eighth. It could have been caught, but not the way I played it. I couldn't decide whether to play deep or play in close to try to cut off a run at the plate on a short hit. And I couldn't get Dark's eye for advice. I guess he doesn't want to give any. So I took my cue from North in center and played in. And Stanton hit the ball deep. I couldn't catch up to it.

Andy Hassler, a lefty, shook me some the way his pitches busted in on me. He and Frank Tanana, another hard-throwing left-hander, are real promising pitchers who don't know how to win yet. Williams will teach them, and when he teams them with Ryan and Singer, Dick will have the pitching to turn the team around. We never did get to Hassler, but beat him in the ninth on two runs off of three hits and not a one of the hits left the infield.

On the winning run, North barged into the catcher, Ellie Rodriguez, so hard he couldn't control the ball and the Angels were behind, 3–2, and beat. We win a lot like this, getting everything out of a game we can. North has been on a tear lately, hitting a lot and stealing a lot, and he won this one for us by running hard. I congratulated him later. The fight's ancient history now.

Tonight we made our own fireworks for the holiday. The Angels let down and we won easy, 9–4, to complete a four-game sweep of the series and leave Williams batting zero for his return. I got a hit a game this series, but no long hits. I'm feeling healthy again, but my timing hasn't come back. The other night, when the Angel left fielder was slow taking the field, I jumped over to the other side of the plate and pretended I was going to hit right-handed and hit to the empty field. It was good for a laugh. When I went back to batting lefty and singled to right, I bowed to the boys from first base. They have been asking when I'm going to start earning my money again. I wish I knew. I'm down to .340. I haven't hit a homer for more than a month. It's beginning to bother me.

Vida lost a perfect game and a shutout in the sixth inning today when Winston Llenas hit a home run, his first of the season. The Blue boy coasted in after that. It didn't bother him. He wants to win, but he can handle losing. He'll give so much now and no more. Well, it's up to him. When he was a rookie, I gave him advice. He's a veteran and doesn't need my advice now. He doesn't want it. Not from anyone. There was a time I thought we weren't close anymore, but the last few weeks I felt close to him again. He's a good guy and good to be with. Baseball's strictly a business to him now. He finds his fun outside of the ballpark. He's single and swinging. He likes the ladies and they like him. Handsome dude with a charming smile. Well, so am I. And I like the ladies, too.

When we got in Sunday night, I called one girl and she wasn't home. I called another and her line was busy. Well, you only get one chance at a time. I called another and she was in and she came to the hotel and stayed awhile. After she left, another girl called. I didn't know her, but someone had suggested she call, so she did, and we talked awhile. Then another girl I did know called and she came over and she stayed awhile. Then after she left, I met another girl. It was just one of those nights. A lot of conversation, you know.

Let's face it, when you are a baseball star it is made easy for you. You are supposed to be a stud and sometimes you give in to temptation and play the part. But I don't make a habit of it because it is bad business; it can take a lot out of you, and it is not the way I really like to live. I enjoyed much more a date I had with a girl at UCLA that I date a lot. We went to a delicatessen and had hot pastrami on rye and we talked. Nothing special, but it is special being with her. She is not just another chick. No one I see more than once or twice is another chick to me. She is one of the girls I know that I really like. I believe she really likes me for me, not for baseball. I am going to stay over a day to spend it with her and I'll fly back to Oakland later.

Friday, the 5th. Cold as hell tonight and me in a damn slump. People wondering when I'm going to hit a homer, wondering this and wondering that. Shit. I hit a home run. I drove in three runs with the home run and a fly ball. That is sixteen home runs, so I am back on a normal pace. Actually, Billy North already had the game won with a two-run homer in the third inning. Catfish shut them out and we beat Baltimore, 6–0. Mike Cuellar didn't have much, while Catfish scattered six or seven hits. He only struck out one or two, but he only walked two. Typical Catfish game. We have been getting good pitching. Recently our pitchers have gone fifteen, sixteen games without giving up a home run.

Finley called up a kid today. A black kid called Claudell Washington. That gives us two Washingtons. This one is from the Bay Area. He was in high school just two years ago. I'm 28 and I can call him a kid. Well, he is, but he's a big kid: six-two or so, 195 or 200 pounds, very muscular. And he swings a 42-ounce bat! That's a big bat. That's six ounces bigger than I swing. That's about as big as anyone in the big leagues swings. Richie Allen swings one that big. I hear Babe Ruth swung one bigger, 46 ounces or something like that. But a lot of the guys don't think this kid can swing this big a bat. That remains to be seen. If he can do it, he can do it. He came up from Birmingham, Double-A, and he was leading the Southern Association in batting, home runs, runs-batted-in, runs-scored, doubles, triples, stolen bases, big bats and about anything else you can think of. He pinch-hit tonight and kind of blooped out. A lot of guys looked at him kind of funny, like, "Hey, man, you swinging too big a fucking bat." We'll see.

Sunday, the 7th. Baltimore beat us the last two games of the series. We can beat them and we may have to in the playoffs. They're off to a bad start, but they're a good team and they should come on to take the other division. They always come on at the end of the season. They have a smart manager, Earl Weaver. They're experienced. And a confident club. They lack our power since Frank Robinson was traded and Boog Powell slowed down. But they have a lot of good hitters and a great designated hitter in my former teammate, Tommy Davis, who will be hitting .300 when he's 300. He lacks power, but he handles that stick like an artist with a paint brush. He puts the ball where he wants it.

I'll never know. It just goes to show baseball men don't know baseball players sometimes. The Giants were blinded by McDowell. Sudden Sam has the speed. He's spectacular. Or was. But he was wild. And he wasn't tough. He didn't know what the hell he was doing out there and you never could count on him. Not on the field or off it. You can count on Gaylord game after game, season after season. You got Sam on the ropes, you had him. You get Gaylord on the ropes, you better be careful or he'll put the ball in your ear.

Monday, the 8th. We beat him. We snapped his string. He was tough, but we were tougher. I guess we just wanted to remind the world who we were. We know who we are. The best. Because we beat the best.

I spent the day with Dave Duncan. We were very close when he was with us, and I miss him a lot now that he's with Cleveland. I picked him up at his hotel and we went out and had some sandwiches for lunch, then went to my pad to chat. He was happy, so I was happy for him. He fucked up with Finley, but people said he was a fool for wanting to be traded. He was sent from a first-place team to a last-place team. Now Cleveland is in first place and he is carried away by it. He's only hitting .195, but I hear he's been getting big hits. People around the team tell me he's really the type of ballplayer they needed on the ball club and means a lot to the team, so I was happy about that.

He told me Perry wasn't the only one producing. He said George Hendrick was really pounding the ball and playing good ball. I'm happy to hear that because George is a guy who used to be with the A's. He has a lot of talent, but also a lot of problems. If he is in the frame of mind where he feels like playing, he is capable of being the best player in the game. Dave was telling me about all the other great players they have, saying they have greater players than we have. He said Buddy Bell was better than Bando at third and Frank Duffy was as good as Campy at short. I said, "Hey man, come on."

He said Jack Brohamer was as good as Green at second. I said, "Hey, man, come on, no one is better than Green." But he insisted.   He gave up on left field because of Rudi, but he wouldn't give up on center field because he felt Hendrick is better than North, which he may be.   But when he started to say Charlie Spikes was better than Jackson in right, we started to laugh.   I told him, "You're just backing guys because they're on your ball club.   You got some good guys, but they're not that good.   You could win your division, but only if Baltimore loses it. If the Orioles play their games, there's no way you can win from them."   I said maybe they could beat out Boston because Boston catcher Carlton Fisk is out for the season, and without him the Red Sox are out of hope.   What I didn't say was I could see Cleveland collapsing completely because they were playing over their heads.

It rained all day, but Dave kept saying the rain wasn't going to save us, we were going to have to go against Gaylord anyway, and I said, "Well, fuck it, we'll face him and we'll beat him." Before the game I visited with Gaylord and I wished him well. I mean I want to beat him, but I want to beat him at his best. I respect him.   I said, "Go out and do your thing and we'll do our thing and we'll see."   And he said that was the way it should be.

It was one of our half-price nights, but even so it was a Monday night, not even midseason—and there were 50,000 fucking people in that damn mausoleum.   It felt like New Year's Eve.   With that many people we were going to play the game, rain or no rain.   So we started in the rain.   And we started with Claudell Washington instead of Billy North.   Finley called Dark from Chicago before the game and told him to use Washington as the designated hitter instead of Mangual and to use Mangual in center instead of North.

Billy was pissed off.   He said, "Haven't I proved myself? Am I a part-time player now?   Why the hell should I be replaced by some kid who's been up three days?"   He had a point.   We won the World Series with him.   We can win another one with him.   Shuffling the lineup like this just creates a lot of animosity.

But Charlie's always shuffling.   The last few days, they've been trying to talk Gene Tenace into catching again so Joe

Rudi can play first base and the kid can play left. Tenace has been saying, "I don't want to catch," and Rudi's been saying, "I don't want to leave left." If they make the move, it will weaken our defense. But Finley doesn't consider defense. He just considers offense. Like those times he pinch-hit every time our second baseman came up. And he wants the kid with his big bat in the lineup. On the other hand, if you never make any moves, you'll never improve.

The kid tripled in the eighth inning, his first big-league hit. Wound up knocking in the winner, too. So how can you knock Finley for ordering Dark to use him? That fucking Finley isn't always wrong, you know.

And no one's right all the time.

Before the game, the writers were all around Blue. They wanted to know if he was worried about pitching against Perry and if he was bothered by the big game. Vida kept saying it was just another game, and he wouldn't pitch it if they weren't paying him for it. He said he couldn't care less about Perry. He really put it down, as if it bored him. Maybe it does. But he did pitch a big game. I felt it, even if Vida didn't.

After Perry hit Rudi with a pitch in the second, Tenace hit a home run to give us a 2-0 lead. I thought Blue would blank them after that, just shut the door on them and we'd win, 2-0. Wishful thinking, I guess. They picked up a run in the fourth on two singles and two walks, but Blue pitched out of a bases-loaded jam. Then Duncan hit a two-run homer in the seventh and they led, 3-2. I've never seen anyone happier than Duncan. Revenge, you know. He was all smiles, running around those bases.

I thought they had us beat then. Maybe they should have. Perry and Blue were both pitching super. Each had given up a big home run, but they weren't giving up much. But we're not beat until we're beat, if you know what I mean. I struck out to start the last of the ninth and it made me madder than hell. I don't know what Gaylord got me with, but he got thirteen of us to strike out with something. It wasn't a spitter. Maybe it was a resinball. The whole goddam game Bando was bitching about Perry putting so much resin on the ball it was blowing dust in his eyes when it got to him. He kept telling the umpire to tell the pitcher to take the fucking resin off the ball. Duncan was getting riled up, but nothing riles Gaylord. Name like a fucking riverboat gambler—that southern sonofabitch will beat you one way or another if he can. But we weren't beat yet.

Joe Rudi, good old Rudi, hit a triple. Herb Washington went in to run for him and when Tenace hit a sacrifice fly, we had the tying run. It was the first game Herb had won for us. You might say he won it. If he hadn't tied it, we couldn't have won it. He scored on that short fly where Rudi wouldn't have. It was the first time we saw where his speed helped a lot and he earned a lot of his money on just that one sprint. He just outran the throw from left.

In the tenth Dark put Mangual into Rudi's slot in left and brought North off the bench to play center. And in the last half he pinch-hit Pat Bourque, who drew a walk and was sacrificed to second. Campy grounded out. But up came Claudell and the kid got that big bat around on a slider and banged the ball through the infield for the hit that brought home the winning run. Here was Claudell, two years ago a schoolboy in Berkeley, a week ago in Birmingham, a hero in his first starting game in the majors—and he was mobbed on the field by all the players. It was like we'd won the World Series. Finley has turned his fucking fireworks back on now, and wow!

I looked at Perry, walking off with his head hung down. They walked off, the Indians, with no one paying them any mind. It had to hurt. It was one they wanted. It was like they wanted to prove something. Well, they didn't prove it and it has to hurt. They've been winning, but they may start to lose now. It may have taken something from Perry, too. He won't win his next fifteen in a row, I guarantee you. Everyone knows now he's not invincible, and they'll be going after him.

Everyone was in our dressing room afterwards, not theirs. I heard they had their doors locked for fifteen or twenty min-

utes, so you can see how they took it. Most of the writers
were around Washington. Well, at nineteen it's a moment to
cherish. Some of them were by Blue. Vida was giving them
the "Man, I just threw the ball, that's all" bullshit. But he
threw hell out of it. He only gave up four hits. He was tough
in a tough game.

A lot of guys were around North. The A's had announced
that Billy had a broken toe, which was why he wasn't playing.
But when he went out to play in the tenth, it gave it away. So
they asked Billy what was bothering him and he said not playing bothered him. He said his whole body was fine, and that
included his fucking toe. Well, that's how Finley fucks up.
He's got guts, but he messed up the right move by making excuses about it.

Afterwards, Duncan and I went out and had a few beers.
Dave was really down. They lost a game they had won.
And they lost something in having it happen. After losing,
his homer didn't matter. That's the way it is. We all want
our homers. But most of us want to win more. If the homer
hasn't helped you win, it hasn't helped you. We stayed up
until two, talking it over.

Tuesday, the 9th. I read the morning paper in bed, and Duncan
called us a bunch of crybabies for bitching about Perry pitching
with resin all over the ball. I gave Dave a couple of pair of
tennis shoes yesterday. Just a little present, you know. I
know he hates the A's because he hates Finley. But I also
know we were his teammates. I thought about him calling us a
bunch of crybabies. I just lay there and thought about it
awhile.

We went out and kicked the shit out of them tonight, 7–0. I
got two hits and drove in two runs. Rudi got two hits and
drove in three. Bourque hit his first home run and Catfish
shut them out on three hits. Well, hell, Dave Duncan or no
Dave Duncan, the Cleveland Indians are not the Oakland A's.

The game wasn't the big deal tonight. With Finley, the big
game is played off the field as often as it is on the field. We
walked into the clubhouse tonight to find that Finley had

phoned and two of our coaches, Noren and Hoscheit, had been
fired and replaced by Bobby Hoffman and—get this—Bobby
Winkles. Well, I'm glad to get Winks, but I'm sorry to see the
other guys go. Here we are 85 games into the season and five
games in first and Finley feels he has to make these changes.
What a fucking shame!

It's almost a year to the day since I blasted Dick Williams and
his coaches, and Finley answered me by extending their contracts. I was wrong. I ripped them because they were stoog-
ing for Finley. Well, there is no other way to work for Finley.
But I was wrong because they did their jobs as best they could
and I said so later.

Noren has been our third-base coach for the last three years
and we won the division all three years and the World Series
the last two years, so he couldn't have made too many mistakes.
Early this season, Dark accused him of fucking up the signs to
make the manager look bad, but there was no way he was going
to do that. If anyone did that it was Dark, because he didn't
know the signs. Noren knew it was coming. Hoscheit knew
he was on his way out, too. But I guess at this point they both
thought they'd get through the season.

Vern was crying when he got the word. I just walked over
and told Irv and Vern that I appreciated all they had done for
us and I'd always remember them and I wished them well.
They thanked me and we shook hands. Writers asked me
what I thought and I said they were good men and we were
going to miss them, but we lose a lot of good men from this
team and we just go on our way. I said nothing around here
surprises me, and nothing does. But it's something I'll never get
used to.

Thursday, the 11*th.* A fellow read me what Noren told a reporter in L.A. Irv said that any time a man was fired by Finley it
has to be figured as a plus. He said Dark once was fired by
Finley for not doing the job—and now he, Noren, had been
fired by Finley for doing the job. He said maybe Finley fired
the wrong man this time, that Dark may carry a Bible around
with him, but he was a hypocrite and no one in the game trusts
him. Noren claimed Dark was out of the game a long time

because no one wanted him. He said he didn't keep up and didn't know anything about the game and the players playing it when he came back. No one else but Finley would have brought him back, Irv explained, and now it served Dark right that Charlie had brought in Winkles to stand by as manager any time Alvin screwed up. Noren said he wouldn't let Alvin manage anything he owned, but the A's would win anyway because the A's were winners. He said Finley let Dark manage only because Finley wanted a manager he could manage. Noren called Dark incompetent, a liar, two-faced and a lot of other stuff.

Pretty rough stuff. A man should show some class when he gets a bad deal. But Irv did get a bad deal and I can't blame him for being bitter. I hope his saying these things doesn't hurt him, because he's a good baseball man. I expect to see him back with Williams in Anaheim sooner or later. Some of our other coaches will wind up there, too. Hoscheit may not go there because I think he's through with baseball. Vern said Finley promised all the coaches raises if the team won again last season, but he didn't give them a dime. He called Finley a lousy owner and Dark a lousy manager. He said he's had it with this sport. Maybe he has.

We had an off-day Wednesday. I didn't want to hang around the house. I can't take the TV. I have watched the Watergate hearings when they were on. I live in the world. But I have lost faith in our leaders.

My brother and I went for a drive in a Porsche Cararra I'm thinking of buying. We went down to Merced and got some clothes for him. Mary went with us and we had a good time. I wouldn't say she's my girl, but she comes as close as anyone around here. She's a good girl and I have a good time being with her. She's good people. We listened to a lot of music and rapped and drove down the highway and let it all out. It was relaxing. We got back and I had to pack in a hurry. I got to the airport late for the plane to New York. I heard later all the guys were trying to get them to take off without me, but they waited for me. Alvin told me, "Big guy, I'll wait for you anytime." I laughed.

The seats in back were taken, so I sat up front in first class.

The guys didn't think a lot of that and let me know it.   I sat with Winkles.   I think it will help me to have him with us because I think he is someone I can talk to and someone I can get things from in reference to improving my game.   I think he's genuinely interested in improving me as a player.   I think he's interested in improving all players.   I think he can be a coach who can help the team.   I know Sal and Gene and Rudi like him.   All the black guys like him.   I think he's going to fit in real well.

He told me he was disappointed that Dalton had deserted him.   He felt Harry had hired him knowing he needed time to make the adjustment from college ball to the big leagues and should have backed him up.   Well, you have to learn not to expect too much from the people in this profession.   Winks learned by his experience.   He called Finley and asked for the job.   It's just the sort of thing Finley would go for.   If Dark doesn't do the job, Winks will get it.   Finley would like nothing better than for Winks and the A's to make Williams and the Angels look bad.

Friday, the 12*th*.   We had two days off and today it's back to the ballpark.   I looked at the schedule and between June the fourteenth and July the ninth we played 23 straight days.   Or nights.   I didn't have to look at the schedule to know we hadn't had a day off in a long time, and I was sick of it.   All the guys were.   It took a big game like the game against Gaylord Perry and the Indians to stir us up.   After you play 20 or 25 games in a row, it takes something special to get you going.   You play 20 or 25 games in a row and you get sick of playing games and you get so you don't give a goddam whether you win or lose the fucking game.   You play 20 or 25 games in a row and—I don't care who you are, Pete Rose or anyone—there's no one who hustles so hard that he doesn't lose interest in it for a little while somewhere along the way.   Anyone who says something else is lying.   There is no other sport that expects you to play every day or every night.   It is stupid for baseball to ask this of us.   It's cheating us and it's cheating the owners and it's cheating the fans.   You just can't do your best.   You just can't play the way they're paying for you to play.

It gets you physically and it gets you mentally. Mostly mentally. You begin to think tired. Like you've been up all night, night after night. Like you don't know where the hell you are or what the hell you're doing. You know, it's sleeping in until noon and squeezing in two meals before you have to be at the ballpark by five-thirty, then spending two and a half hours practicing to play the game, then playing the game from eight to eleven, then going out for three or four beers and some lousy pizza or rotten tacos and then dumping yourself back into bed. And then it's getting up and doing it again.

It's Finley acting up or somebody bitching. It's the bus to the ballpark. It's the cold in Oakland and the heat in Kansas City. It's the dressing rooms and the hotels. None of 'em bad, none of 'em good. All the same. The waiting rooms and the airplanes and the freeways. It's talking to the same writers and answering the same questions over and over again and reading the same crap in the newspapers. It's signing the same autographs for the same kids and being hot and sweaty by the time you work your way through the crowd and out into the night. And everyone thinking we're having a thick steak and a swinging party, but by the time we get out anything any good is closed. It's being so tired you just want to get to the sack to crash, but figuring you got some time to yourself, so maybe you go hunting for a chick so you can go dance or screw or something.

After awhile you're playing a part when you're playing the game. You try to look like you're hustling, but you don't know what the score is. You have to keep punching yourself up. It's monotonous, man. You can't ask for a day off to go fishing or something, because it would make the manager look bad if someone got hurt or he needed a pinch-hitter. They may give a guy a game off here and there, but if he's got to be at the ballpark five hours, it's no goddam good.

No one else in any other job goes 20 or 25 straight days at work without a day off. Most work five days and wouldn't give up their weekend off for anything. It's amazing how good a day off is for us. Just so you don't have to go to the ballpark and think baseball. The day before a day off a ballplayer just wants to get the game over so he can get to the day off. We just had two days off and now I feel good again. We play four games in three days in New York, but I look forward to the games. That's all I wanted, a couple days off.

Sunday, the 14*th.* After losing two straight at Shea Stadium, we had two meetings today and went out and won two games. Friday night, Pat Dobson held us without a hit for five innings, held us to two hits over nine innings and beat us, with Holtzman, 3–0. Dobson's a pretty good dude, and most of the guys like him. Oh, they wanted to hit him, but they couldn't. We hit the ball hard but got nothing out of it. We thought the balls were soft. They're making them somewhere different this year and they are different. Some of them are so soft you can knock them out of shape. You mash the ball and it dies.

We thought we'd bounce back against Dick Tidrow yesterday afternoon, but we were wrong. We had him 3–0 after I hit my seventeenth home run, but Blue couldn't hold it. Lately, Blue goes good for four, five innings, then comes apart. When he came apart in the fifth, Dark came out to get him and Vida walked off the mound and walked right past him and threw the ball behind him on the ground, and it made Dark look bad. I can understand Vida being upset, but his conduct wasn't very professional. Vida'd given up eight hits and three or four walks and thrown a wild pitch and let them tie it up. Well, it just seemed to fall apart completely after that.

This morning Tom Skinner conducted our Sunday chapel services. He was with the Washington Redskins six or seven years and he can relate religion to athletes. I invited a number of the players who do not always come to these sessions—and they came. One thing we talked about was how when two people meet and have sex, God is not against that as long as they are not using each other and abusing each other. He went into the word "community" and said that in a way we all were living in a commune and we have to learn to live together without abusing one another.

The session lasted a lot longer than usual, about 45 minutes, which left us only about 10 minutes to get ready for the game, but it was worth it. Guys asked him how you avoid the temptation of running around on the road. Tom went into the fact that we shouldn't think we're unique in being tempted and giving in from time to time, but we have to maintain a balance between the pleasures of life and making the most of our lives. It was Dark who got the topic turned to how important the community of the ball club was and how we had to have a good Christian feeling on the team with the guys pulling for one another. Winkles and Adair joined in this, too. Anyway, everyone seemed to get something out of it.

Then, before the game, Alvin called his own meeting. He said it was a shame one or two guys with a bad attitude can have such a decaying effect on a team. He talked about the way Holtzman and Blue were bitching and how it was spoiling the attitude of the pitchers. He said he made a mistake with Vida by taking him out too early, but Blue made a mistake the way he went out yesterday. So now they were even. He said when he went out there he didn't want to play catch. Alvin said some guys weren't hitting and weren't hustling as a result, which wasn't professional. He singled out Billy North and Billy stood up and argued with him in front of the team, but it just made him look bad. Alvin said he didn't want to hear it. "I'm the manager of this ball club and I expect to be respected accordingly. If you want to be the manager, phone Charlie and ask for the job. Until you get it, don't manage for me and don't second-guess me!"

This was one time Alvin didn't quote from the Bible, but it sure as hell was a sermon, and it sure as hell was a good thing. With the exception of Billy and maybe Vida, the guys all agreed it was a good thing for Alvin to do. It was time he took charge and stopped eating shit. I did think it was bad for Dark to single guys out for blame in front of the other guys and I told that to the writers who asked about it later. They seemed surprised I'd defend North, but, hell, he's a teammate. I know how it felt when Finley chewed me out in front of the team earlier. Not that Billy didn't have it coming, but in private, not in public. Well this is a business and you got to grow up fast. You're playing for money, not feelings.

I still don't know about Dark. He has impressed me by

keeping his cool and sticking with players who have put it to him. He's been going through a learning period, but he doesn't deal with game situations very well. He's not giving the players what the manager is supposed to give. I wonder why he doesn't charge out on the field and argue on behalf of his ballplayers more. He doesn't back them up. I wonder if he has any emotions. Well, this sermon showed some emotion.

We went out and we ended the Yankees' six-game winning streak. I can't swear it was the sermon that did it. I know we're a better team than the Yankees. We were losing the first game, 3-2, after six, but got five in the seventh and went on to win, 7-3. Bando hit a three-run homer. Then North hit one and Bando hit another in the second game and we went on to win that one, too, 6-1, to sweep the doubleheader. Bando busted out of a bad spell and afterwards I told him I'm just glad he's on my ball club.

Wednesday, the 17th. We swept three straight from the Orioles and we seem to be streaking now and pulling away from the so-called contenders again. Monday night this guy Garland—a rookie named Wayne Garland—nearly no-hit us. Now I respect all players in the big leagues because if they didn't belong they wouldn't be here, but we're the best and he didn't seem that tough to us and for eight fucking innings he held us without a hit. We were sitting there in the dugout watching him work and we couldn't believe it. Well, it was unreal and reality returned in the ninth inning. Greenie, just reinstated off the disabled list, singled to right to start the ninth and that kid sort of sagged and we had him. We loaded the bases. Bando doubled to lear them. They got Grant Jackson in to pitch to me. I figured he'd lay the first one over, so I went for it and drove it deep between the outfielders for a double to score Sal. A fly ball and a wild pitch brought in two more. We came from 0-4 to win 6-4.

Last night we almost blew a four-zip lead. Holtzman was coasting along on a shutout when he gave up two hits and two runs in the eighth with the help of an error by Rudi, who let the ball go between his legs in left. Dark brought in Fingers and he fanned Earl Williams for the second out, then got Don Baylor to ground to Bando for what should have been the third out. But he threw the ball away and instead they had the third run. Fingers just stiffened and struck out Brooks Robinson to end the inning. He is a tough sonofabitch. Then tonight we won, 2–0, and I accounted for both runs. Blue pitched better than he has and, with Fingers getting the last out, we whipped Mike Cuellar, who is cute and tough to whip. I'd been in a little bit of a slump again, but I busted out with three-for-four. I stole a base, too.

What made it fun was my family being there. I left about fifteen tickets for my mother and father and sister and everyone else in sight. My father drove up from Philly. Family means a lot to me. I feel for Cookie Mangual. He's left the ball club to be in Puerto Rico for his father's funeral. His father died of cancer and we sent flowers and our feelings.

We've won five straight and the way I figure it, 19 of our last 25 or 26. We swept a top team. And life is fine—except your father dies, like Angel's did, and you remember you're a person first and a ballplayer second.

Saturday, the 20th. We had a lousy flight into Cleveland and it really ticked the guys off. We flew commercial and couldn't get a flight out Wednesday night, so we had to fly out Thursday morning. We got in close to noon, got settled, and then got out to the ballpark for that night's game. When they don't give you a travel day, the team should give you a charter so you can get in and get your rest. We're in a pennant race and they save $2,000 by making us go the hard way. Sometimes I just don't know what they're thinking about.

We won, anyway. We beat Perry again. This time we beat him 3–2. Catfish won his sixth straight. Perry lost again trying for his sixteenth. It's been ten days since we stopped him and he's struggling now. We got big hits at the right time. One was by Claudell Washington, who whipped Perry last time. For a kid like Claudell, it's Gaylord who? He doesn't know he's not supposed to hit him, so he hits him.

It was something else last night. It went the other way.

Dick Bosman pitched a no-hitter against us and we lost, 4–0. It almost seems like we get no-hit once every season. Jim Palmer no-hit us in '69. Clyde Wright the next year. I don't know if anyone turned the trick in '71 or '72. I remember Jim Bibby did it to us last year. It seems like we were bound to be no-hit this year. About ten days ago, Pat Dobson no-hit us for six innings. Four or five days ago, Wayne Garland no-hit us for eight innings. Tonight, Bosman goes all the way with it. These are guys that haven't been stopping a lot of people. Bosman's been bombed this season. But he's a good guy and I was glad for him.

He didn't overpower us or anything, he just kept putting us out. He didn't have super stuff, but he didn't throw any bad pitches. When we hit the ball hard we hit it at someone. My last time up, I hit one so hard it should have shook the second baseman, but it didn't. A guy goes along pitching an ordinary game and suddenly about the sixth or seventh inning, you realize he's got a no-hitter going and you can't believe it. Well, he damn near pitched a perfect game. In the fourth, Bando hit back to the pitcher and he got off balance going for it and threw wild to first. It was an error and the only runner we got on the entire game.

As I passed Bosman coming in from the field for the last inning I patted him on the butt and I wished him luck. I said, "Go get it." And he got it. Afterwards all the writers asked me about it and they made a big deal about it in the papers this morning. Well, hell, why not wish him well? He's a good dude and he's been struggling. If we could beat him, right on. If I could hit him, I would. I wasn't going to cry about it. I'd have been sorry if some flukey hit had robbed him of his big game. I mean, if you're gonna lose, why not lose to a no-hitter? Fuck it. If he can get it, let him have it, let him have the whole thing. You know, get the headlines, get a bonus, get something to write home about. I don't know why the big deal about one player wishing another one well. Players don't do enough of it. They think it, but they don't do it. Well, hell, be human. No-hit game or no no-hit game, it's just one game. Billy North came into the dressing room after the game and asked me how many hits we'd gotten. Gene Tenace came up to me and said, "Nice hitting." We know where it's at and this one game ain't it. There's another game today.

Sunday, the 21st. We were on national television yesterday afternoon and that made it special. You get worked up because you know you're being watched by a lot of fans. It works me up because the All-Star Game is coming up and I know the people say here's three and a half million votes, let's see what he can show us. I guess I'm a showman. Maybe "showboat" is the word. Holtzman started for us and got knocked out early. We were losing, 6–0, after four innings, but we started to scratch back and knock Jim Perry out. North got three hits and knocked in two runs. Rudi got two and knocked in one.

Suddenly it was the eighth inning and we were behind only 7–6. I hit a ground ball into center field. As I reached first, I saw that Hendrick wasn't hustling on the ball. I never broke stride and I slid into second ahead of the throw. I felt they wouldn't expect me to steal third, so I decided to go. The catcher's throw got away from the third baseman when I slid in hard. I jumped up and hurried home and we had a tie game. I felt good about it and so did the guys, who gave me the "nice goin', Reggie," business.

I needed that lift. I manufactured a run the way a slugger isn't supposed to be able to do. I got good write-ups about it and I heard later that up in the booth Curt Gowdy and Tony Kubek marveled at it. It puffed me up and made me feel like I could do anything I wanted if I put myself to it.

They got the run back in their half. We got two to go ahead in the top of the ninth, 9–8. But they got two to win it in the bottom of the ninth, 10–9. Well, we got beat, that's all. We battled back and had made a sensational game of it, one of those games which stands out above all the others. We'd been beat, that's all. I'd showed my stuff. I'm sorry it wasn't enough, but sorry don't do it.

We got 'em today, 6–3. Ted Kubiak, filling in for Bando, who has a sore ankle, came through with the single to put us on top to stay. That's why this is a good club. We bounce back

from disappointing defeats.   We have cats who can come off
the bench and come through.   We're a team.   North tripled to
score Kubiak and we were home free.

So it's on to Pittsburgh and the All-Star Game.   It's an honor,
especially since I got more votes than anyone else ever.   I figure
I've won acceptance as a star.   After a fast start, I've slowed down
a lot.   I only drove in six runs in June.   It's been a struggle in
July.   I'm down around .320 and the homers have been few
and far between.   I do have 60 ribbies, but only 17 homers.   I
got a lift from last year that's still carrying me along, I know.   I
get a lift from my personality, too, I think.   I'm a colorful
player on the field and outspoken off the field.   I've been on the
big magazine covers this season.   A TV outfit, Laurel, is picking me up at the All-Star Game and will follow me around right
through the World Series for a documentary that'll run next
year.   It may bring me as much as 20 grand if enough stations
buy it.   I'm well known now and I'll get votes I don't deserve.
I got almost three and a half million votes.   I got more than
Henry Aaron and Johnny Bench and I thought they were the
most well-known athletes in the world.   They're gonna make it
no matter what they do and maybe I will now, too.   I've established myself at that level.

What really knocked me out was when Joe Reichler asked me
to get to town early because his league, my league, the American League, wanted me there to receive the media and represent the league.   That's a big honor.   I bitch about a lot, but
right now I don't know what more I could want out of life.
Well, a family.

Tuesday, the 23rd.   Because of his bad leg, Bando couldn't go
to the All-Star Game.   Catfish, Fingers, Campaneris and Rudi
were going, but took Monday off before the game.   Finley didn't
offer to pick up the tabs for any wives to make the trip to
Pittsburgh, so the guys were willing to wait.   I flew in Sunday
night.   Johnny Bench was in early too, and we had time to talk
that night.   I really like him.   He's not only a great player
who produces under pressure, but a great guy who'll rap with
you.   We went to his room and had a party.   You know, a
couple of beers and a lot of words.

He said he thought that back in June, when his Cincinnati club was ten or eleven games back of Los Angeles, the Reds were beat. But now that they'd cut the lead in half, they were going to catch the Dodgers. The Dodgers collapsed with a big lead last season and look like they might again this season. The Reds don't have the Dodgers' pitching, but they are more mature. They're still hungry, too. They've won a lot the last few years, but while they've been in World Series, they haven't won one. The Dodgers seem to have a lot of talented young players, but I don't know if they've got the stuff to stand up under a stretch run. So I'm backing his Reds.

Yesterday at our Players' Association meeting we spent a lot of time doing a little business. We voted a new three-year contract for our rep, Marvin Miller, who has done a good job for us. And we discussed supporting the NFL Players' Association strike. We don't know all of the things they want and we know that some of the things they want seem silly, but we sort of feel we should back them on their strike because they backed us on ours.

At the hotel during the day I gave a lot of time to a lot of writers. That night we had a workout at the ballpark and the American League officials were upset because we had only 7 guys show up, while the National League had 28, which is maybe why they win this game every year. When you win, you want to play it, I guess. Afterwards all the writers wrapped themselves around me to hear what I had to say, which wasn't a hell of a lot. I felt like I was a novelty, the only guy in town who could speak the English language. I felt like saying, "Hey, man, why not talk to somebody else? Why not talk to Gaylord Perry, who won 15 straight games? Or go over to the other room and talk to Henry Aaron, who hit 715 home runs? Hey, Johnny Bench is here, you know. Don't ignore those guys." But I didn't. I just said I want to thank the three and a half million people who voted for me, who must think I'm a pretty good ballplayer.

They had a luncheon today, the day of the game, and I got to visit with old friends among the players and meet new players I didn't know, like Mike Schmidt of the Phillies and Steve Garvey of the Dodgers. Gaylord Perry was sitting next to me and we got to talking to the Dodgers who were nearby, Jimmy Wynn and Ron Cey and Garvey, about how the Reds were going to catch them.   We called Bench and Pete Rose down and they joined in, saying how The Big Red Machine was going to run right by The Little Blue Bicycle.   Then another Red, Joe Morgan, sneaked in behind Garvey and said, "Boo, here we are, right on your shoulder."   It was all in fun.   The Dodgers took it well and gave it back in turn.

I received a trophy for being the biggest vote-getter.   I was happy to get the opportunity to point out that my dad was in the audience.   God, he felt like Paul Bunyan.   I felt good about that, but bad that when I asked for five tickets for my father and a few others, I had to pay for them.   I know the money goes into the players' pension fund.   I also know I did a lot for them and they could have done a little for me.

I can afford tickets.   I put out $300 for tickets for family and friends, who think I get 'em free.   It's just that I did everything they asked of me and when I asked them for something, they didn't do a damn thing about it.

Richie Allen knows how it is, I guess.   He doesn't do a damn thing for anyone in baseball.   Sometimes he doesn't even do what he's supposed to do.   We get to the ballpark early and there's a big crowd there and a hundred television cameras and a thousand writers and the only one who's not there is Richie Allen.   Everyone, including the players, is walking around bitching about him: "Who the hell does he think he is?"   "Doesn't he think he owes the game anything?"   "I wouldn't want him on my team."   All that crap.

And then he walks in 25 minutes before game time and the same guys who'd been bitching fall all over him, practically kissing his ass: "Hey, Richie, good to have you."   "Hey, gimme five, man."   I see this sort of thing all the time and don't like it.   I'm sure Richie sees it.   I'm sure he doesn't like it.   I'm sure it explains the way he acts sometimes.   And Allen is cool.   When the writers ask him why he shows up at ten minutes to eight for an eight-fifteen game, he says, "Oh, is the game at eight-fifteen? I thought it was at eight.   I guess I'm early."   Which was funny.

Well, it's not really a funny situation.   He does owe the game more than he gives it. He's paid $250,000 a season to play the games, but if he doesn't feel like playing, he doesn't play. The other night, his team, the White Sox, had a doubleheader. He showed up in the sixth inning, hit a home run in the eighth inning, then didn't play the second game. And he didn't play the next day, either. Then he played the next day and got two hits. I stand in awe of his ability. He probably is the best hitter in baseball. I really believe if he wanted to, he could hit 60 home runs every season. He doesn't care to. And I can't understand that.

He wants to go his own way, which is all right. But if you take their money, you got to do it their way. I guess I don't feel about him the way I did. I guess it hurt me when he went out of his way to point out I'd never hit .300. I respect his talent, but not the way he uses it. Management cheapens itself by letting him get away with it.

With the kind of interest he shows, it's no wonder we got wiped out again. We got whipped, 7–2. It was the third straight All-Star Game we got whipped and the newspapers say it's eleven out of the last twelve now. You can't put too much on one game, especially an All-Star Game. But when you add up the games like that it shows you something. I think we've got the best team in baseball, but clearly they've got the best league. We could win any game, but we are not going to win *most* of the games because, by now, we do not expect to win.

It is a fun sort of game, but it is really only fun for the National League. They look forward to it and compete with confidence in it. A guy like Garvey's never been in it before, but he got the first hit and scored the first run, doubled in the tying run during the rally that put them on top to stay and made a super stop at first base to protect their lead. He was voted MVP of the game, but a lot of guys did jobs for them. Reggie Smith hit a homer. Lou Brock got a hit, stole a base and scored a run. He's sensational and he's going to surpass the record for stolen bases set by Maury Wills about ten years ago. Brock's about 35 and I only hope I can go like he is when I'm as old as he is. He got one shot at showing us something and he showed it.

They got good pitching, too. They stuck it to us. We got only four hits. I didn't get any. Lynn McGlothen struck me out on three breaking balls. Breaking balls! I mean this is the All-Star Game, man, throw the ball and let the batter hit it! He went at it like it was the World Series. Which is why they win. We went at it like it was a meaningless exhibition game, which is why we lose—that, and the fact they've got more good ballplayers. Frank Robinson says it's because they've got more black ballplayers. Let's face it, they were the first to have more black ballplayers and they've always had more. I don't know why, but it's the way it is. Most of the top players are black. There are some super white players, but most of your superstars are blacks. Maybe because they grow up hungrier, needing sports more than whites.

The American League players feel inferior to the National League players. I could feel it. They were waiting to be beaten, so they were bound to be beat. I felt bad I didn't get a hit. It's the sort of showcase I like, but you can't always do well when you want to. I did what I could do. Late in the game, Mike Marshall popped the ball into short right field and I thought I could catch it if I went like hell for it. I went like hell and I slid on my stomach and I made a goddam good catch and I felt that repaid the people who voted for me.

It's embarrassing to be beat the way we are every year in this game. And I'm ashamed of the stars of my league who put it down because they think they can't win it. I believe we'd be better off playing the Oakland A's against the National League. What the hell, we're the World Champs.

Saturday, the 27th. Back home, we beat Minnesota two out of three. Thursday night, Bando hit two home runs and Blue pitched a three-hitter and we won, 5–1. Blue gets to the point where he sees he has to go if he's going to win 20, so he does. It's all inside of him. Friday night, Larry Hisle drove in three runs with a home run and a sacrifice fly and they had us down, 3–0, but we came back to beat them, 5–3. Campy singled with the bases loaded. This put us seven games in front, which is our largest lead of the season. I guess it was their turn to win one and they did tonight, 6–1. Ray Corbin won over Catfish Hunter. These things happen.

Tonight I decided to stop seeing Mary for awhile. I wasn't really going with her, but I told her I was cooling it. I've been dating other girls and she's been dating other guys, but she's been throwing it up to me. So maybe it's best to forget it for awhile. She's a nice girl and I like her a lot, but I don't want to hear about her boy friends. I got ball to play. I got to keep my mind clear. July's almost gone. We're getting down to it now. I don't need any hassles.

Monday, the 29*th.* Chicago came in and we whipped the White Sox in both ends of a doubleheader Sunday afternoon and made it a sweep of the series tonight. That makes it six victories in our last seven games and twelve out of fifteen or something like that and we have a nice eight-and-a-half-game cushion to fall back on. Tenace hit two homers, Rudi hit one and Campy hit a two-run double to back up Holtzman in the opener. The second game was a mess with nineteen or twenty walks, but we won it, 3–2, as Bando doubled in two runs and I singled in the winner. It was my first RBI in two terrible weeks. The day lasted seven hours. Tonight, we came from 0–4 to an 11–5 lead and then had to hang on to win, 11–9. It was one of those games that lasts less than three hours, but seems to go on three days.

North got three hits and drove in four runs. He was quoted as calling me an "enigma and a paradox." Well, I am on record here and now as calling *him* an enigma and a paradox. I can't figure him out, any more than he can figure me out. I have found out that he played awhile this season with a broken bone on top of his left foot and I guess that explains some things.

We made four errors today. I made one of them. Angel Mangual made one. All of us make 'em. But Mangual just simply dropped a fly ball, which was funny. It got in the sun, but he could have caught it. Maybe his mind wasn't on it. He's a puzzle, too. He's a great human being. He has a great knowledge of life. I consider him the sort of friend who would be with me through thick and thin. But I have been disappointed in him as a player.

His first year up he battled Rick Monday for the center-field job and beat him out. Which is why Monday was traded to Chicago. It was a great deal for us, since it brought us Ken Holtzman from the Cubs. But then Cookie hurt his leg and when he came back he wasn't the same. Cookie would drop fly balls and Dick Williams would chew him out, and Cookie would swing the bat like a girl and strike out. Williams was smart, but he made mistakes, too. He made one with Cookie. Dick just took Cookie's confidence away and it's never come back. This game is mostly mental.

Wednesday, the 31*st.* Last night I hit two home runs, my first in two weeks. Tenace hit two, Haney hit one and we got fifteen hits and trounced Texas, 11–3. The funny thing is they started one of the best pitchers in baseball, Jim Bibby, who is eight feet tall, weighs 400 pounds and throws the ball 800 miles an hour.

Before the game, Bobby Winkles talked to me. He said I seemed to him to be playing tense because I was worried about not hitting. I don't want to say, oh, well, hell, I got great talent, I'll come out of it. I don't want to count on it. But, as I told the writer, Ron Bergman, later, when you play the game for ten years, you get to bat 7000 times or so and if you get 2000 hits that's .286. But that also means that's 5000 times you've gone without a hit, and 0–for–5000 is .000. Bergman ran to figure it out, but I'd already figured it out. Winks didn't hit those homers off Bibby, but I believe he helped me hit them.

This afternoon, the tables were turned. Jeff Burroughs hit a home run and a single and drove in three runs and they clobbered Catfish and nosed us out, 7–6. Some days the best hitters beat the best pitchers and some days the best pitchers beat the best hitters. Burroughs is beautiful. He's strong and he has a strong stroke. He'll be hitting home runs long after I'm gone.

Sport magazine is the latest to latch on to me. They're doing two stories on me for an issue that will be out World Series time. One is by Murray Olderman, who lives out here. They took five hours to shoot photos of me. Then Murray wanted to do his interview. I said not now, man, I'm tired. He said that maybe we could talk a little. I said he could hang around the house awhile if he wanted, but I'd appreciate it if we did the interview another day. He said okay. I had him up to the house. I introduced him to my secretary. I fed him lunch. A girl stopped up for a few minutes and I introduced him to her. We just lounged around and chatted a little. After awhile he cut out saying he'd get back to me. I appreciated his putting off the interview because I was beat.

The other story is by George C. Scott, believe it or not. Because he played General Patton in the movies, they wanted me to pose as Patton for the cover photo—you know, "General of the A's." They wanted me to put on the helmet, field glasses, pearl-handled revolvers and other stuff that dude wore and sit in a jeep. I pointed out it would make me look like a fool. They begged me. I could have said no, but I didn't. I guess I am a fool. I posed.

Scott flew up with the magazine editor, Dick Schaap, from Los Angeles to Oakland in a chartered plane Tuesday. We talked for about half an hour before the game. I don't know how much he could have gotten out of that. He didn't take notes. He's not a writer. But it was one interview that was as interesting for me as for the writer. He talked about himself as much as I talked about myself. I could relate a lot to what he said. He said he loves acting, but he doesn't like all the stuff that goes with it. He said he doesn't dig stories probing into his private life. He doesn't like belonging to the public. He said he hates people tugging on his shirttails all the time and taking from him and wearing him out mentally so he isn't free to do his work the way it should be done or live his life the way he wants to live it. Well, I can sympathize with that. He must be bothered much more than I am because his face is better known.

I asked him if it was worth the $500 or $600 to fly up in his own plane, instead of the $20 it would have cost to come commercial, and he said I was fucking right it was. He said he didn't give a damn if people thought he was trying to act big-time about it, it was worth it to him to have a peaceful flight. He mentioned he was quitting after this last movie he's just made. At least as an actor. Maybe he'd direct, but he was getting out of the spotlight. "Fuck it," he said. "I'm just gonna quit."

Well, we're different personalities, and I sort of like the spotlight, but it burns me, too, sometimes. And sometimes I think I would be happier if I left, too. I'd miss the money, though, let's face it.

That night I felt like I was on stage. My first time up, Bibby threw me a good pitch on the inside part of the plate and I swung hard and made good contact and rode it out. The next time, he threw me a hard slider that hung right over the plate. I just crushed it and it was gone, too. So I showed Scott something. He seemed to know the game and I was glad to give him something good to write about, because I haven't been doing much to write about lately. He thanked me and I thanked him and he went his way and I went mine.

7 ☆ AUGUST

Friday, the 2nd. We're a different team when we're in Chicago than we are anywhere else because Charlie's always around. This is his hometown. He operates our team by telephone from this town. You know when he's in Oakland, because all the dudes in the front office have their shoes shined and they sit up straight at the desks and all the broads are running around like they're real busy. We're a different team anywhere Charlie is—and in Chicago he's always here.

Campy Campaneris is on the disabled list again. He was out a week or so the middle of June and now he's out again. He's always hurt a lot. He hurt his ankle this time. He kept saying he could play and Dark wouldn't play him and the next thing we knew Campy turns up on crutches like he's crippled. Dark wanted to use young Phil Garner at shortstop in the first game of the Chicago series last night and he listed him on the lineup card. Then Finley came into the clubhouse and two or three minutes before the game Dark had to make a change, using Teddy Kubiak at shortstop instead of Garner.

We came from 0–3 to tie at 3–3 before they got four runs in the last two innings to win, 7–3. Holtzman started. Odom came in and went right out. Then Knowles came in and got racked up. It's been a bad year for Darold and it looks like he's on his way out, which is sad, but it's the way it is. He's 32 or 33 and he's been with a lot of teams in the majors for about ten years. He's been with us three years now and he's been a great reliever for us. He was at his greatest last year, when he pitched in every one of the seven World Series games for us. Many people thought he should have been MVP of the Series over me. But when he's bad, he's very very bad.

He's a big, strong left-hander, but he won't use his strength. He's what we call "a nibbler." He won't throw the ball over the plate. He'll only throw for the corners, and he misses a lot. He won't challenge the hitters. We call him "Thirty-Two" because that's his uniform number and he always goes to three-and-two on the count to every hitter. This season he started out walking a lot of guys and then he'd have to come in with a pitch and they'd hit it. Now he gets a call only every seven or eight days, and he's pressing and he does badly. He's gone from hero to goat in a hell of a hurry, which is what this game really is about.

Bando hit a home run and drove in all three of our runs in the first game. He's in one of his streaks where every time he gets a hit it gets us a run or two. He doesn't get many hits, but what he gets gets us runs. He probably drives in more runs per hit than any batter in baseball. I was sitting near Sal when Charlie came up to him and said, "You'll take a hundred and twenty next year, huh?" meaning a hundred and twenty grand. Sal looked at him and said, "I don't know, I just don't know." Charlie just smiled and walked away. We thought it was kind of funny, him just giving in like that. But that's the guy: He's high on Sal today. But tomorrow? And he's down on Knowles. And on North, too.

Billy has been in heat. He's had six hits in the two games here. He's raised his average 70 or 80 points to .270. He's catching the balls in center. But his running has been rotten. He'll steal one base and get thrown out twice. He's been thrown out nine times in his last twelve. So Finley told Dark to take the steal sign from him. And it burnt Billy up. He wants the freedom to go whenever he wants. Billy broadcasts when he's going, but when he's running right he can get away with advertising. He just hasn't been running right.

Tonight we were losing, 2–1, in the eighth, when North singled with two out.   He got the sign to go and stole second.
Then Bando got one of those hits that gets us a run.   Herb
Washington went in to run for Sal and stole second.   Then I
singled up the middle off Terry Forster, the toughest left-
handed relief pitcher in the league, and that brought Herb
home with what turned out to be the winning run.   This was a
game that base-stealing and speed won for us.

It was also a game Herb Washington helped win for us.   For
a while, Washington was forgotten.   He'd go in, go for second,
get caught, and go back to the dugout.   Once in a while he'd
make it and sometimes he'd score.   But for a month or so now
he's been making his presence felt.   It's tough because when he
goes in everyone knows he's supposed to go.   But now he's
learning the lead he can take and the pitcher's moves he can
make his move on.   He's been stealing four out of five bases he
goes for and scoring runs about half the time he's on base.
He's putting pressure on the opposition and he's helping us.
I've changed my mind about him, but so has everyone else.
Finley was right.   Or Dark or whoever it was.   Now that I
agree with them, they'll probably change their minds and let him
go.

The good thing about Herbie is that he's a good guy and
part of the team.   He's taken a terrible ribbing.   He's going to
be a rookie the rest of his life because he's never going to get
the times at bat you need to pass that point.   And regulars
don't like being lifted for runners.   But Herbie has taken it in
good spirits and now he feels good enough about this business
to needle back.   He's fit in.

How many times does the 25th man on a baseball roster win
five or six games a season for you?   Billy has also helped
us win five or six.   He helped us win tonight.   Vida did, too.
Pitched a four-hitter for his fifth straight victory.   He's settled
back to business, pointed at 20 again.   He has 13 now.

Chicago, Chicago, toddling town.   A girl called me the
morning I got in.   It was a quarter to ten here.   But it was a
quarter to eight back there where I came from.   She woke me
up and tried to turn me on.   She said I wouldn't remember
her but her name was Lynn and she'd been out with me and

some friends in Los Angeles a little bit back.   I didn't remember her.

She said, "You weren't very nice to me, but I was with you.
We went for a ride in your white Cadillac with the red interior
and we drove around the Valley.   And it was real foggy and we
listened to your tape recorder."

I said, "Oh, is that right?   What did I have on that night?"

"A plaid suit."

I said, "Lynn, I love you, but I don't know you and you don't
know me.   I'm sure you're a nice girl, but you're not telling the
truth.   I'm not in Los Angeles a lot.   And when I'm in on
baseball business, I don't drive my car.   I drive a Grand Prix,
not a Caddy.   Every car I buy is black and I wouldn't dream of
owning one with a red interior.   I don't own any plaid clothes.
I'm sorry, sweetie, but you got the wrong guy."

She said, "OK, I'm sorry, too."   And she hung up and I went
back to sleep.

Then, about three that afternoon, she sent me a dozen roses
with a note which said, "I'm sorry, but will you please join me
at O'Hare Airport for lunch.   Meet me at the Sheraton Hotel
there.   I'd like to buy you a drink and make my mistake up to
you some way."   The flowers were funny, but I didn't meet her.

Then another girl called.   She's been calling me all the time,
wherever I go.   She says she's black and working for whites
who are wealthy, but she is poor.   She says they treat her bad
and she wants to make a good life for herself.   She says she's
22 years old, going to college and getting good grades.   And
since I make so much money and give so much of it away to
charity, why couldn't I contribute to her college education
and—by helping her—help my race get ahead?

She always says, "What's twenty-five hundred dollars a year
to you?"   I tell her it's a lot to me and I work hard for it and
while I give some of it away, because I should share my good
fortune, I give it to family or friends or people I know or causes
I believe in, I just don't throw it around.   But she keeps calling.   She won't take no for an answer.   I get a lot of calls like
this.   I don't know how they get my number, but they do.

I also get a lot of calls from the Lynns of the world who want
to meet me and maybe be my girl.   And if you think they're

ready to just jump in the sack with me, you're wrong. They want to go through the whole business of romancing first. So I don't pick up on these calls. They could be bad trouble anyway. Troubled girls looking to take you in some way. And I don't pick up girls much, anywhere. I've taken hundreds and hundreds of plane flights, and out of all those flights, I've met one girl I still see today. I meet girls the way other guys meet girls—through friends and at places I go regularly. I'm not looking to meet a lot of girls, anyway. I know a lot of girls already.

Monday, the 5th. Two doubleheaders in two days here in Minnesota. It's tough and we were satisfied to settle for a split. There was a big crowd of around 35,000 on hand Sunday, biggest of the season here, and it's nice to play in front of a lot of fans. Mangual and Rudi hit home runs with men on and we won the opener, 10–4—Catfish's fifteenth victory. Bando homered in the second game, but we lost, 2–1. Abbott lost it to Bill Butler.

Dark got a phone call before the game again and made some changes. Charlie listens on radio and when they announce Dark's lineup, Charlie calls in with his. One game it's Kubiak at short, the next game Maxvill. One game Rudi's in left, the next game he's on first. One game Tenace is on first, the next game he's behind the plate. In doubleheaders I'll play right one game and be designated hitter the next.

I got seven hits in the first three games of this series. I got a triple in the first game and doubles in the second and third games. I also got a home run in the third game, which was the first game of Monday night's twi-night doubleheader, and it won the game for us, 2–1. I am beginning to swing the bat better now, but it is still not what it was in April and May.

I hit a hell of a fastball for my 20th home run in the eighth inning to break a 1–1 tie and beat Bert Blyleven. He has a hell of a fastball. And he has the best curveball I've seen in baseball. It's like a ball rolling off the edge of a table. Even if you know it's coming, you can't hit it. I mean they could dig up Ruth and Gehrig and all the big names—and none of 'em could hit it. But he can't control it yet, so you can let it go.

You can wait for the fastball. He can blow it by you a lot of the time, but you can hit it some of the time, too.

He doesn't know how to set up the batters yet. He's a great big, strong kid with marvelous stuff, but he hasn't learned how to use his strength. He's only 22 or 23, and he's losing more games than he wins. I think he's struck out more men than any other pitcher at this point in a career. But he's not a man yet, he's still a boy. This is not a game for boys with quick bats or strong arms, it's a game for men who know how to use what they have. This game makes a man out of you. He may become the best pitcher in baseball. Or Ryan may. Or Busby. Or Bibby. Or Blue. All have the ability. It depends on who grows up the most.

Holtzman has grown up. He gets more done with less ability than a Blyleven or a Blue or a Busby or a Bibby. He beat Blyleven in the first game of tonight's doubleheader with the help of Fingers. The pitching was poor in the second game. Hamilton started for us and he was wild. We fell short, 4–3. Rod Carew singled in the winner for them. Carew is the best average-hitter in baseball. He's not a big guy and he doesn't swing a big bat, but he's the smartest hitter in baseball. And he handles the bat he does use the best of anyone I've seen in this sport. He doesn't hit home runs or drive in many runs, but he hits singles and doubles. He's the sort of player you want hitting in front of the hitters who drive in runs. He's the best bunter in baseball and the best at hitting behind the runner on the hit-and-run. He realizes his limitations, which a lot of players don't do. A lot of players who aren't suited for it swing for the fences and wind up hitting fifteen or sixteen home runs and .250. Carew swings for hits and winds up with five or six home runs and .350. He's not yet 30 and he's won three or four batting titles and he'll win another one this year. The best thing to do is do what you do best and he does his thing and I do mine. I get more headlines and make more money so my way works, but he is underrated.

Thursday, the 8th. When we got into the dressing room after the last game in Minnesota, Vida was already dressed and he didn't look like he was feeling well. Dark went over to him and asked what was wrong and Vida complained of pains in his chest. He went with us to Texas and went to the hospital there for a checkup. Finley was informed, and apparently he told them to take every precaution with the player. Later, we found out he even flew his son back to New York to get an EKG they had taken of Blue once, so they could compare it to a new one now. Of course Charlie's just been through a heart attack so he's sensitive to this sort of thing, but he's good about these things, anyway.

The first night we were in the ballpark in Dallas, Vida telephoned to say he was feeling fine. Finley told us not to visit him in the hospital, to let him rest, but it did appear he was all right. Today Vida rejoined us and said he felt fine and all the tests came out all right. He said he suspected he just suffered from some bad pork he'd eaten. There was a story by a doctor out of Texas that a lot of muscular black males suffer heart trouble because of their excessive chest development. Vida didn't think much of that and neither did I. To me it's just a lot of hocus-fucking-pocus. I don't like the connotation it puts out. But I hope Blue is all right.

The first game in Texas on Tuesday night, Blue Moon came off the bench and out of the bullpen to fill in for Vida. And he did fine, though he was defeated, 1–0, by Fergy Jenkins. John hadn't started in a hell of a long time, but except for a couple of bloop-hits that led to their only run, he could have had a shutout. He's been struggling and suffering and it was nice to see him do so well. Of course, Fergy Jenkins always does well. He's what I mean when I talk about a man who's learned how to do his job. He doesn't have to strike you out to get you out. He wouldn't walk anyone if he just wanted to get the pitch over the plate. The umpire was giving him the outside corner, so he kept throwing an inch or two off the corner and he kept getting the strike call. We bitched about it, but as long as he's getting it, that's what he'll take. They call that on the soul, on the brother, right there on the black.

If Fergy throws two inches outside and you go for it, next time he'll throw three inches outside. He's the only pitcher

who has ever dominated me with control.   He doesn't throw
hard.   He doesn't have a great curveball.   He doesn't have a
great change-up.   But he has a lot of good pitches he can put
wherever he wants.   And he can set you up for any pitch he
wants you to try to hit.   He had won 20 games six seasons in a
row when he had an off-season last year.   You'd think after all
he'd given the Cubs, they'd give him an off-year, but instead
they gave him away for nothing.   He won 20 games a year in
the National League, so he'll win 25 in the American League.
He is a pitcher's pitcher and a batter's nightmare.

We won the last two nights, 8–4 and 10–2.   I hit a three-run
homer off Bibby in that 8–4 game.   It was my third straight
home run off of Bibby.   They made a lot out of it in the papers, but I don't want to make too much of it.   He could strike
me out the next three times.   He can overpower me or anyone
when his heater is humming.   He throws so hard he scares you
sometimes.   He throws a lot of wild pitches and hits a lot of
scared batters.   But he is wild and he only has a fastball.   And
when he's not humming 'em over, he has nothing else to get
you out with.   He is an exciting .500 pitcher.   He wins big, but
loses big, and he loses as many as he wins.

With Blue out, they brought Knowles in from the bullpen
and he pitched about as good a game as Odom did the day
before.   He can be a great reliever, but he's subject to slumps
and a reliever has to be consistent.   I've seen him walk eight or
nine guys with the bases loaded.   But last night he didn't come
in in a tough spot, he got to start fresh and he held them for
five innings.   He was out of shape so they brought in Fingers
to finish up, but Fingers wasn't sharp.   Fortunately, he didn't
have to be because we'd built a big lead.

Odom has scuffled with me, with Vida, with almost everyone.
He doesn't mean anyone any harm, but he likes to kid and he
doesn't like to be kidded and that combination causes trouble.
He's had a sore arm so he hasn't been the great pitcher he
figured to be.   He's had to scratch to stay around, and he's
become insecure and very sensitive.   Everyone knows the way
he is and they forget his flareups fast.   Fingers is another need-
ler, but he's been getting a little sensitive about being needled,

too. He's having difficulties in his marriage. Still, he's doing his job.

He wasn't needed tonight, because Catfish performed and when it's the Cat, it's usually nine innings. He gave up nine hits, but only two runs. Well, that's the Cat for you. He only struck out one, but only walked one. We got ten runs and so he just coasted. He's not going to waste it when it's not needed. Rudi drove in five of the runs with a home run, a double and two singles. He drove David Clyde out fast, a kid who has been rushed much too fast. Rudi is still our steadiest player, and it is a crime that he is playing for only 55 grand, which is a raise of only five grand from the great year he had for us last year. The arbitration board bombed out on this one, because Joe has a value to a team that only his teammates know.

I feel for Rudi, because he's probably my best friend on the team. He is quiet and I'm not, but we work together. He is married, but we are together a lot, and we seem to get a lot out of each other. I admire him as a man as well as a player. He was really beat up by Finley and the arbitration board and it stole part of his pride from him. It's too bad. He's carrying a heavy weight around. He wants very much to knock in 100 runs, but the stats don't measure this man. If I had to pick a Most Valuable Player in this league right now, it would be between Bando, Rudi and myself. And if I don't get back in the groove I'll be out of the running to repeat.

If Luis Tiant keeps pitching the way he has been he has to be considered for MVP. Pitchers have the Cy Young award, so Tiant would have to win 25. And I don't think he will. I don't think the Red Sox will win their division. I know Texas won't, but if Texas finished second, Jenkins could be considered. Or Burroughs. He's ahead in homers and RBIs now. He really is outstanding. You have to be really outstanding to be considered when you're not with a winner.

Texas could finish second. They have Burroughs and they have Jenkins. They don't have many great players, but Billy Martin gets the most out of his players. He gets fired because he's always getting into hot water and he's always getting into fights. But he's a fighter and he's a winner. He paid me a compliment one time. He hollered at me that I could play for him anytime. I'd like to sometime. I played for Dick Williams and I'd like to play for Billy Martin because they're two of a kind. One thing's sure: When others are fading, Texas will still be trying to catch us.

Sunday, the 11*th.* We played in Texas Thursday night and flew home to Oakland to open a series with Boston Friday night. We won in Texas, but we lost at home to Boston. Bill Lee beat us, 6–2, and it wasn't that big a deal, but Finley decided to make a big deal out of it with Dark. Saturday morning in the clubhouse, I walked by Dark's office and he was in there with Finley and Bando. Alvin called to me, "Hey, Jack, come on in, you ought to be in on this." So I went in and they were talking about the fact that the first game we play when we get off a plane at the end of a homestand or a road trip, we always seem to play bad. Alvin explained that he didn't like the drinking on the plane. And Charlie said, "Well, if that's what it is, we'll just cut out the drinking on the plane."

Dark doesn't drink so it's easy for him to say you shouldn't drink. And it's easy for Finley to ban drinking on planes. He did that before, but after a while the rule got relaxed. But I didn't think it was fair to a team which had proven itself by winning a World Championship. On the other hand, I know some of the guys don't handle drinking too well.

I said, "I don't drink so it won't mean much to me, but some of the guys do and I don't know how they'd take this. I do drink a little beer and I don't see where a little beer would hurt."

Finley said, "All right, we'll ban hard liquor and limit the drinking to a little beer." Dark was willing to settle for that.

We went out and won that day behind Blue, 5–3. It was his first start since his heart-attack scare. He was well rested, and he said he felt stronger than usual. And he just went out and knocked the bats out of their hands. He outmatched the Red Sox. It was his 15th win of the season.

This afternoon Juan Marichal showed us another kind of pitching. He held us to three hits in eight innings and beat us,

2–1. It was another tough loss for Abbott, but he lost to a
master.   He's 35 now and I guess he hasn't got what he had
when he was with the Giants, but Marichal can still show you
something.   He's still got that high kick that looks like he's
stuffing his foot in your face before he pitches.   He's got as
many motions as Luis Tiant.   And as many pitches.   And he's
smoother, prettier.

He teases you with fastballs, keeps changing speeds on you
and throws a zillion screwballs that break every which way.   He
can't throw as hard as he used to, but he doesn't have to.   He
makes you look so bad, he just takes the heart out of you.   I
guess he's had a sore neck and a sore hand, but if he's going
out, he's going out in style.

If Marichal and Tiant can continue to pitch like this, the Red
Sox have a shot at the playoffs.   Boston has another top
pitcher in Bill Lee.   Carl Yastrzemski and Rico Petrocelli give
them a lot of punch.   They've got a good team.   The only
thing is that their catcher, Carlton Fisk, is an important part of
the team and he's out now for the season.   I thought they
would miss him more than they have.   I still think they'll slow
down without him.

The only reason they haven't slowed down so far is Yaz won't
let 'em.   Yaz is the guts of this team.   He's a better ballplayer
than people realize.   People badmouth him because he pops
off sometimes.   But without Yaz, this is an ordinary team.   I
really respect him as a player for what he puts on the field.   He
puts it all out there.   He's one of the most valuable players in
baseball year after year.

Wednesday, the 14th.   Before Monday night's game, the series
opener with the Yankees, Finley called a clubhouse meeting
and Dark informed the players of the ban on hard drinking on
the plane flights in the interests of improving team performance.   Dark said, "The rest of the year we'll have to sacrifice
a little to keep things going.   All of you want to give one hundred
percent when you come to the ballpark, but some of you wind up
giving seventy percent.   From now on, I want you to give one
hundred percent of one hundred percent."

One player wrote "100 percent of 100 percent" on a piece of

adhesive and taped it to the back of his uniform. Some of the
guys were sarcastic about the meeting. One said that hip flasks
soon would be back in style. But most of the guys took it with
good grace. We're not the only club to put in such a ban.
Some of the Yankees told us they have a ban on drinking.
But, hell, there's talk that Alvin's going to take an ax and run
around busting up saloons. And it isn't as if Finley doesn't
drink himself. Finley keeps saying over and over, "Sweat plus
Sacrifice Equals Success." It's the slogan he lives by and tries
to beat into everyone's head. Good old "S Plus S Equals S."
The players say, "Shit Plus Shit Equals Shit." Which is true,
too, I guess. We're really past the point of pep talks, but Charlie
thrives on 'em.

Pepped up, we went out and won two out of three from the
Yankees, which put us nineteen over .500 at 69 and 50, which
is enough to take us into the playoffs if we can keep it up.
Monday night we won, 3-2. Hunter beat Dobson. Tuesday
night we won, 6-1. Holtzman beat Doc Medich. North and
Herb Washington ran wild. Wednesday night they beat us,
4-1. Blue lost to Rudy May, who throws hard but is inconsis-
tent. We should have beat them in this one, too.

The Yankees don't know how to win. I told that to a writer
and it'll probably raise a stink, but it's true. They shouldn't be
behind Boston in their division, but they are. Boston has a
good team, but the Yankees have a better team. The Yankees
have a hell of a lot of talent, you know—Munson, Bobby
Murcer, Medich, Mel Stottlemyre, Sparky Lyle. The Yankees
have a lot of good ballplayers, but they don't have a good team.
They don't seem to have a lot of spirit. They don't play with
confidence. They don't do the little things that you have to do
out on the field to win. They don't seem to sacrifice for one
another.

Take Bobby Murcer. I think he's a hell of a ballplayer, but
he's not a team player. I don't think they have a leader, and
he should be leading them. They're playing in Shea Stadium
and it seems to have psyched them out. It's a bigger ballpark and it seems to have them scared. Especially Murcer.
We used to marvel at his swing, but now he's swinging like a

lady. He keeps saying he can't hit homers in Shea Stadium, which is shit. With his swing, he should be able to hit them anywhere. He's mixed up in his head and it's affecting him physically. It's too bad, because he's a hell of a talent.

The Yankees could catch the Red Sox, but I still believe Baltimore will win the Eastern Division.

Campy came back off the disabled list Monday night. He said he didn't want to, but Charlie wanted him to so he did. Charlie was worried about shortstop. He saw a couple of ground balls get by Kubiak, so he ordered Dark to substitute Dal Maxvill. But he has no confidence in Maxvill, though Maxvill is a master shortstop. He can't hit, but you don't need a hitter at shortstop, you need a fielder, and Maxvill's a fielder. He's a better fielder than Campaneris, but Charlie only looks at the hitting. It's great to be able to bring in a Maxvill when a Campaneris is out. We have a great bench. Kubiak is a great guy on the bench. He knows he's just an extra man. He doesn't bitch about it. He makes himself useful and when his chance comes, he does a job for you. When someone gets hurt, he's ready.

When Fosse got hurt, Haney was ready. He's only hitting .160 or so, but you don't need a hitter at catcher, you need defense and he's a great defensive catcher. Fosse isn't any better defensively, though he's a lot better with the bat. Fosse was considered the American League's answer to Johnny Bench as a young catcher, until Pete Rose bowled him over in the All-Star Game and wrecked his shoulder a few years ago. That's where he hurt his shoulder, not breaking up Billy North and me. It makes good copy, but it's bullshit. Fosse's OK. He's an enthusiast. And he can swing the bat. He's recovering from his operation. He'll be back before long and will be welcome.

We've got bats on the bench. When Cookie Mangual and Claudell Washington aren't playing they can pinch-hit effectively. This kid Washington's going to be a wonder. He thinks I have a wonderful life now. He envies me. I tell him everything I have now, you'll have a few years from now —when I no longer have it. He has the swing to be a super-

star. Jesus Alou is as nifty with a bat as any ballplayer.
Boogaloo—we call him "Boogaloo"—could get a base hit in a
dark alley off a pitcher he couldn't see.

There are guys who would love to play every day and don't
and guys who do and wish they didn't. Campaneris is a funny
guy. He's hurting all the time. The writers write that when
we lose a game, we lose because he's out. The ballplayers don't
like that because it's bullshit. He helps us win, but we can win
without him. There's only two or three guys this club couldn't
win without for a prolonged period. I'm one. Bando's
another. Joe Rudi, probably. Dick Green, possibly. Campy's
a hell of a player. He can get hot and carry this club for a
while. But then he can do nothing for a while—and the club
can get along without his help. He's not the best shortstop in
the field, but he's the best all-around shortstop in the league.
But we can get along without him—because we have to do it
so much.

He comes back Monday night and goes hitless and says he
doesn't feel right, so Tuesday and Wednesday nights he's back
on the bench. And he sits there without making a sound. He
sits off by himself. He's not close to anyone on the team. I
don't think anyone on the team knows him. I don't think anyone understands him. He's withdrawn. I try to understand
him. I don't dislike him. I do sympathize with him. The way
I see it, he still doesn't speak English well. He doesn't read
English. He doesn't seem to hear you when you speak to him.

He's from Cuba and he feels like a foreigner in this country.
He has a wife and child, and he feels he couldn't get a job in
this country except for baseball. I don't think he knows what
he'll do or where he'll go when he's finished in baseball. He's
making 70 grand a year and he wants to make it as long as he
can and protect his position in the game as long as he can; he
doesn't know what there'll be for him later.

A couple of years ago in the playoffs, when Lerrin LaGrow
of the Tigers was throwing baseballs at him and Campy threw
his bat at him, he was just trying to protect himself the only way
he knew how, trying to protect his position. He seemed
shocked when they suspended him. It scared hell out of him,

and he went and sat in the corner of the bench all by himself and went into a shell. He worries about himself. He worries when he gets a hangnail. He worries when he gets a pimple. He has the lowest tolerance for pain of any player I've ever known. When he's hurting, he doesn't want to be playing. Well, it's all he's got and he feels he's got to protect it.

Actually Maxvill makes a better double-play combination with Dick Green. Green is the Brooks Robinson of second basemen. He holds our defense together and you win with defense as much as you do with offense. Last Sunday he took the bat right out of Boston's hands. With the tying run on second, Greenie was playing 40 feet out in the fucking outfield. Danny Cater hit a single into right-center. Only Greenie was standing in right-center, and he caught the ball and took them right out of the game. After the game, they asked Green what the hell he was doing out there and he said he was waiting for Cater to hit the ball to him. It always looks like an accident when Greenie happens to be where the ball is, but it's no accident; he knows this game and he goes where the ball is going to go.

He's a goofy sort of guy, always screwing around off the field, but he's fun to be with. He's tired of the game. He doesn't get out of it what he should. After every season he retires. And before the next season, Charlie talks him into returning. Charlie knows the season Greenie doesn't return is the season the A's will be in trouble.

Sunday, the 18*th.* The A's had a day in my honor yesterday. I had a lot of last year's awards to get. Finley called me and asked me if it would be all right to have a day in my honor so I could get my awards, and I said yes. He picked this Saturday and it drew this tremendous crowd of 10,000, but it was very nice. I invited about 20 of my friends and they all came. Lee MacPhail, the president of the American League, almost didn't come. He came late, after Joe Sargis of UPI had given me the plaque MacPhail was supposed to give me for being Most Valuable Player in the league last year. I also got a trophy for being voted Player of the Year in both leagues.

A representative of the City of Oakland gave me $250 to give to my favorite charity. I'll match it and give it to the Muscular Dystrophy Association. I'm chairman of the fund-raising board in my area. And the Oakland A's players gave me $300 to donate to a charity, which I really appreciate and which I'll probably give to a black charity. Because they were the team in town, the Tigers' John Fetzer and Jim Campbell gave me a really beautiful clock, which I'm going to put over my TV at home. And Charlie gave me a home entertainment center —you know, stereo, radio, TV, the works. It felt nice, because it was the first thing he's ever given me.

Believe it or not, he also gave me an autographed eight-by-ten picture of himself. It says, "To Reggie Jackson . . . Someone I'll always admire . . . With great Respect, Charlie Finley." I'll put it on the stereo. I'm sort of proud of it. And I gave a hell of a speech. Outasight.

Everything was nice, except we lost the game. But it was good to be alive. Just alive. The same guy that sent me the death threat last year just sent me another one. The cops and the FBI know it's the same guy because the notes have been in the same handwriting. They also lifted the same fingerprints off of them, and they're all mailed from the same south San Francisco area. The letters are addressed to Monte Moore, but they're intended for me.

This one was received during the Boston series, but I didn't say anything about it because I didn't want to talk about it or to think about it. I think I was supposed to get knocked off during my day, and now my day is done and I'm still here. I thought about calling the day off. Finley said I could do whatever I wanted to do. But George Williams, the head FBI guy out here, and the other FBI guys said to go ahead with it; they thought it would be all right. I trust them because I know them by now. I use 'em every year.

The day of the game, two of the guys picked me up at my house and drove me to the ballpark. They followed me around all day and brought me back home. There were 20 plainclothes guys all around and I had my bodyguard, Tony Del Rio, around. All right, it's probably a kook. But kooks kill too, don't they?   More important people than me have been assassinated in recent years.

I'm in the spotlight.   I can't laugh it off so easy anymore.   I can't let it scare me off, either.   I think I showed in the last World Series I could perform under this sort of pressure. This day I went hitless, but I might have anyway.   They tell me they've talked to four or five suspects, but they haven't pinned it on anyone yet.

My life has been kind of funny lately.   Slug and his family have been spending the summer with me.   I have really loved having them, but it has upset my routine, too.   It was good rapping with him.   It was good playing with the kid.   His wife cooked all the time, which was real nice.   But I'm not used to having a wife around anymore.   And a kid.   I'm used to having a woman here when I want one here.   Having family here cramped my style some.   Still, it was good for me.   It wasn't all giving and not getting.   I needed some lawn furniture, so Slug went out and bought some stuff.   I needed my hi-fi fixed up, so Slug set up the speakers and stuff.   His wife kept the kitchen going.

It was nice, but it changed my way of life.   I didn't realize it, but it affected my play.   It cut into my concentration.   Well, that's the way it is.   You don't just live at the ballpark.   Now they're going back home and my life is going back to the way it was.

Friday night, Hunter hooked up with Mickey Lolich, and Lolich got the better of it.   They scored a run, but Tenace homered to tie it up.   Lolich may have a beer-belly hanging over his belt, but he can still bring that ball to the plate in a hurry and he's still tough to take.   But in the sixth inning he hung a slider over the plate and I hit home run number 22 off him with one on and we were ahead, 3–1, and breezing.   You know, that's enough offense, boys.   Catfish will hold them and that will be that.   Then Jim Nettles, who just came up a couple of weeks ago, hit a three-run homer off Catfish.   We were stunned.   Nobody hits a three-run homer off Catfish in that situation.   And *Jim Nettles?*   Then the next hitter, Bill Freehan, who got nine homers all year, hits another one and we were done. Back-to-back homers off Hunter, four runs, and we were finished.

Saturday we lost, 4–3. Campy singled with one out and they brought in John Hiller. Campy was supposed to steal, but he didn't run. He said his leg hurt him and he couldn't run. He was limping, but Dark didn't put in Herb Washington to run for him. It burned up Finley. He went down to the dressing room later and he bawled out Dark for not bringing in Washington and he bawled out our trainer, Joe Romo, for not going out to check Campy's leg. Today Romo ran out every time Campy or anyone else got on. It was funny as hell. Romo was doing what he was told to do. But what he did was run out to examine the runner seven or eight times every time one of them scratched his ass.

After Saturday's game Finley held one of his marathon meetings with Dark and the coaching staff. I'm told it lasted five hours. I'm told no one talked but Finley. I'm told Finley told his staff this was a better team with Rudi in left and Tenace at first instead of catching. This is funny because it is Finley who has wanted Rudi at first and Tenace catching.

Oh, yes, he also figured out that Odom should replace Abbott as the starter during Phil's next turn, because Abbott had a bad start that day. So he's being sent down. Well, it's not the first time he's been sent down this season. He'll be back. He's Finley's fucking yo-yo. The other day Finley ordered Pat Bourque down so he could call Bill Parsons up, then changed his mind in a matter of minutes and canceled his order. Bourque laughed and said, "It feels like I never left." Well, it's not really so fucking funny when you're treated like a yo-yo.

After the game I went into the clubhouse and the writers were there and they were telling the players they had figured out why we had lost nine out of seventeen. They were wondering if we needed to get some help like Cleveland did when they picked up Rico Carty, or like this or that team did when they picked up this guy or that. I gathered them around my locker.

"Look," I said, "before you go spreading shit all over this clubhouse and instigating trouble on this team, let me tell you some things: We're not going to play .700 ball all season. We

don't have to be told we're in a little bit of a slump, we just have
to read the papers.

"We've got the best team in baseball. We've proven that before and we'll prove it again. The numbers will add up right
at the end, which is the only time you have to add them up.
We don't have to go to Japan to get Sadahara Oh, or whatever
the hell his name is. We don't have to go to Mexico for anyone. We don't need anyone we haven't already got. All we
need is to relax and keep our cool—and we'll come out on top
at the finish."

Well, it came out in this morning's paper that the A's are
losing, but Reggie says if they relax and keep their cool they'll
be all right. This afternoon we were in a tight game with the
Tigers for seven innings. In the eighth inning I hit a three-
run home run and Tenace hit a three-run home run and we
scored nine runs and we won, 13–3. I had a single and a double besides my home run and drove in four runs.

I told Charlie today, when I passed him in the walkway, he
had nothing to worry about. I told him all the five-hour meetings in the world weren't going to do for us what we could do
for ourselves. And he said, well, when we seemed to be developing a problem he wanted to do what he could for us to
solve it.

He does do what he can do, which is better than doing nothing. Maybe he butts in too much, but he cares and I guess
that's better than being one of those owners who doesn't care.

Wednesday, the 21st. Pat Bourque hadn't had a hit in eleven
at-bats, when he singled to drive in two runs Sunday. So
Monday he was gone, traded to the Twins for Jim Holt. It was
strictly a trade of left-handed pinch-hitters. Bourque had become family and we'll miss him. It is one thing to be Reggie
Jackson and another to be Pat Bourque. It is easy to say this is
a great game when you drive in 100 runs a year and make 100
grand a year and get your face on national magazine covers.
But it must be hard to feel that way when you are bounced
around and never get a good chance and no one knows you
and you must move your family a couple of times a year.

Finley's last night here and he saw us lose to Milwaukee, 1–0.

Billy Champion and Tommy Murphy stopped us cold. I
guess we used up all of tonight's hits yesterday. There's no
other way of explaining it. It was a tough loss for Vida. He
allowed only four hits, but one of them was sent downtown by
good old George Scott.

I gave Charlie and myself a scare when I popped up with a
man on in the ninth and, in throwing my bat toward the back-
stop, saw it sail three rows into the stands behind home plate.
It just missed Alvin's wife and hit a boy. I guess Alvin was
scared, too. The boy was, but he wasn't hurt. Finley rushed
to him and took him into the manager's office. I met him
there and gave the boy and his friend a bat and an autographed
baseball each. Finley gave them tickets to all the remaining
games at home and a tour of the clubhouse.

The only office worker at the ballpark yesterday wearing a
tie was the one who had to pick Finley up at the hotel and drive
him to the airport for his flight home to Chicago. Then all of
a sudden all was calm. Dark relaxed. The players heaved a
sigh of relief. Tenace hit a grand slam, and we won, 7–1.
Hunter had a three-hitter for his eighteenth win. Tonight
my two-run homer, number 24, was about all we got off
rookie Kevin Kobel, and the Brewers beat Blue Moon and us,
5–3.

Friday, the 23rd. Before we left for Boston, people around
town were talking about how we were starting to struggle.
Well, hell, our lead has fallen off to four and a half. But
we're still in front. We've cooled off and Kansas City has gotten hot, but we'll get hot and they'll cool off. On the flight to
Boston, Dark huddled with his coaches and they talked things
over, with Finley's shadow at their shoulders. They came out
of it asking me if I'd hit third instead of fourth for awhile.
There's a lot of class to hitting cleanup, but Babe Ruth batted
third. Well, all right. It's getting interesting now. The
money's on the line now, and when that happens, I'll put my
money on us.

Boston has sold out their ballpark for three straight nights.
We're in pennant races. Everyone's excited. I love it. This
is what baseball is all about. I'll get out to the ballpark early

every night.   Fenway is a joke of a little ballpark with that left-field fence so close you could reach out and touch it, but at least they put people into the seats in this town.

Tiant had the 35,000 fans dancing in the aisles tonight as he shut us out, 3–0, on six hits for his 20th victory.   That man did everything but stand on his head and throw.   He threw over-hand, underhand, sidearm.   He put on a fantastic, tremendous show.   Even being beaten, you had to appreciate it.   Blue was beaten again in a game that he worked well enough in to win. Kansas City settled for a split of a doubleheader, so our lead was cut only half a game.

Sunday, the 25th.   We beat Boston two in a row.

Saturday night the Catfish cut them down, 4–1, on four hits. When we need one, he wins one.   They had won five straight, but they didn't win this one.   Kansas City won too.

Sunday afternoon they made a mistake.   Marichal was scheduled to start, but they turned to Moret instead.   Rogelio Moret, a Puerto Rican.   He one-hit the White Sox his last start, so they used him.   And he has the talent, but Marichal has the experience.   It was a tough time to turn to a kid.   Moret is so skinny, you can't believe it.   Seven feet tall and 100 pounds. Throws hard, too.   No-hit us for five innings.   But we got to where we could time him, and when we put pressure on him, he popped.   Rudi ripped a grand slammer.   Meanwhile, Holtzman shut them out on five hits, 5–0, for his fifteenth vic-tory.   We went whooping and hollering into the clubhouse.

K.C. won, too, but we're OK now.   Afterwards Rudi was rattling on about his five RBIs and ribbing me about being 0-for-five and he got the other guys going on me.   But I just told them I'm a team player.   To prove my point, I treated Rudi to dinner.   Only he picked up the tab because, he said, five ribbies have to give handouts to 0-for-fives.   But we lost the dinner.   The food was 0-for-five just like me.

Monday, the 26th.   We were the backup TV game tonight. Interviewing me before the game, Maury Wills asked me if I watched the scoreboard to see how the other teams in our divi-sion were doing.   I told him I sure did.   I said there's two kinds of players: those that watch the scoreboard and admit it, and those that watch it and lie about it.

Billy Champion pitched against us tonight. We thought we'd take him, because we owed him something, but he put it to us again. Abbott was called back up for the third time this season, but Dark started Odom anyway and he pitched well enough. First it was one-nothing, then two-nothing, and the game was getting on. I came up in the eighth with two on and one out. I hit the hardest ball I've hit in a helluva long time. However, I hit it right at Pedro Garcia at second base and he turned it into a double play. It should have tied the game. We were really down in the dressing room later. Then we found out Kansas City lost and that gave us a lift.

Wednesday, the 28th. Before the game last night, Finley came into the clubhouse. I can picture it. It's a short drive from Chicago and he drives up with friends telling them he'll talk to us and turn things around. He's such a supersalesman he thinks he can sell wins to ballplayers. Somewhere along the line, every season he turns up to give us the Knute Rockne rah, rah, rah. He said we weren't hungry, we were fat and complacent. What he forgets is that he's always telling us how he keeps us hungry by not making our contracts too fat.

Finley said the pitchers were doing their jobs, but the batters weren't doing theirs. According to him we need more determination and desire. He said determination is in the head and desire is in the heart. I was sitting by Bando and we both almost burst out laughing. I whispered to Bando that I don't need no determination, I don't need no desire, all I need is a couple of fucking base hits. Charlie put on a real good show, he looked good in front of his friends, and we appreciated it. I mean there are times when he just seems like a good old guy who doesn't know any other way to win than to try to talk us into it. All he cares about is baseball and winning World Championships. He keeps talking about winning five in a row, which is the record. He wants that in the worst way. If he has to sell the team, it will hurt him.

Some of the guys have no sympathy for him and I can un-

derstand their feelings.   Greenie and Tenace and some of the
other guys were cutting him up after he left.   On the other
hand, maybe the message did reach the guys even if they
wouldn't admit it.   Tempers flared in the game, which we won,
3–2.   Geno got thrown out.   Fosse went in for him and caught
six innings and seems to be coming around.   It was a wild one,
and we won it with two runs in the eighth.   Holt pinch-hit a
single and Herbie ran for him, and stole second.   Campy won
it with hustling base running.   Campy showed me something
with his hustle.   There are times his enthusiasm is suspect and
times he performs like a tough sonofabitch.

Another guy who's showing me something is Fingers.   He's
had a hard year.   Privately, not professionally.   He and his
wife Jill have broken up and gotten back together a couple of
times.   I understand there've been some bad scenes.   He was
ready to move in with me for a while.   She was ready to divorce him.   I think they're back together again now.   I don't
know how solid it is.   I haven't talked a lot about it, because I
don't think it's my place to talk about other players' personal
problems.   But now there's a point to talking about it.   I want
to point out how well a professional like Fingers can perform,
even when he's having personal problems.   Rollie went to
Alvin and assured him he could perform despite his problems.
He asked Dark to keep using him just like always, and he has
come through.

A lot of guys are coming through for us, but I'm not.   I have
been hitless in three straight games now.   I thought I was swinging the bat better and was about to go on a tear, but now I
don't know.   After the game last night, I felt real down.   It's
one of the few times in the last few years I felt low like this.
Oh, I'm up and down, but this season is really getting to me.
I got off to such a good start.

I behaved badly last night, brooding all night.   I have a
friend here from Chicago, a girl by the name of June.   She
hasn't been around me that much in these situations.   I don't
usually like having anyone around me at these times.   I guess it
was an experience for her.   She took it in stride.   She's good
people and she was sympathetic and she helped me get out of

my bad mood. I guess I'm entitled to my moods, but I'm glad they don't last long.

This morning the sun is shining and I have a smile on my face and I feel like I can cope with my problems. I'm just going to have to try harder, going to have to concentrate harder. I'm just going to dig in and do better. The Brewers better beware tonight.

Sunday, the 1st of September. I hit two tremendous home runs Friday night and I do seem to be off on a tear now. I don't know when I've wanted home runs more. And the two I hit broke up a hell of a pitchers' duel between Catfish Hunter and Jim Colborn. Hunter won his 20th. I remember that once in spring training I was slow getting into the batter's box against Colborn and he said something about me getting the hell in the box and it made me mad. It's funny how a little thing like that can stick with you and turn you against a guy. He's a good pitcher and he handles me pretty well, but I always try extra hard against him, which is maybe why he does so well with me. The harder you try, the worse you do sometimes. The more you concentrate, the better you do. It is easy to say you should concentrate all the time, but it is hard to do when you go to bat 500, 600 or 700 times a season.

I was happy to help Hunter. Several of the A's were talking about the Cat after the game, and we agreed it was a shame he signed a two-year contract for 100 grand this year. It may take 100 grand to sign Blue next year. It will take more than 100 grand to sign Holtzman next year. Bando will be well above 100 grand. I'll be somewhere between 100 and 200 grand. When we win another World Series, we're going to grind Charlie O. down. But The Cat will have won 20 games for the fourth straight season and he'll still be stuck at 100 grand.

No one is better than The Cat, and no one has gotten less out of it. He is not happy about it. I don't blame him. It is Finley's place to keep his stars happy, but he'd rather keep them hungry. I won't be surprised if Hunter raises hell after this season. If Finley got the best of Catfish in business, it is not right. Finley is a businessman, Catfish isn't. If Finley was

fair, he would offer to renegotiate Cat's contract.   But Finley is
not fair in matters of money.

In Detroit, I visited with Dave DeBusschere, the basketball
star who's quitting as a player with the Knicks to become general manager of the Nets.   Dave couldn't believe I really was
making only $135,000 a year. He said he was making around
$290,000 a year and he wasn't even a superstar.   He said Walt
Frazier was making $330,000 or so and Kareem Abdul-Jabbar
was making more than $500,000 a year.   It's only because bas-
ketball has a rival league and competition for talent that its
salaries are so much bigger than those in baseball.   We agreed
it would be nice if those guys would get that rival baseball
league going, because I'd like to see competition for my talent.
When athletes get together they always talk about money.
We can't be bulled about salaries, because we know what
everyone makes.

I did not get a hit last night because I only had one shot at a
hit.   Joe Coleman walked me four fucking times, and he beat
us, 7–3.   A writer told me he asked Coleman why he walked
me four times and Coleman said he'd have walked me five
times if it took that to beat us.   He said he'd thrown a homer to
me on a three-and-one pitch the last time he faced me and he
wished he'd thrown a fourth ball instead of something I could
stroke.   He said when I hit a home run like that, it electrified
my team, it charged the club up, and we went on to take him
apart.   He decided I wasn't going to get anything good from
him from then on.

I take that as a hell of a compliment.   The fact is, in talking
into the tape recorder for this book, I have talked about the big
hits I have gotten or the big hits I have not gotten.   But I have
not talked about the walks I have gotten, and I have been getting some most games.   I will wind up with around 100.   It is
a compliment to me and it shows the pitchers are afraid of me,
which is half the fight right there.   Bando gets a lot of walks.
Tenace, too.   And Rudi.   All good hitters.   I get more than
most.   And a walk is as good as a hit.   A single, anyway.   But I
am not a singles hitter.   I'd rather have my swings.

This afternoon I got two hits, scored a run and drove in a run off a good pitcher, Mickey Lolich. And we won, 5–3. Bando and Tenace hit home runs. Campy stole two bases. Hunter won number 21 and Fingers saved him in the late innings for his sixteenth save. Well, the money is on the line now and the A's want that bread. We have the longest boardinghouse reach around. Here it is September and we are in the stretch run. The pennant, the playoffs and World Series are within reach.

We finished August with a record of 77 and 56, so we are 21 games above .500 after—what, 130-some games? We are in good shape with the end in sight. Kansas City has started to lose, as I suspected they would, so I no longer am looking at the scoreboard so much. Our lead is back up to six or seven games and I feel we are on our way again. I think I am straightened out now and can contribute to the club the way the MVP should through the last month of the regular season. If someone wants to take a run at us, let 'em. This club can handle all challenges.

8 ☆ SEPTEMBER

Monday, the 2nd. We're home now. I took a girl to the Empress of China last night and I stuffed myself with a five-course meal. There were some people there from Israel and we chatted with them and they wrote my name in Hebrew. If I can learn how to do it, I might sign my autographs that way. That would shake up the kids, count on it. I just needed to get away and relax. The season has only one month left now and it has already lasted three years. Because of this book, I have not been away from baseball one damn day, even off-days, and there are not many off-days. Today was not an off-day because we have a game tonight. And because that fucking Libby—the guy I'm writing this book with—was in town to fill in some holes, as he calls them, in my tapes.

I am talking into my handy-dandy little portable tape recorder now. I talk into it before games and after games. I talk into it at home. I talk into it while I am eating, while I am going to the john, and while I am in bed. I am a guy who likes to talk, but I am just about talked out. When I stop talking into my handy-dandy little portable tape recorder, Libby shows up with his handy-dandy little portable tape recorder, and he tells me to talk into his.

I took him for a ride in the Porsche Cararra I just bought. I tried to scare him by driving about 100 miles an hour on city streets, but he didn't seem scared. I am disappointed, but he has done books on race drivers, so maybe speed isn't what scares him. Cars relax me. I put my money in cars. Five cars now. Twenty-five grand in dough. Speed turns me on. I told him I didn't buy a Ferrari because I was afraid I would be tempted by the extra power. He said I could get killed as fast by hitting a pole at 100 miles an hour in my Porsche as at 120 in a Ferrari. I'll buy that. I believe I'll get killed in a car crash at 100 miles an hour some day. That is the way I'll go. There are worse ways. He asked me why I didn't get tickets for speeding. I told him most of the cops know me and don't stop me. If they don't recognize me and do stop me, they don't give me a ticket when they find out who I am. The cops in Oakland are kind to me. Everyone should have a home-town in which he is a hero.

There are things I want to do this last month of the season. My batting average is down near .300 and I want to keep it above that. I need fifteen ribbies to drive in 100 for the year and I want them. I need three homers for 30 and I want at least that many. But I will take the base hits because I want to steal fifteen bases, so I can wind up with 30 of those, too. In San Francisco, they made such a big fucking deal about Bobby Bonds hitting 30 home runs and stealing 30 bases in the same season that I want to show them how easy it is. I am not putting Bonds down. He does a lot of things well, but that particular thing isn't so outstanding.

Thursday, the 5th. We won two out of three from the Angels, but the satisfaction was taken out of it by Finley. Charlie fucked it up as usual. It was Dick Williams's return to Oakland and as his Angels were being beat in the ninth inning of the first game Monday night, there was a message put up on the scoreboard which read: "Goodnight, Dick." Maybe it doesn't seem like much, but it was rubbing in a defeat on a guy who won a lot for us. I waved to the press box, trying to tell them to take it down. As Joe Rudi said, Dick has too much class to be treated this way, but then Charlie doesn't have any class. All the guys were angry and agreed it was bush. I went into the

Angel clubhouse later and apologized to Dick on behalf of the players.

He smiled and said he understood. I guess he does, because he's been down that road with that man. I said if it happened again, I would walk off the field. The writers printed it and I guess Finley didn't want to test it. He put the same message up, again, after the second game Tuesday night, but this time he waited until after the game.

Monday night we won, 6–4, and I hit my 28th home run and a single and stole my sixteenth base. Dick Green told me he was glad he was on my team. This was my fourth homer in five games, and it came with one on in the first inning, off Frank Tanana.

Williams's Angel losing streak went to ten in a row Tuesday night, when we won, 7–0, by knocking out his best pitcher, Nolan Ryan, in the fifth inning. Holtzman pitched the shutout, giving up only five hits. Ryan allowed only three hits, but he was trying so hard for strikeouts he walked eight and the hits beat him. If he tried less for strikeouts, he'd get more victories.

I got a lot of heat because I patted him on the butt after I made out my second time up, but I didn't tell anyone why. The first time up, he walked me. The second time up, he called for the catcher, Ellie Rodriguez, and sent him back to the plate to tell me he was going to throw me fastballs right over the plate. He was losing 3–0 at the time, but he said he wanted to get the best fastball and the best power together and see who would win. I didn't know whether to believe him, but he delivered. He just threw fastballs. Bam, bam. And I hit one, wham. I sent it on a line to left. I thought it was going to drill a hole through the seats and wind up outside the ballpark. But I didn't get it high enough and it was caught in front of the fence. I was disappointed, but I called it a draw. He had got me out, though I had hammered hell out of the ball. I knew he knew it. Running back to the dugout, I went by him and gave him a pat on the ass to let him know he'd given me a display of guts I admired. He didn't say anything. He didn't have to.

The next time up, he wasn't going to give me one I would hit

out. He threw hard, but he didn't throw a strike. He threw
one right at my right eye. You know, he cranks up and seems
to get a running start and that ball is nothing but a blur.
When he aims one at you, it freezes you with fear, because it
could kill you. All I saw was this white blur coming right at me
and it froze me for a split second before I got the hell out of
there. I went down flat, just in time. I was burnt by the heat
of the ball as it went by.

I was so shook I thought that if he threw three straight
strikes I'd let him have them. We were ahead and I wanted to
wind up alive. But, you know, I figured, well, fuck him. I
don't want to back down. I don't want to start a trend that will
have every pitcher in the game going for my head to back me
down. So, I grit my teeth and dug in and was ready to swing
at anything good. He didn't throw me anything good. He
threw me two maybes that were called balls, which made it four
balls and gave me my walk. I never moved a muscle in that
batter's box, but I breathed a sigh of relief afterwards. He left
after that.

We lost last night. We got ten walks and still lost, which is
ridiculous. We lost, 5-2, as Blue pitched for the fifth straight
time without winning one. Well, Williams finally won one.
There were only 3,200 people in the mausoleum and I guess
it was hard for the guys to get up to beat a team they'd beaten
ten straight times.

I'm only a couple of homers behind Richie Allen for the
league lead. It doesn't look like Dick wants to play, much
less hit homers. If he doesn't want it, fuck it, I'll take it if I
can. I didn't hit any homers last night, but I hit a single and
stole two more bases. And the last time up, I hit the shit out of
the ball.

I also got a lot of credit for a good catch I made. Joe
Lahoud hit one that looked like it was going to get out, but I
was going to get it if I could and I did. I made a better play no
one noticed in the first inning. There was a man on second
when Bob Oliver singled to right-center in front of me. I cut it
off, turned, and made a perfect throw to the cutoff man,
Campy. If he had turned and thrown home, we would have
gotten the runner at the plate, but he didn't.

The thing is, this is the time of year we're headed for another pennant. I feel like I'm being judged and I'm playing my ass off. You have to overcome frustrations. In the first inning, I hit a slow ball in the infield and I ran hard and beat the ball to the base. And then I didn't get the call. I came back to the bench and a couple of guys said, "Nice hustle." Well, fuck that. I want to hear "Nice hit." I've had fifteen fucking calls like that this season and I'm fed up with them. I don't get on umps unless I really get mad and I sympathize with them, but it looks like they're fucking bored right now.

Sunday, the 8th. Baseball shouldn't be boring to any of the A's anymore this season. We just lost three out of four to Texas and we're paying for playing lousy, because Billy Martin's boys suddenly are only five and a half back now. You shouldn't be bored by your business. If you are, find something else to do. Quit fucking around. Do the job. We can get it done, but not the way we've been doing it. We build up big leads in the standings, then blow them by being bored and playing bad. It's stupid.

Thursday night we won, 3–0. Cat's always all business and it was his 22nd win of the season. I got a hit, drove in a run and stole another base. I only need ten more now. This one put Texas eight and a half back. We must have let down, because they got up and got on us. Friday night Bando hit a three-run homer to put us ahead in the eighth, but Burroughs singled in the tying run in the ninth. Then in the eleventh, Dark had Fingers pitch to Burroughs with first base open and a man on second and he singled in the winner, 5–4. Fuck!

Last night Rudi and Tenace homered, but they just stomped us, 8–2. This afternoon, Jenkins turned us off for the fourth straight time, 5–1. He was heading for 30-straight scoreless innings. When I singled to start the ninth, Rudi singled and Fosse scored me with a sacrifice fly. But that was the only hit I had in three games and the only run we got in this game. Now everyone is getting edgy.

Last night Knowles came in, pitched a couple of innings, gave up a couple of hits and got the hook from Alvin. Well, we were losing, 8–1. It seems Dark could give him a chance to get his stuff together, you know. It wasn't surprising to see Knowles steam. Darold walked off with Alvin, arguing with him. When I got to the dugout after the inning, I asked the bat boy what was said.

He told me Darold was saying, "When in the fuck are you going to let me pitch? How the fuck can a pitcher pitch well when you let him pitch only once a month?"

And Alvin replied, "I'll let you pitch when you start pitching better."

Darold spat, "No one stops you from managing when you manage bad."

Maxvill told me they stood toe to toe for two or three minutes and damn near came to blows before Knowles stormed back to the clubhouse.

When I got into the clubhouse after the game, Alvin was storming around, real angry, really looking for Knowles, but Darold had already got the hell out of there. It was real. It was life. It was exciting. It was the A's. It was the World Champion A's in the living, breathing flesh. It was us in the raw and it was real! Haw!

Well, it's stretch-drive time and we're in a pennant race. I still don't think anyone can match us stride for stride through the stretch. There's a race over in the other division, too. The Yankees and Orioles are driving like there's no tomorrow. Well, there isn't. Our year ends in September. You do it then or there's no October. Lou Piniella of the Yankees says my statement that they were losers steamed 'em up and got 'em going. He told that to the newspapers.

The only thing wrong was that wasn't what I told the newspapers. I told them the Yankees didn't know how to win. There's a difference. I said this bunch of ballplayers on the Yankees didn't know how to win because they hadn't been winners and they weren't sure of themselves, that they were suffering from lack of confidence in themselves. But I also said they had talent and if they won enough to get a good feeling about themselves, they could become big winners. Man, you got to listen to what a man says when he speaks! Well, if they could get going because of something I said, it just goes to show you they had something there they weren't using.

Boston's now lost eight or nine in a row and the race is over
for them.   But Baltimore's won eight or nine straight and
they're running right for the top.   Well, the race starts for
them in September.   I think we'll see them in October.   And
maybe the Dodgers in the World Series this time.   It looks like
The Little Blue Bicycle's going to stay ahead of The Big Red
Machine this time.   They say they're the best team in baseball.
Bullshit!

Monday, the 9th.   We had a twi-night doubleheader tonight with
Kansas City to wind up our home stand.   It was a half-price
family night and it drew more than 50,000 fans.   Seeing all
those people in the seats stirred us up and we swept two without giving them a run.   Vida and Cat pitched the shutouts as
we won, 3–0 and 7–0.   Vida gave up two hits and Catfish four.
It was Vida's first shutout and 15th win of the year.   It was
Cat's 23rd win.   Tenace hit a home run in the first game
and Rudi and Bando hit homers in the second game.   We beat
their two best pitchers, Busby and Splittorff.   I got one fucking
hit in the two fucking games.   But we won two, so I'm satisfied.
     I've hung the nickname "Bambi" on Herb Washington.   He's
getting there, but he doesn't have it all together yet.   The
other day, he pinch-ran and was picked off first, but the ump
called him safe.   The batter hit a routine fly ball and Bambi
took off before it was caught.   He ran right past second base
and never touched it.   He heard us hollering for him to go
back to first, but when he ran past second, he missed it again.
He got to first and the ump said he was safe even though the
other team raised hell.   Then he went to steal second and was
thrown out, but was called safe.   We were rolling with laughter
in the dugout.   The way we figured it, he had set a new all-time
major-league record for making four outs in one inning, but he
was a hero for stealing second.   He is so fucking funny.   He
has taken the needle and now he is giving it.   He is on me, on
Bando, on Rudi, on all the All-Stars, and he doesn't know one
end of the bat from the other.

Tuesday, the 10th.   We're flying to Minnesota on the first off-day
we've had in two weeks.   One of the players came up to me

and told me that I think Tenace and Bando are my friends, but they're not, because they're always talking bad about me behind my back. I always felt I got along especially good with these two guys.

I asked Geno about it and he said, "Hey, Buck, I don't know who's feeding you that crap, but whoever did isn't telling the truth. I like you and respect you and root for you and you know it."

Sal said, "Hey, look, you know we're the same kind of guys. If we didn't like you, we wouldn't talk about you behind your back, we'd tell you to your face and we wouldn't have anything to do with you."

I believed him because that's the kind of guy he is. They both wanted to know who the sonofabitch was, but I'm not saying, although maybe I should.

It's funny, but we're grown-up men who act like kids sometimes. Maybe it's because we play a kids' game for a living. But I think it's because we live so close together. There aren't many professions where people live together as close as we do. We not only do our jobs together, but we share dressing rooms and hotel rooms. We're cramped on planes together. We're away from home and our families, on the road together half the season. We're like a family and everyone knows all families have fights. You live too close together too long, and you rub one another wrong once in a while.

In any group of 25 guys, there are bound to be guys who don't make it together. We're winners, so at least we respect one another. But sometimes we let one another down. I mean, we depend on each other to do our jobs. If I don't drive in a run, maybe Cat loses a game he should win. Or Campy makes an error that costs Blue a win. Every little thing we do is added up in rows of statistics and sometimes it's someone else's fault that the numbers aren't what they should be and that hurts. We're performers, we have egos and we're sensitive. Our bread depends on the numbers.

We've found out we can be outspoken and still win, so we pop off. We've found out we can fight and still win, so we go to blows. It's too late to stop us because no one tampers with success. We're tough and we run around trying to live up to our reputations.

There's a lot of little stuff, a lot of needling that goes on, that no one outside the team knows. For instance, Darold Knowles used to wear a ten- or fifteen-dollar raincoat that was so bad you couldn't believe it. After a while, the guys got sick and tired of it. We were riding on a bus when Bando grabbed it and tossed it to Tenace and Tenace tossed it right out the window. Everyone laughed, even Knowles. About two weeks ago in Detroit, I ripped a pair of sunglasses off Bando's face and tossed them out another bus window. I mean they were bad glasses. They were $3.98 glasses and he makes $100,000 a year. He's got no business sporting such shades, so I got rid of them for him. He just laughed. Everyone laughed.

But, sometimes, maybe it goes too far and it's no laughing matter. Like with Rollie Fingers's wife. Now, we needle guys about their wives all the time. It's all in fun. Most of the guys got ladies they're sure of. But Rollie and his wife have been having their troubles, and the needling is out of line.

The other day Catfish cut this cartoon out of the newspaper, showed it around, and then taped it to Rollie's locker when he wasn't there. It showed a man and woman together in bed, with the woman saying to the man, "I told Alvin we were washed up, but I said it soft in case I want to make up with him." We all thought it was funny. But when Rollie saw it, he didn't think so. He tore it down and asked who had put it up. We wouldn't tell him because we all figured we shared in it. He asked me if I did it and I said I didn't. I told him no one was going to admit it. To the day he reads this, he won't know who did it. But it doesn't matter that Cat did it; we were all party to it.

Rollie stood up in the center of the room and said he wanted to make an announcement to the team. He said, "I'm sick and tired of jokes being made about me and my wife. My personal problems are private and I intend to keep them at home. I'm doing my job at the ballpark, I'm not letting anyone down, and I deserve a little respect. Fun's fun, but when it goes too far it stops being funny, so forget about me and my wife and get down to business or there's going to be some head-busting that this team doesn't need!" That was it. No one said anything. Then we went out and went back to work.

Alvin didn't get into it. I've watched Alvin all year and I've decided he won't lose us enough games to lose us the championship. He makes more mistakes than most managers, but after all is said and done he seems to have the personality to deal with a domineering owner and pop-off players better than most. Since we have the players, he will win with us. He's stood up to the most severe stresses through this season and he's still standing. And I respect him for that. I wish he was a smarter manager. He probably wishes I was a better ballplayer. We're the best we can be. He told me privately the season has taken a lot out of him and if Finley offers him the job again next season, he won't jump at it and may not take it.

It is a long season. It is a fucking long season with all the ups and downs and all the squabbles we seem to pack into every year. I figured it out and we have played 20 games the last 21 days. We are all worn out. I am, I know. I feel I have little left and I long for a rest in the worst way. We are all reaching for something extra to get us by.

Some players pop pills. Maybe I shouldn't talk about this, but I want to tell it like it really is and not leave things out. If I was dishonest, I wouldn't say it. I have taken pills — boosters, greenies, bennies, whatever — and a lot of the players take them. I will not say who. It's a long season without enough days off and with travel on most of the days you are off. Most of the time you travel without a day off between games. You play a night game, then fly all night so you can be somewhere else to play another game the next night. Worst of all, you sometimes play a night game, then fly all night and have to play a day game the next day without any real rest or sleep. You may be hurting from injuries. By August and September, we all are suffering from some things only rest will heal. And there is no rest to be had. We are paid to perform, and we have to play and we have to produce — so some players do what they have to do.

The owners don't want to know what we go through, because if they did they wouldn't be able to work out the schedule the way they do. The fact is, they don't give a damn about us as people. To them we are just players and they pay us and they want to see performance. The fans don't care. Reggie Jackson's got to be Reggie Jackson day after day, night after night. He hustles or they boo him. It is mentally tough sometimes to drag yourself out of bed and go to the ballpark to play one more of the 160-plus games we play every season in six months, and it is physically tough sometimes to play them hard.

Some players take pills because of the unreasonable schedule the owners force upon them. I took pills when I was a young player and didn't know how to handle the pressure. I do not take pills now, I have not for a long time and I will not in the future. I haven't taken any for four or five years. I wouldn't run the risk of getting caught if I wanted to take them. I don't happen to want to myself. I know they have to harm you in the long run and I will preach against them. I sympathize with the players who take them, but I can't condone it. I'm sorry for some of the things I did in my youth, but I've grown up now and I don't do these things anymore. But I'm not going to pretend a problem doesn't exist when everyone in baseball knows it exists. Certainly the players know it and perhaps if it comes out the situation can be corrected. I realize the overhead, including the players' salaries, has gone up and the owners have to get their money back. But giving the players one day a week off might improve performance, bring in more fans and relieve the pressure.

If somebody big in baseball wants to jump on me about it, that's their business, but they better not pretend they don't know it's going on. It *is* going on, and if they don't know it, they should. They condone it by not doing anything about it, which makes them as guilty as we are. They set the standards and they know damn well what we have to do to meet them. And the only thing that makes me different from some players is that I'll admit the truth where many others won't. Some will, some won't. But a lot of us are into it.

Thursday, the 12th. We split in Minnesota. We should have swept. Glenn Abbott was pitching against Joe Decker in the first game and Bando and Rudi had hit homers so we were ahead, 3–1, when suddenly Dark decided to take Abbott out in the eighth inning. He brought in Fingers. Then he brought in Lindblad. Then he brought in Odom. A fucking parade. They tied it. Then in the tenth, Dark brought in Knowles, and Harmon Killebrew won it with a two-run homer, 5–3.

Before tonight's game, Hunter came to me and told me that half his 100-grand salary was supposed to be deferred. It was supposed to be sent directly to his insurance company as a sort of an investment for the future. Finley had agreed to it when Cat and his agent negotiated his contract. But Finley found out he would have to pay extra taxes on a salary split like that, so he turned around and refused to do it this way. Cat called his attorney and he was told that if Finley didn't live up to his contract, Charlie would be in violation and Cat would be a free agent. He told me because I'm player rep and I should know what was happening between the players and the owner.

I told him I'd hate to lose him, but I could see where he'd be tempted to get in a position where other clubs would bid for his services. Man, how much money would a Hunter be worth on the open market? He told me he wanted to stay with the team, but he wanted to get what he had coming to him from Finley, and, if Finley failed to honor his contract, he'd have to pay a hell of a lot more for his services on a new contract than he had on the old one. He and his attorney have notified Finley they will sue if it's not settled. Finley has been calling Cat ever since. Finley says he'll pay, but not the way he's supposed to, and that's the only way Hunter wants it.

Finley keeps reminding Cat of the time he was a kid and Finley loaned him the cash to buy a farm. Cat keeps reminding him that he was hassled so much about it he finally sold part of the farm and paid off Finley. Cat says Finley somehow manages to call on the day he's due to pitch. Cat's sure he's hassling him so he will pitch poorly. This is hard to believe, but Charlie's hard-headed when he feels he's being screwed. The only thing he'd rather win more than a game is an argument. Cat feels Finley is trying to beat down his bargaining power by getting him beat. He'll pitch tomorrow in Texas. If the telephone rings, it'll be Charlie.

We won tonight, and we beat one of the best. Holtzman beat Blyleven, 2–1. Holtzman gave up four hits, Blyleven six. At one point, when Blyleven took the mound to start an inning, he had to wait for his second baseman to take the field. I shouted, "Hell, go ahead and start, you've struck out six straight, you don't need a second baseman." He looked at me and laughed. I had the last laugh, but it was a weak one. I was hitless for the third straight game and North had to bust his butt on the bases for the run to beat that guy.

In the clubhouse, the phone rang and it must have been Charlie calling. I heard Holtzman say, "I'm tired, how come I wasn't taken out of the game? I'm too tired to talk." And he just hung up and went off to get dressed and get the hell out of there. He's sick of being taken out of close games, because he's supposed to be tired. He hates Finley and won't play his game. Super Jew is a lot of man. He won his eighteenth tonight and he'll get 20 unless Finley fucks him out of it some way. And he'll be a big guy in the playoffs and World Series, as he always is. He's a businessman who hates his boss, but does his job.

Sunday, the 15*th.* Flying into Texas, the players felt Alvin was showing some fear. He hasn't gone into a tough series for a long time and he seemed to be nervous. Most of us feel no fear. We've been in a lot of tough series before and we've won most of them.

It did hurt us when Hunter lost the opener to Jenkins Friday night. Anyone can lose to Jenkins, but Hunter is supposed to win the big ones and usually does. He pitched well enough to win, but he got beat, 3–1, because we didn't get him enough runs. We had Jenkins on the ropes in the third. North and Campy singled and I came up with the bases loaded and hit a pitch deep to left. I thought I hit it far enough to be a home run, but it wound up a caught fly ball. It brought in our only run, which wasn't enough.

Hunter had 22 straight scoreless innings when they scored in their half. Lenny Randle tripled two men in with a fly ball that hit at the top of the center-field fence. Later on, Cesar Tovar doubled, was bunted to third by Randle, and scored on a sacrifice fly by Burroughs. After that, Jenkins just put it to us. Now he and Cat have 23 wins each.

Afterwards our guys were arguing about who is best. We all love the Cat, but we can be objective. Some guys feel Fergy is better. Some say Jim Palmer. Others say Tom Seaver. They don't bring the Blues and Busbys and Blylevens into these arguments because they haven't established themselves the way the older guys have. We all hate to have to bat against Ryan more than anyone else, but you can beat him as bad as he can beat you. You don't beat a Hunter or a Jenkins very much —and almost never bad. If I had to choose, I'd take Hunter. I know he can be at his best under the pressure of a playoff or World Series. I just don't know that about Jenkins.

Blue told Bando he was nervous before last night's game. We got him a lead in the first inning off of Jackie Brown. Bando walked. I doubled into the left-field corner. And Rudi knocked us both in with a single. They got a run in their half to make it 2–1. Then I homered in the fourth to make it 3–1. I felt good about the game then. But we didn't win. They came up in the fourth swinging. They got one hit, then another, then another, then another. For some reason, Dark brought in Bill Parsons, a young pitcher we had picked up, and he walked a man. Then Alvin went to Fingers. Before he put the fire out, they had five runs. The roof had fallen in. We wound up losing, 8–3.

With that loss our lead was down to four games. And I began giving Texas some serious thought. They've become a ball club that can make the plays. They can beat us if we don't make the plays. I felt it was important we win today, Sunday. A sweep might set us on our asses and start us doubting ourselves. Sunday was a super day because it was a ball game that meant something.

Before the game, Bill Glass conducted our religious service. He is the former All-Pro football player from the Southwest who is devoting himself to Christ. However, he stressed sports more than religion in his talk. Alvin asked him how much he felt attitude had to do with winning, and Bill said it had everything to do with it. He said that in 22 years of football, no one ever taught him how to get up for a game. He said he learned the power of positive thinking. He said he learned that if you let defeat in your thoughts, you could be beat. But if you pictured triumph in your mind, you could win. I went away picturing triumph in Texas.

Before the game, Bobby Winkles was with Dark and he told us he'd heard how tough we were in tough games and he was tired of hearing it and he wanted to see it. No one got mad at him or anything, but we went out and showed him something. We were down to Abbott against Bibby, so the Rangers had to be big favorites, but we had the bats and the bullpen to turn things around.

They got an early run, but North singled Bando home with the tying run in the second. I walked and Bando homered in the third. I got a hit, stole a base and scored our last run on a single by Claudell in the seventh. Abbott performed real well into the fifth. When he got into a little trouble, Fingers came in and stopped them cold. Fingers pitched almost five full innings, permitted only three hits and shut them out. We won, 4-1.

We felt a little like we'd won the pennant. They needed the sweep, but we wouldn't give it to them. We won only one of the three games, but we won the big one, and asserted our right to remain on top.

You know the cats that are going to come through when you need it. When you bring in Fingers from the bullpen, you bring in the best. He just set a team record with his 66th relief appearance. Maybe he doesn't work as much as Mike Marshall, but our starters don't need him as much. I'll bet you one of Finley's fucking orange baseballs that when we need relief in a big game, Rollie will give us as much as Marshall will give L.A., and maybe more.

When you need Bando or Rudi, they'll be there. Bando hit the 100-RBI mark in Minnesota, and Rudi will come close. Bando's hitting a big .250. One of the writers told me that he drove in 42 runs with his last 42 hits. He won't waste his hits. Neither will Tenace. He's hitting a big .215, and he's driven in 65 runs. He doesn't get many hits, but he has 100 walks already. He's the only .215 hitter in the game who's always on base. If he's not driving in a run, he's there to be driven in.

We have a lot of ways to beat teams. We score enough to win. I've got 22 steals now and I've been thrown out only five times. Billy and Campy and Herbie steal more, but get thrown out more. But they do steal. We've got around 150 steals, which is a team record. We're always in position to score. We're a power team that runs, which is rare. I feel the Rangers respect us a little more tonight than they did this morning.

Monday, the 16th. We have our second off-day in about a week, but we passed part of it on a plane on the way to Kansas City. When we got in, I did get to play nine holes of golf, my first since spring training. I shot a 42, which is fair.

Later, I relaxed with Rudi, shooting the breeze over who will win the Most Valuable Player award in our league. It has not been a year when one man has been outstanding, as I was last year, and as Dick Allen was the year before. Neither of us will win it this year. We have not been dominating forces this year. And Allen removed himself entirely by retiring recently. He'll be back, but the man is a puzzle.

I believe Jeff Burroughs will win the award. He has had the best season of any individual other than pitchers and his team will finish at least second, which surprises some. However, I do feel he is only an offensive player, strictly a hitter, really. Personally, I feel the MVP should contribute in many ways to his club. Also, I think the player that most helps a team win the championship should win the award.

We will win the championship, but our votes will be split. I will get votes because of my prominence, but I have not been the MVP of this team this season. I have done things no one notices. My steals, for example. I lead the team and I'm among the league leaders in runs scored. I've produced a lot of runs. But after my fast start, I have not had an outstanding year.

I'll get votes—but *I* wouldn't vote for me. I would vote for Bando or Rudi. Bando has been our MVP over a stretch of seasons, but I would vote for Rudi this season. Both are really underrated. They make a team win, which is what MVP means.

The pitchers have their own award, but if you get right down to it Fingers is as valuable as anyone in this league. Hunter, too. We would not have won anything without Hunter. I think I would give Catfish the Cy Young Award, the Most Valuable Player Award, the Academy Award and the kitchen sink.

Tuesday, the 17th. Well, here we are in Kansas City and here I am ready to cut someone's throat. I am on the cover of *Sport* magazine dressed like General Patton and inside the magazine I am undressed in a rotten article. It has been out awhile, but I have just started to get static about it and I am just beginning to be burned up by it. I have had bad stories about me, but this is the worst. Not Scott's story. There was nothing in it anyone else couldn't have written. It was a waste of time. But the real waste was the other story by the other writer, Murray Olderman. I trusted him and he betrayed my trust. He never did get back to me. We talked a little that day, but he never did a real interview. He made up a story.

They begged me to pose as Patton and when I did, I was afraid I'd be ridiculed for it. I didn't expect the magazine to ridicule me for it. He started off his story poking fun at me for posing as Patton. And went on from there. I talked about wanting to impress my peers and he kept referring to this over and over in a way that made me look ridiculous. I talked about religion and he made some sarcastic reference to my having a Bible on my television set, and girlie magazines strewn around the room. He talked about my girl as if she didn't have any clothes on and I was screwing her on the couch in front of him. She's a nice girl, she was dressed and we behaved decently.

You don't have to believe me, read it for yourself. But I wish you wouldn't. There's not much that's true in it. Athletes always bitch about stories, but I don't. I don't expect everything written about me to come out the way I want it. I don't expect everyone to write nice things about me, but I don't want the sort of sarcastic treatment that makes me look like something I'm not. I'm not a hypocrite, but his story suggests it.

He dug out a bunch of old stories about me and quotes from me and used them without asking me about them. I don't know if this guy Olderman's a good writer, but this was a bad story.

I feel let down and disappointed. I don't know why I go to the time and trouble to satisfy the media. I don't want to do it anymore. People say I owe it to the game, but I don't owe the game my self-respect. Maybe I owe something to the good writers and broadcasters, but one bad story will be remembered more than ten good ones. You stick your neck out, you can only get your throat cut.

Thursday, the 19*th.* We lost two out of three in Kansas City and it is no wonder with Charlie becoming manager again. He took over in Texas and the telephone wires have been humming ever since. He knows the game, but he doesn't know how to play it. You can't have a game run his way and his manager's way, too. Alvin lets him have his way. I guess he's got no choice.

Charlie's playing musical chairs with second base again. The last game in Texas, Ted Kubiak started and Jim Holt pinch-hit. Dal Maxvill went in and Cookie Mangual pinch-hit. Dick Green finished up. In the first game here, Maxvill started, Holt pinch-hit, Kubiak went in, Mangual pinch-hit and Green went in. In the second game, Kubiak started and they let him hit. But when he got on, North ran for him. Green, Maxvill and Trillo followed. In the third game, Trillo started, Mangual pinch-hit, Kubiak went in, Holt pinch-hit, Maxvill started, Alou pinch-hit, and Green wrapped it up.

It's stupid and it leaves us short-handed. When we had a man on second and needed a run, we didn't have a pinch-hitter left. It unsettles the ball club. Poor Campy doesn't know who the hell to throw to on double plays. He could throw it in the dugout and let whoever's turn it is take it. Or send the ball to Chicago for Charlie to handle. We're not playing baseball, we're running relay races. We're gonna cut the handle off the bat and hand it to the first second baseman in and let him pass it on to each new one as he goes in. If we win in spite of Finley, we're some ball club.

We lost, 2–1, Tuesday night. They got the winning run on a ball hit over second which Campy had to handle because the second baseman wasn't sure he was supposed to pick up the ball. Hunter lost to Busby in a real good duel of good pitchers. It was tough to lose it. I didn't get any hits and we didn't get the Cat any runs.

I got a hit, stole a base, scored a run and drove in two when we won last night, 5–4. Rudi's single drove in the winner. Holtzman hung up number nineteen, with help from Fingers, who hung up save number eighteen. Texas split with the Angels as a couple of early home runs did in Jenkins. That helped and our magic number went down to eight. Any wins by us or losses by them adding up to eight and we're in.

We didn't get one of them tonight. We lost while Texas won. I banged two doubles and a single and stole another base, but we lost, 4–3, in ten innings. I had come out early to hit for an extra hour. Wes Stock threw to me, while Winkles, Dark and Bobby Hoffman watched. I appreciated their interest.

John Mayberry of the Royals was out early and started razzing me. I was annoyed at myself, so I got annoyed at him. I told him to go to hell and get lost. To show you what kind of man he is, instead of getting insulted, he came over and watched and told me my timing seemed off and we talked about hitting to the opposite field. I always hit to left with power, though I haven't been recently.

We talked about the way I was swinging last year and especially the way I swung in the All-Star Game here in KC last season. I had seven or eight real good swings against Tom Seaver. John said they had some films of the game up in the office. He took me up. We were there 30 or 40 minutes watching me swing, swing, swing. I saw that I was driving my shoulder toward the pitcher, sort of charging him when I swung. We missed batting practice, but it was worth it to me and really kind of Big John.

I went to Alvin and talked about it, then went into the clubhouse and thought about it. I figured out fucking up my shoulder fucked up my form because I wasn't moving into the pitch with my shoulder like I should. I did tonight, but once your form is fucked up, and you start fooling around with it, you're in trouble.

We lost a game we should have won tonight. We were losing, 2–0, when Campy hit a single and Rudi hit a home run to tie it up. It was his 20th homer and when he touched home my man hollered, "I finally got the sonofabitch!" It was also his 95th RBI, so five more and he'll finally have the 100 he wants so bad. I doubled then, but it was wasted. Next time up, I singled, stole second, went to third on a bunt by Bando and scored the lead run on a single by Tenace. I felt I'd made the run happen. I felt we'd hold the lead.

But Blue lost it in the ninth with two out. Cookie Rojas hit to first, but it got through Tenace. Freddie Patek ran for Rojas, went to steal second and went to third when Fosse's throw went into center. Dark brought Fingers in. Orlando Cepeda, pinch-hitting, bounced the ball up the middle to score the run.

With one out in the tenth, I drove a double off the left-center wall. Bando walked. Then, with a two-and-two count on Tenace, I went to steal third base, when Tenace hit a fly ball to center. I was already past third, so I scrambled back toward second. I touched third on the way back, but I didn't think the umpire saw it. I beat it back, touched third again and took off for second. I got there too late; the throw doubled me off and ended the inning. I felt lousy about it.

Then in their half, with one out, Al Cowens singled and Dark pulled Fingers and put in Lindblad. He loaded the bases. He got Mayberry on a pop for the second out, but Amos Otis got him for a single that won the game, 4–3. We went down to the dressing room disappointed and depressed. The dressing room developed into a bad scene with a lot of bitching. Billy North was under the impression we should have won the game and he was bitching about how bad we played. I knew he meant me, though he didn't name me.

I talked to Dark about it and he understood, but he said Finley was on the phone afterwards and he really reamed out Winkles, who was coaching at third. Which shows how you can't tell what's happening from a radio. Winks did his job right. I ran on my own.

Vida was bitching about being taken out. He said, "I don't know what Dark's thinking about sometimes. I think he hides behind his Bible. I think he's hiding right now. Where the hell is he?"

And Johnny Odom asked Wes Stock, the coach, if he should dress tomorrow. Wes wanted to know why the hell shouldn't he dress.

John answered, "What's the use of me being in the bullpen, a right-hander, when they leave Lindblad, a left-hander, in to pitch to Otis, a right-hander? Should I dress? What the hell should I dress for?"

Stock sighed, "Hey, man, don't ask me, ask The Man."

I didn't like it. I didn't like it at all. Too much tenseness. Tension everywhere. Someone should have straightened the guys out, but who? I already got my ass in a sling this season for trying to straighten a teammate out. I spoke to Bando about it later and he admitted he should have done something about it. He said he should have cleared the clubhouse and let the guys know they were overdoing it. Don't get on one another. Stay together as a team. He's the captain of this club and it's known that he has the authority to do this sort of thing. But he didn't. And he felt bad.

He felt he'd been afraid to act because he'd been bitching himself and had blown up once. I'm the player rep. I tried to get out of it at midseason, but the players insisted I keep it. But when I asked for an assistant, one player after another turned me down until I got to Bando. He has a sense of responsibility. He felt he let the team down this time. It was a drab bus ride to the airport. Forty minutes of misery with no one saying anything to anyone.

Saturday, the 21st. I talked to Finley today, here in his hometown. The film company that is doing the documentary on me had asked if I felt Finley would sit still for an interview. I told them I didn't see why not, he owed me that much. But when they asked for it, he turned them down, and they got mad and told him off. They called my agent in New York, Paul Goetz, to complain. He called me to say he'd try to straighten it out, but I shouldn't let it bother me, I should just play ball. Then Finley called me to say he just didn't want any of that stuff until we clinched the pennant. I let it go.

We lost last night, 2–0. We got only three hits off Bart Johnson and none off Terry Forster, who bailed Bart out in the eighth. Forster was wild, but we couldn't take advantage of men-on situations.

I almost turned it around when I hit a ball about 400 feet to left-center witn Campy on second, but Carlos May made a catch over his shoulder, and that was that. It was a very disappointing defeat for Abbott.

Finley doesn't handle defeat too well. He said he had been talking to Dark all day yesterday until three this morning and now he was talking to him again. That's a lot of talk. I wonder how much Alvin heard? I wonder how much sleep he got? I wonder how he can sleep? But Finley tells me, as if to show me he's on top of things and doing things for us, that he was concerned we might blow the pennant. I told him I didn't want to hear that from him, I don't want him to talk about losing. I said "losing" wasn't a word in my vocabulary and I was surprised it was in his. He laughed and it let up on the tension a little.

Saturday night, the 21st. Hunter handled the White Sox and we whipped Wood, 3–2, tonight. Mangual tripled in the tying run and Washington singled in the winning run. I didn't get a hit. We only got five hits, but we won. Hunter gave up six hits and two of them were home runs, but he won. Cat will do that. He'll give up homers with no one on. He doesn't strike out a lot of batters; he makes the batter hit the ball. But he bears down with men on. This was his 24th win, which ties the team record set by Blue a couple of seasons back.

It was Wood's nineteenth loss. He'll lose 20. He lost 20 last year. He won 24, but he lost 20. It doesn't do anyone much good to win 24 if you lose 20. You have to look at the plus. He was plus-four. Fuck that. This year he'll be minus. They keep thinking he can pitch every third day and they won't admit they're wrong. They've got to get their thinking straight.

Texas lost, so our magic number is six.

Sunday night, the 22nd. I pulled a hamstring muscle in my right leg going for a hit at the end of today's game. I was chasing it when I went up against the wall. I pulled up and I heard the muscle pop and felt the pain. The same fucking muscle I pulled earlier in the year. I don't think it's as bad as some I've had, but it comes at a bad time. We have about ten days to go in the regular season and about two weeks before the playoffs start. If I sit them out, I won't be at my best when I need it most.

I am sitting here on the plane on the flight home and my leg hurts like hell and I am mad at life. I had a hell of a shot at 30 stolen bases and 30 home runs and 100 RBIs. Now I may not make any of them.

We lost today, too, 3–1, to Jim Kaat, who has won five straight and is in fine form. Kaat won his nineteenth, while Kenny Holtzman stayed at nineteen. Ken Henderson, who is a good all-around ballplayer, helped them to their last two runs with a triple and a single. One funny thing happened when Kaat struck me out my first time up. I asked for the ball, which some thought sort of strange. Maybe I am sort of strange. It was my 1000th strikeout and I wanted it to put in my trophy case at home along with the ball I hit for my 1000th hit. They're both big parts of my baseball career, you know. I want it for laughs.

Before the game, Finley came into the clubhouse to take a picture with some of his stars who have led his team to its run of titles. It was for the cover of the World Series issue of *Sports Illustrated*. It was supposed to be me and Bando and Cat and Rudi, Campy and Geno and Vida. Maybe someone else . . . I forget. Oh, yeah, Kenny. Only Kenny and Vida weren't there. Kenny begged off because he was pitching, but he would have begged off for some other reason if he'd had to. He didn't want to be in the picture with Charlie. Vida didn't beg off, he just refused. He was asked and he said no. Alvin asked him and he still said no. Charlie asked him and he said no to his face. Ol' Blue said he didn't want to be in no picture with fucking Finley. I admire the man for not copping out.

I have mixed feelings about Finley, but I don't mind being pictured with the man. I'm proud of this nucleus of players who have won so much. They took the players they could get. Finley got right in the middle of it, all smiles. Finley would have taken the picture alone if he'd had to. Fact is, he'd have preferred it that way.

So here I am sitting on this flight headed home for the last home stand of the regular season and I just want to get the season over with and be done with baseball for another year.

We were having a good time kidding around in typical A's fashion when this stewardess screwed the trip up for me. I was listening to music when a beautiful lady behind me leans forward and says how much she likes the music. We start a conversation and I invite her to sit in the empty seat next to me and eat her dinner with me. She comes up and we're rapping and listening to the music and waiting for our food, when this stew comes up and says the lady is not allowed to sit there and has to return to her seat. I ask her why, and she starts to sound off and we start an argument.

There are regular passengers on this plane and they know we're players, I'm sure they know who I am, and I feel about a foot and a half high. I'm embarrassed for me and this beautiful lady. I try talking nice to the stew, but she won't listen.

She doesn't talk nice to me, so I said, "Look, honey, if you want to get shitty, fine, but there's no way in the world you can be shittier than I can be."

She says if I don't shut up, she's going to talk to the captain. I tell her to talk to the captain. She goes and talks to the captain. She comes back and tells me that if she has to tell the captain about me again, he's going to come back and talk to me.

I ask her, "What's he going to talk about, baseball, beautiful ladies, or lousy stewardesses? What's he going to do, pull up to a cloud and park and tell me to get off?" She storms off.

I am sitting here now waiting for the bitch to come back.

There are ballplayers who get out of line in public places, but I am not one. I seldom drink and I seldom let myself get out of line in public. This time, she was the one who was out of line. She maybe had a bad day and was taking it out on her passengers. She is human, too, and I am not going to report her for being a bitch. If she reports me to Finley, fine. I will not back down and apologize when I am in the right.

I am sitting here relaxing and talking into my handy-dandy little tape recorder. I have had my meal, and my beautiful lady has returned to her seat. I am waiting to see if that shitty stewardess wants to talk about it some more. I am ready and raring to go. Hey, it's typical Oakland A's! It's sort of fun. I dig it. It makes me forget how much my leg hurts.

Monday, the 23rd. The doctor looked at my leg and told me it didn't look too bad, but I might be out about two weeks. I told him I would be back in the lineup before that, that I was going to be playing before the playoffs and in the playoffs no matter what. Even if he had to shoot my leg so full of pain-killer that I wouldn't be able to feel if I had a leg or not. I missed one World Series with a pulled muscle and I felt so bad about it that Rudi had to feed me by hand and I cried myself to sleep. Fuck it, I'm gonna play! He said he'd see what he could do.

Thursday, the 26th. Well, we clinched a tie for the title in our division. We won two out of three from Minnesota, and the last one clinched the tie. Tuesday night, Tenace hit a grand slam, his 25th homer of the season, to help Blue win his 16th, 5–1, but Blue will fall far short of 20 this season. Wednesday night, Abbott got beat in another tough one, 1–0, as Blyleven pitched a four-hitter. So we turned to the Cat tonight and he collected his 25th as we topped the Twins, 2–1. He has won 17 of his last 21 decisions and he has pitched 23 complete games. He is the complete pitcher. Combined with the loss of a doubleheader by Texas to Chicago, we are six ahead with six to go.

I didn't play the first two games of the series. I didn't even suit up. Finley came in for the kill and he invited me to sit in his box with him. I did and it was enjoyable. I was impressed by his knowledge of the game. He made it clear that he could call the shots if he wanted, but he had decided to let Alvin manage the clinches. Although he second-guessed him a lot sitting in the stands, he let him manage. And his second-guesses were good ones. He talked about the ballplayers as they came up and he knew their ins and outs. When Jimmy Holt pinch-hit and his average was shown on the board as .233, Charlie said he wasn't hitting that for us, he had only four hits in 33 times up. I looked at the stat sheet to check him out and Holt was 4-for-35. I said, "Hey, you kinda know what's going on, don'tcha?" and he smiled and said, "I sure as hell do." And he does.

He said he was going to get us a designated hitter for next season—Billy Williams or Willie McCovey.

The second night I sat with him, he had invited about 15 kids, black kids, to sit in the box right next to him as his free guests. He had them brought all the peanuts, popcorn, hot dogs, soda pop and candy they could eat. He was very nice to them and I was very proud of him. It saddened me later to hear some of the writers and other people putting him down for doing it, saying he was putting on a show. That poor bastard can't win for losing. Sure, he's wrong a hell of a lot and there are times I hate him. But he's right sometimes, too. And this was one of those times I loved him. I think he was sincere, and I think it was a nice thing to do whether he was or not. And he does it a lot.

The next day at batting practice, Geno came to me and said, "Hey, man, when you gonna come back to the bench and watch the game with us?" I said a lot of the guys didn't dress when they couldn't play and they cut out early, that I'd only been sitting with Finley because he asked me.

Geno replied, "Well, Buck, you ain't a lot of the guys. You belong with the ball club more than with the owner. I believe it would look better if you were on the bench." I could see the sense in that. I thanked him for his advice and I said I would follow it.

I think it was nice of him to be thinking of how things look for me. I don't really care how things look. I like to do what I want to do, but I was grateful to Geno. I decided to go along with him to show it. I sent my apologies to Charlie, suited up, and sat on the bench. I was glad I was with the guys when we clinched the tie for the title. Not that we celebrated, but I belonged there.

Friday, the 27th. Tonight we wrapped it up. In the fourth inning of our game with Chicago, the final score of a loss by Texas flashed on the scoreboard and that was that. We hollered a little. Not a lot. The crowd cheered. Crowd! Seven thousand and some. Typical crowd in Oakland. As soon as we wrapped it up, Dark yanked all the regulars out. Except Rudi, who he knows wants to get his 100th ribbie bad. That made it hard on Holtzman, who was going again for his 20th win. He even took Holtzman out after five. We lost, 3–2, and so Holtzman took the loss. If he'd stayed in and the regulars had stayed in we might have rallied and won.

Kenny couldn't have cared less. "Fuck it," he said afterwards, "I'm used to this kinda crap. No one's gonna go out of their way for me here." He said it without emotion. He just dressed and left.

I got to pinch-hit. I didn't get a hit, but I got to get into the game the night we clinched our fourth straight divisional title. That is a real accomplishment achieved by a real club and I had a strong sense of satisfaction. I think all of the players were proud of it, but they took pains not to show it. Something went out of us somewhere along the line. It'll never be for us what it was or might have been and should be. It is sad, but that is the way it is. We are all businessmen now, doing a job. We want to win and we win. But we don't do it with a lot of joy.

Later, the writers expressed shock that there wasn't more of a celebration. Finley came into the clubhouse. He had provided 40 or 50 bottles of champagne, but we didn't drink a lot of it or spray it around or raise any hell. I think Finley was disappointed. And Dark. It was a big thing for Dark, but he just said we've got the really big games ahead of us now. Some of the guys drank some of the champagne. Most of them just took a bottle home with them. They just went home. I went home, Sal went home, Joe went home, Vida went home. The Cat cut out. We all just cut out and went about our business. When I was leaving, someone said our clubhouse looked like a church on Monday.

9 ☆ OCTOBER

Wednesday, the 2nd. Frank Robinson was named manager of the Cleveland Indians. It has been rumored for a while now and I knew it was coming, but I was afraid to talk about it or think about it for fear it would jinx it. I am sort of surprised, because I really thought his best chances had blown on by. When he was traded from the Angels to the Indians, I thought he was on his way out of baseball and I felt bad about it. I could not feel better about anything than I do about this. Not just because he is baseball's first black manager in the majors, but because there is not a better man in baseball. He has only a fair team, but if they give him a fair chance, he will be a great manager.

Well, our season is finally over. Now that the preliminaries are out of the way, the real season starts. I wanted to play a little to test my leg and try to get my timing right, but after I played the last two games of the Chicago series as the designated hitter, I sat out one of the games in Anaheim. I got a couple of hits and I feel like I'll be OK. Championship play charges me up, anyway. I can be the designated hitter during the playoffs. My leg should be better by the World Series. I'll have to take the field, because the National League won't let us use the designated hitter. My leg hurts like hell, but I'm not telling anyone about it. I say it's getting better fast. I hope to hell it is.

We won two out of three from Chicago. After we lost the first one, we won the last two. Both clubs were coasting, but the games meant something to those guys who were going after something individually. Rudi drove in a couple of runs, which left him needing three in the last couple of games for his 100. Blue won his seventeenth. He's lost fifteen.

In Anaheim, we got shut out by Frank Tanana in the first game, 2–0, and we lost the second game, 3–2. While Rudi drove in both our runs, he fell one rotten ribbie short of his 100. I was kind of looking for something too in the last game— my 30th homer. I didn't get it. I was in the on-deck circle to hit if the last batter got on, but he didn't.

Richie Allen won the home run title by default. He didn't even play the last three weeks, but his 32 held up because I didn't hit enough to catch him before I went out of the lineup. And because Burroughs didn't hit any down the stretch at all. I wound up with 29 homers, 25 stolen bases, 90 runs scored, 93 driven in, and a .289 average. I fell short of everything I shot for. It was that sort of season for me. Not a bad season, but not what I hoped it would be. Burroughs won the RBI crown at 118. He hit .301 and wound up with 25 homers. It will be enough to win the MVP for him, I'm sure. Carew led in average at .364, which is something else.

I'm studying the final stat sheet now. We didn't have a .300 hitter and were last in the league in hits. But we scored the runs to win the games we needed. Rudi led us at .293, Campy hit .290, I was third and the kid Claudell was fourth at .285. We were the only ones on our team even within reach of .300. But Bando, hitting only .243, hit 22 homers, drove in 103 runs and scored 84. And Tenace, batting only .211, hit 26 homers, drove in 73 runs and scored 71. Rudi hit 22 homers, drove in 99 runs and scored 73. North hit .260 and scored 78 runs. .Tenace led the league in walks with 110, while Bando had 86 and I had 85. North led the league in stolen bases with 54, while Campy had 34, Bambi had 29 and I had 25. I was thrown out only five times and had the top percentage in the league. Bambi scored 29 runs with his 29 steals, which isn't bad for a guy who never got to bat.

Catfish won 25 games, lost 12, had 6 shutouts and an earned-
run average of 2.19. Jenkins was 25–12 too, but his ERA was
higher at 2.82. Hunter will win the Cy Young, I figure. Holtzman wound up 19–17. The next to last game they let Hunter
start and go three and then put in Holtzman for three. I
couldn't understand why they didn't let Holtzman start one of
the last two games and go at least five innings and give him his
last shot at 20. They didn't, and he seemed completely uncon-
cerned. I think he figures Finley ordered it that way and, if
that's true, it's too bad. But I don't know that. Dark might
have done it different, but it is Dark's job to get his pitchers
ready for the playoffs and he did get Ken in one of the last
games. With a little luck, he could have won it. Vida finished
at 17–15 with a 3.25 ERA. Fingers was 9–5 with 18 saves and
a 2.65 ERA.

They're only numbers. They don't show what we have inside of us that wins for us. The only numbers that matter are
the 90 that represents victories and the 72 that represents losses.
We could have won more and lost less, but we didn't have to,
which is why we didn't. We finished five in front of Texas,
eight in front of Minnesota, nine in front of Chicago and 13 in
front of Kansas City. All those hot cats cooled off. We cool
'em off. Perry, who was 15–0 when we cooled him off, must
have gone 6–13 after that because he wound up 21–13. A lot
of guys won 21 or 22, but Hunter and Jenkins were at the head
of the class with 25.

The numbers that matter most are behind the dollar signs.
We voted on shares before the ball game the other night and,
as usual, it was cutthroat. The rules are that if you're with the
team the whole season you get a full share and there's no vote
on it. If you're sent to another team in your league before the
season ends, even if it's at the end of the season, you get nothing because they don't want to tempt players to throw games
to their old teams. But if you were there awhile and didn't go to
another team or if you're there at the end, your share depends
on the vote. And the rule of thumb, frankly, is, fuck you!

We're more generous than most teams, but we swear by that
rule, too. It's wrong, but that's the way the guys are in these

cases, they're very tough. The more you split up the shares, the less you get. We voted 27 shares last year, and when we won it all, these came to a record of almost $25,000 each. We were more generous this year. We voted 31, so we'll wind up with less.

We voted half-shares to the coaches who came on late, Winks and Hoffman, and a quarter-share to one player who joined up late, Jim Holt. Two coaches, Hoscheit and Noren, who were fired, were voted $2,500 each. Manny Trillo, who was the center of the Andrews controversy last season but didn't last long this season, was voted $2,000. Pat Bourque, Deron Johnson and Gaylen Pitts were voted a grand each. Tim Hosley was voted $250. Several other players who were with us only a little while, including Johnny Summers and Vic Davalillo, were voted $100 each. Our trainer, Joe Romo, our travelling secretary, Jim Bank, and our equipment manager, Frank Ciensczyk, were voted half-shares. The clubhouse kids were voted fractional shares.

The real rhubarb came from a full share we had to give Bob Locker. It's nothing against Bob, but the fact is he never pitched a pitch. He was put on the disabled list in March and was left on there. Technically, this made him a member of the team. Charlie said it was his fault, because he didn't drop him before May 15th. Finley decided to be a nice guy and let him have an operation on his arm and see if he could come back later.

Billy North bitched the most about it. Bando bitched, too. Sal said, "I'm suffering all season at .240, trying to drive home some runs, and I got to carry this guy on my back? It's just not fair." It isn't, but it's just the breaks and all the bitching in the world won't change it.

I'm trying to get my head straight for postseason play. The Orioles won, as I thought they would, and they will be a problem in the playoffs. But I don't think we really put ourselves into this season. We didn't have to. I think we've got something saved. We will beat Baltimore in the playoffs. And I think we will beat Los Angeles or Pittsburgh in the World Series. It won't be close. I think it will be the Dodgers and I think we will drub them because we are sick and tired of hearing about how they have become the best.

I am worried about my leg, but otherwise my mind is clear. I am still steaming about the article in that magazine. I have told myself that the next time I see Olderman, I will tell him off. He's the kind of cat who comes around for the big ones, so it'll probably be in the playoffs or World Series. I have told myself I'll wait until he's with a crowd of writers waiting to interview me and then I will tell them that I won't talk until that guy goes. I want to embarrass him the way he has embarrassed me.

I told this to the players. I told Libby. He thought I shouldn't do it. He said I have this super public image that will last long after my career is over, and if I do this thing, I could spoil it. He's probably right. I may not talk to Olderman at all. I want to embarrass him, but I may not.

I'd just as soon not do any interviews at all from now on, but Libby brought this writer from Long Beach around, Rich Roberts, and asked me to talk to him, so I did. He came around after the last game when I was unwrapping my leg. I said I thought it was a shame that, at my age, I will have to wrap my leg in bandages the rest of my career. I told him I was sick of the season and wanted to get it over with, that I wanted to go on to the other things besides baseball in my life. I was hurt and depressed, and down mentally, like I am at the end of every season. I'd had it with all the hassles.

Maybe I said some things that won't sound right, but I said what I felt and I hope he gets it right. I feel the letdown and I won't lie about it. I am down. But I know the playoffs will bring me up. And the World Series. When they turn on the spotlight, they turn on Jackson.

Friday, the 4th. We open the playoffs tomorrow and the pressure is building. I feel it, but it doesn't bother me. I respect the Baltimore Orioles, I don't fear them. I know they are capable of beating us, but I don't think they will. But they can win if we beat ourselves. I am concerned that the Oakland A's are taking this too lightly, as if it will be easy. If we do not take it lightly, it will be easy. If we do, it will not be.

I remember all too well when they beat us in the playoffs of 1972. They were a good team, but we were better. However, their team had been in the pressure of postseason play before and we had not been and that defeated us. We got afraid of losing, so we lost.

I remember, after the last out of the game, I couldn't believe we had been beat. When you lose, everything you've won all year seems to be lost. I remember sitting on the dugout steps with my head in my arms long after the other A's had left. I was sick inside. It was like my world had ended. I had waited so long, but for what? For this? Finally, I knew I had to get up and go, so I got up and went up those stairs. They felt as steep as a mountain and a mile high. When I got into the clubhouse, there was a lot of talk from the press and players about "next year." I said, "Fuck next year. Next year may never come. We had our chance and we may never get another one."

Next year did come. We got another chance. And we made the most of it. We beat Detroit in the 1972 playoffs. But I tore up the muscles in my legs and I was on crutches during the World Series. It was terrible not being able to play while the team was beating Cincinnati in that World Series. I couldn't eat and I couldn't sleep. It was like being an outsider. I must admit it hurt me a little when the A's were able to win without me. I was happy for the team, but sad for me.

I didn't think I'd get another chance, but last year I did. This time I made the most of it. I was the Most Valuable Player of the World Series, just as I had been of the regular season. Everything finally fell into place for me and fit together. But Finley fucked it up by fucking up Mike Andrews. All our spirit just sagged and what had been a joy became a job.

Finley is in town, of course, and he has assumed command. For instance, Fosse is going to catch. There was some thought that Tenace would catch and Claudell would play left and Rudi would play first, but Finley says Fosse, so Fosse it is. Finley will let Greenie go all the way at second, which is the best thing possible for us defensively.

We have more power than Baltimore and power does matter. Baltimore does it mainly on defense and pitching. They have a better defense than we do. They have more starters than we do. But we have better pitchers. And the Orioles don't have anyone coming out of their bullpen as rough as Rollie.

I don't underestimate them. I respect them. But they are not as good as they were a few years ago. And we are better now than they were at their best. We have proven it.

I do not think this series will go the distance. We are all healthy, except for me. And I will play right field. There was some thought that I should be the designated hitter with Claudell in right, but Claudell is just a kid and we want to go with the lineup that has won for us in the past. Dark asked me if I could play in the field and I said I could. But I am not sure. I haven't tested my leg. It feels all right right now and I want to play. Finley must have told Dark to play me, so I will play.

We worked out today, but I took it easy. We had a meeting and we went over Jerry Adair's scouting report on the Orioles. Scouting reports don't mean much, but every little bit helps.

Mike Cuellar is starting for them tomorrow. As Adair said, we have to be careful not to get soiled, because he throws a lot of crap. He doesn't throw hard, but he throws a screwball and every other kind of screwy pitch at you. He must be 40 years old. He must have been in baseball 20 years, and every year now he wins 20 or close to it. But Catfish will start for us, so we have that going for us.

The big buildup has begun. It seems like every newspaper and radio station and television station in the world had guys at the workout today. I must have answered ten thousand questions, but I didn't say anything. You know, I said I respect them and all that kind of crap. I said I felt we would win the playoffs but I'm not going to say anything that will rile the Orioles up. Now I'm sitting here in the dark at home hoping I'm right. I need my rest, but I don't think I can sleep. I'm too worked up.

Saturday, the 5th. We lost. Hunter got knocked out. Four and a third innings. I can't remember the last time I saw something like that. I was surprised he could get knocked out that way, that early. It stunned me. It stunned us. We depended a lot on him. Well, he's entitled to a bad game, even in a big game. But it hurt.

I got hurt, too. Warming up, running around the bases, rounding second base, I felt my muscle pull a little. It hurt, but I didn't say anything to anyone. I hate to tell you what I said to myself. Son of a bitch, it scared the fucking hell out of me, and I am still scared! I played, but I couldn't run real good. I'm sure Finley saw it and Dark saw it. I'm sure I'll have to be the goddamned designated hitter tomorrow.

They hit three home runs. They have no home run hitters and they hit three home runs. Two of them, by Brooks and Blair, didn't carry much more than 330 feet. They landed just inside the left-field foul pole, but they counted. It wound up 6–3. Campy drove in all three of our runs. He had three hits. I didn't have any hits. I usually hit Cuellar, but I didn't today.

We didn't have a sellout, but we had forty-some thousand and we let the big crowd down. We let ourselves down. In the eighth inning, I ran for a fly ball that fell foul and the fans booed me. I couldn't run, so I couldn't reach it. The fans know this. They're not deaf and dumb. They know I'm hurting. The boos really hurt. Hell, I have busted my butt for this team and no one wants to know about it now, when I've got a bum leg. It isn't fair and I feel bad about it, but that's baseball. That's sports. That's the fans. Maybe they don't think I have feelings. Maybe I'll go boo them at their place of business tomorrow.

No, I got my own business to take care of. The A's do. Back to business. We all know what we got to do now. It's hard to say a defeat is good for a team, but it may make us see we were overconfident. We have not played the baseball we can play the last six weeks or so and we have carried this lackadaisical attitude into the playoffs. Now we know we've got to bend our backs and pick up that burden.

The Orioles have been playing flawless baseball, I believe.

They have won ten in a row now, because they won their last nine before the playoffs. They always seem to have nine or ten in a row going into the playoffs. Maybe they have lost so little lately they think they can't lose. We have to make them taste defeat. Holtzman will hurl for us tomorrow. Playoffs, World Series, they're just games to him. Pressure doesn't mean anything to him.

Dave McNally will pitch for them. He has been pitching for them for ten or twelve years. He throws hard, but with control. He won 20 games for them every year for a lot of years, but he has not won 20 for some years now. Because he is a hard ball thrower, he feels the age in his arm more than Cuellar. He is not as tough as he once was.

I have a lady here and I am going to try to relax. I don't want a lot of people around distracting me. I don't have my family here. I invited my father because he wanted to come, but I won't feel bad if he doesn't make it. I don't want the distraction. It's time for business. The fun and games will have to wait.

Sunday, the 6th. Holtzman handled them just perfect and we put it to them, 5–0. So we are even and we are on our way now. We played the way we can play. We have been reminded that if we do our jobs, we will win. Holtzman was super. Super! The Jew was just super. He held them to four or five hits. They only had one or two hits until the last two innings, when he was weakening a little, but he had determination to do the job. I think if Finley had signaled for Fingers this time, Holtzman would have hit him in the mouth.

Kenny kept them off balance with off-speed pitches all day. His curve was breaking beautifully. McNally was throwing hard, but not that hard. It was scoreless until Grich dropped Bando's pop-up in foul territory in the fourth. Bobby won't drop many, but this one gave us the opening we needed. Sal then socked one into the stands and it hurt them more than just one run. It was like they had given it to us and it hurt them. We're a team of opportunists; if you give us an opening we'll go right through it. A couple of innings later, North

walked and, with two out, Rudi tripled off the right-center-field
fence to make it 2–0. Fosse then hit the ball into the left-field
seats with two on in the eighth and that was it, 5–0.

Afterwards, Fosse was the happiest player in the dressing
room. He's had a rough road back from injuries, but he's a
good ballplayer and he made a big hit. I was happy as hell for
him. It didn't seem to mean anything at all to Holtzman. He
just put it down. He told the press that it was his job and he
had done it. He even said he was ready to retire after next
year, his tenth year. He's one guy who might really do it. He
said he had given baseball as much as it had given him and he
was sick and tired of the travel and the hassle over salary every
year. What he meant was he was sick and tired of Finley.
When Charlie came in to congratulate us, Kenny wouldn't
even look at him.

Now it's on to Baltimore, and I believe we'll win the next two
and wrap it up. I was the designated hitter today, but I didn't
hit again. I am becoming concerned, because I want to contribute. I am swinging good, but I can't guide the ball and I'm
not putting it in the right places. As long as we win, it's okay,
but I won't feel right about it if I don't play a big part in it.
I'm not cut out to be a bit player.

Monday, the 7th. Today's newspapers stressed the pep talk Finley gave us before yesterday's ball game. Fuck, I had forgotten
about it, that's how much it meant to us. I don't even think I
talked about it when I talked into this tape recorder yesterday.
He came into the clubhouse in his kelly-green sports coat
about 20 minutes before game time and talked about the difference between determination and desire, whatever the hell
that is. Some of the guys heard him and some didn't. Well,
hell, determination doesn't win for you, talent does. You need
determination, but without talent, it ain't gonna get you around
the block. We won, not him. Kenny won, not Finley. Kenny
and Sal and Joe and Fosse, not Finley. It's a fucking shame for
the newspapers to give the credit to an owner and not a ballplayer. Why fuck Fosse? It meant so much to him. We won

on the field, not in the clubhouse. We won on the players' talent, not the owner's talk.

Finley had Miss California as his guest at the game. Her name is Luci Anne Buchanan, she's from southern California and she was second or third in the Miss America contest this year. As far as I can see, she could have finished first, because she's a fox. She's some kind of pretty. Nice people, too, but she smiles too much. She threw out the first pitch and I met her in the VIP room at the stadium after the game and escorted her to her car. I asked her if she got tired of smiling so much, and she smiled and said she did. She said Finley told her that since she had been good luck for us, she had to go to Baltimore with us, as his guest, to bring us more luck. Finley's no fool.

Frank Robinson came to my place for dinner last night after the game and it was good to be with him. He's been through playoffs and World Series and he knows what they are for a player. We talked about how important these next few days are to our careers. We also talked about how wonderful it is that he finally is going to get to manage in the majors. It is a big thing for blacks, but it's something that should have happened long ago, not only to Frank.

He said he is not going to hire an all-black coaching staff or an all-white staff. He said color isn't going to come into it. He doesn't want "yes men." He wants cats who can contribute. He wants to succeed, so he can be considered a good manager, not just a black manager. He knows it is going to be tough. He has a good team, but not the best.

He feels he has some good players. He hopes to help Hendrick become the ballplayer he should be. He figures Perry will help, because he is a pro and a top pitcher. He told me the thing with Gaylord, who said he wouldn't play for Frank unless he was paid more than Frank, was blown out of proportion. He had talked to the guy and he knew the guy would give him all he had, because it was his job. He doesn't care what Perry said, as long as he performs. He said he didn't want to trade a 20-game winner.

Frank said he wouldn't play if he had his way. But he does want the 20 homers he needs for 600 and the 100 hits he needs for 3000. Cleveland's front office wants him to play, so he'll probably play. He figures it will be hard to play and manage at the same time. But it should not interfere too much because he can be designated hitter.

You could see that he's proud to be named the first black manager. But it's pride more for blacks than for himself. There is pride for himself simply in his becoming a manager, in overcoming a bad background when he was a wild kid and an undisciplined player. He has made people respect him. I respect him. I take pride in knowing him.

We talked about Simon Gourdine becoming deputy commissioner of the NBA and maybe becoming the commissioner when Walter Kennedy retires. Simon's not only black, he's young. He has to have shown them something special. When I heard about it, it warmed my heart. I didn't realize how happy I'd feel about something like this, until it happened. I guess color means more to me than I'll admit to myself.

It relaxed me to rap with Robby. It took my mind off the tough games we have to go. We have to go against Jim Palmer, who is tough. He's been hurt, but he's healthy now. Healthy, he's as good as they come. It's a big game, because a 2–1 lead in a five-game series is a hell of an edge.

Blue goes in the big game for us. It's an important one for him, for his pride. Laddie's had tough luck in big games and it's hurt his pride. The press has been unfair to him. Very unfair. They've stressed this side of his record more than they should. But, I'll tell you, the players have been talking on the plane flight, and we have confidence in him. Maybe we shouldn't, but we do. He has so much ability above and beyond the average that you always think he's going to throw a shutout, and when he doesn't you don't understand it.

We feel he's due. He's overdue.

Tuesday, the 8th. Well, Laddie laid it on them. He overmatched them. He knocked the bats right out of their hands. He wanted it so bad he just took it. He shut them out on two hits. I don't think he's going to be beaten in big games very much from now on. He just made up his mind to forget the past, and he just went out there and threw the fucking ball the way he can throw it.

He had it all, even complete control. He didn't walk a batter. He had a good fastball, and a good curveball. He could pick his spots and hit them. He looked like his old self today. Better, because he has become more of a complete pitcher. He doesn't just try to throw it past them now, but he threw it past them for nine innings today. He had Baltimore beat all the way. Greenie made a couple of errors behind him, which is unusual, but Blue bore down.

He had to be good, because the other pitcher, Palmer, was good, too. Blue never had any breathing room. Palmer didn't give us much. He looked as good as ever to me today. He threw not only a good fastball and curve but also a good slider and change-up. We only got four fucking hits off of him.

Sal slugged a fastball into the seats in the fourth and that was the ball game, the way Blue was working. I got my first hit of the playoffs in the ninth inning. I was o-for-ten and beginning to be concerned, so this single was almost like a home run. They called time and came down to ask me if I could score on a double. I said I could. I didn't think I could, but I didn't want to be taken out of the game.

I was wrong. I wanted to stay in. I excused it by telling myself it was a close game which might get tied and my bat might be needed later. But I was wrong. The man gave me the respect of asking me how I was and I should have respected that and told him. But then Rudi made the third out, so my staying in didn't hurt.

You want to stay in. Geno wanted to stay in when Bambi was sent in to run for him after he walked in the seventh. When Washington got thrown out trying to steal, it made the move worse. Tenace threw his helmet down the dugout. As luck would have it, it landed at Alvin's feet. Alvin picked it up and threw it away. It rolled out of the dugout, right by the box seat where Charlie was sitting. Now that was luck. That was funny. But it wasn't funny to Charlie, who leaned over, looking into the dugout with one of those stares that could kill. And it wasn't funny to Alvin or to Tenace.

Geno popped off afterwards. He stormed into the dressing room and he told the writers he thought it was a horseshit move. And it was. He pointed out that you don't take out your team's best defensive first baseman—and one of its best hitters—for a runner in a tight game. He was right. Dark does what Finley wants and this is what Finley wants. Geno said he didn't blame Herbie, but he did blame Dark. And he blamed Finley even more, because everyone knew it was his move. He explained that Herbie should have been held back to run for a man like me, who can't run right now. True.

He was hurt and hollering that he wanted to be traded. Right now. Right out of the playoffs. Today, anyway. Well, that's the A's for you. We're back in form, popping off and having fun. All we need now is a fight.

Vida held up our standards later. He was completely cold. Just like Holtzman had been the day before. Kenny and Vida pitch back-to-back shutouts and throw icicles back-to-back in the interviews later. Laddie didn't even want to talk to the writers afterwards. He said it was just a job he'd had to do, and he'd done it. And if they hadn't been paying him to do it, he wouldn't have done it. As far as he was concerned, it was just another game. They couldn't believe he could be so indifferent.

He said, "If you'd taken the fucking I've taken, you'd also act cold." A writer asked him who had fucked him. And he said, "Ah, man, I just don't want to go into it," and he walked away.

The reporters all assume he means Charlie. And he does. But he also means them, too. He feels the writers built him up and then tore him down. He feels they weren't with him when he needed them. And he means the fans, too. He wants to know where they went, and where his friends went, when he went bad. He knows who his real fans are, who his real friends are, now. He knows I'm a friend and a fan. Anyway, I hope he knows it.

We still have one more to win. We'll win it tomorrow. We won't celebrate it. We'll just go on to the World Series and win that. It looks like Los Angeles, though they lost today. They won the first two. They're at home and they only need one more to top Pittsburgh. It looks like it'll be the Dodgers, and I look forward to that.

I was happy because my family was at the game. I bought a bunch of tickets for my mother, my sisters, my brother-in-law, my nieces, my nephews. They were all here rooting for me. After the game I went to dinner with them. It was nice. It's family and it's nice, but I can't take too much of it. It takes too much out of me, and I have to keep my mind on my job.

My mind is mixed up. I don't like being designated hitter. It's like being half a player. I wrap my leg before every game. I spend every spare minute in a whirlpool. I should sleep in the whirlpool. I can't sleep at night. I stay in my room away from people and watch a little TV and try to relax, but I can't. I can't relax and I can't sleep. I doze off and I wake up. I doze off and I wake up. And I lay there thinking. It would scare me except it's always this way in the playoffs and World Series and it goes away when they're over.

I'm not scared, but I am wound up tight. We all are. Charlie can see it, I guess. He brought the broad to Baltimore, the Miss California—Luci Anne or whatever her name is. And he brought her down to the dugout just before the game, which was something highly unusual. But she had that smile on and she talked to the players and let them tease her and she kissed some, and hugged some, and all the tension seemed to evaporate. It was fun—good, clean fun. Some of the guys were so excited they forgot to take their batting practice. Look, she's just a lady, but it was something unusual and it relaxed us. Charlie was just showing off, I suppose, but it broke the routine.

It'll be the Catfish against Cuellar again tomorrow. I don't believe Cat can have another bad game. Maybe I shouldn't say this, but I think he's fabulous and I am counting on him to come through for us. We have held them scoreless 22 or 23 innings now and the Cat will carry on. I don't think Cuellar can beat us again. Not twice in four games. He's not that good. The pressure is on him. If he fails, they're finished. California, here we come.

Wednesday, the 9th. Cat cut them down. We won on walks and we're on our way to California. We won on one hit and eleven walks, but we won and that's all that matters. We beat the shit out of them, 2–1. Hah! Cuellar wasn't exactly wild. Cuellar was careful. Most of his walks were in the middle of the batting order. He wasn't going to give the big bats a big pitch. He walked nine and Ross Grimsley, who relieved him in the fifth, walked two. I got three walks, Bando got three and Rudi got three. I got the only hit.

Cuellar walked Sal and he walked me on a three-and-two pitch with two out in the fifth. He threw a wild pitch and we went to second and third. With first base open, Weaver had Rudi walked intentionally to fill the bases. It set up a force play at any base, but it was a bad decision; you don't intentionally load the bases when your pitcher is walking batters. Cuellar walked Tenace and we had a run. When he threw two bad pitches to Washington, Weaver got him out of there. He had a no-hitter, but he was being beat by his walks.

Two innings later, Ross Grimsley walked Sal. I brought him home with the breathing-room run. Like I said, it was our only hit of the game, a double. I drove it on a line a long way and I thought it would go out, but it didn't quite make it. It was hit to left, to my opposite field. It hit the top of the wall, just above Don Baylor's glove as he leaped for it. I'm satisfied it got to the wall and got us an extra run.

Hunter had his stuff together and he shut them out on three hits for seven innings. He got the hook after Baylor opened the eighth with a single. It was a quick hook, but the Cat didn't complain about it. He knew he had a rested Rollie ready to relieve. Dark brought in Fingers from the bullpen and he did his job. We were worried when they threatened in the ninth. Blair worked a walk off Fingers, and Grich singled with one out. Tommy Davis forced Grich at second, but Boog

Powell singled Blair home with two out. There was bedlam in Baltimore. With the tying run in scoring position, Baylor tried to bunt, but he couldn't reach the outside curve Rollie broke off on him. He then fouled off a couple of pitches and missed another for the third strike. We began to breathe again.

I let out a holler and we ran in happily, the American League champions for the third straight season. The first question asked of me was how I felt about facing the Dodgers. Curt Gowdy and Tony Kubek asked me. The question was totally unrelated to this ball game or to this moment. We had won a big game and another pennant and we wanted to enjoy it for a moment before turning to the World Series. We didn't care if the Dodgers won or lost. They could have substituted the 1927 Yankees and we couldn't have cared less at that time.

We even celebrated some. We slung around a little champagne, but not much. Maybe because it's expected of us. Play the game of baseball and go home. First, however, we had to shake Charlie's hand. He walked around holding it out to us and we had to do something with it. Then we had to go to dinner with him. He threw a party at some restaurant here in Baltimore. He had about 70 people there. We figured the bill had to be about $3000. That meant he had to leave a $600 tip. That was our fun for the night, figuring out how Finley would be fucked by the bill. It's too bad, because he was trying to show us a good time. He meant well, but it doesn't matter to most of the players anymore. We went home early. We have to get up in the morning to fly to Los Angeles.

Friday, the 11*th.* Hey, the A's are here. The real A's and they are real. The fighting A's and they are fighting. And suing one another. Mike Andrews says he's suing Finley for two and a half million bucks for the slander that prevented him from remaining in baseball this season. Well, it was good to hear from Mike. One of the first questions Finley was asked after the playoffs was had he heard from Mike. He asked what kind of a fucking question that was. Now he knows. It's in all the newspapers.

Along with the fact that the Catfish is suing Finley for 50

grand. Well, not exactly for 50 grand. He doesn't want the money anymore. He wants to be a free agent so he can bargain for a new contract. And not necessarily with Finley and the A's. Finley says he offered him the money. In cash, or a check. Catfish says he didn't pay it when he was supposed to, the way he was supposed to. I've been waiting for it to happen since the Cat told me about it. But I didn't expect it to come up at this time, just before the start of the World Series. I suppose the Cat considered it a slow day for sports news.

There was a fight, too. Fingers versus Odom. One round. Bam, bam. I was sitting in the whirlpool in the clubhouse listening to the guys get on one another before the workout yesterday. So help me, I was sitting there listening to the guys get on one another and wondering why the hell they don't have more fights than they do, when all of a sudden they're having one.

The guys are always getting on one another—in the back of the bus, in the dugout, in the clubhouse. They're always taunting teammates about their baseball abilities.

Like after Bando boots one, Fingers will say, "Hey, steel-glove, when you gonna get a new mitt?"

And Sal will say, "Rollie, I could run a train on the rails you serve up. They hit the ball back at you harder than you throw it." Which is all right. Until it gets personal. Odom might call Sal "a fat wop," so Sal has to call him "a dumb nigger."

It's funny, but one black can call another a nigger, and not like it when whitey does it. A wop can call a wop a wop, but they don't like it when a polack does it. It's the words like "wop" and "nigger" and "polack" and "greaser" which rub some guys wrong. I don't use them much.

Guys kid other guys about their wives, but some guys get angry if they're worried about their wives. Or if they've been screwing around, themselves. A guy will get to the clubhouse late and another guy will ask him what took him so long. The first guy will explain, "I had to wait until you left, so I could get into your wife."

And the second guy will laugh and say, "Jeez, thanks, if somebody didn't service her, I'd have had her on my back the rest of the home stand."

He's not going to say that if he's worried about her.

Rollie had asked the guys to cool it but Blue Moon didn't. Rollie was riding Moon, so John said, "Hey, man, you better beat it back to the hotel. Your wife might be in bed with somebody by the time you get there, if you wait too long."

Fingers was furious. There was a shopping cart in the clubhouse they use to haul uniforms around and he shoved it at John. He told John to shut his fucking mouth. John said something I didn't hear. Rollie went for him and John grabbed him around the waist and they wrestled around and went down. And that was that.

Some of the other players pried them apart. Not poor Ray Fosse. He was sitting alongside them. When they started up, he jumped up and ran for the showers. He broke up my fight with North and he wasn't about to get into another one. No real damage was done in this one, though Fingers hit his head against a locker and got a cut. He was taken to the hospital where five stitches were taken to close the cut and then he came back to the ballpark. Odom twisted his ankle. He may be sidelined a day or two.

Dark didn't see it, of course. He was having a meeting. I think Finley found out ahead of Alvin. He has an espionage system that tops them all. I swear he's got the ballpark bugged. Nixon needed him. The fight had hardly finished when the phone was ringing and there was Charlie calling to find out about it. He asked to speak to Sal and to me, wanting to know what had happened. Sal told him the tale, I confirmed it. I didn't express any opinion about it.

Finley talked to Dark and then Alvin called a meeting. At first, Finley wanted them to tell the press they were just fooling around. Then he called back to say they should tell the truth. He figured if they tried to cover it up and the truth came out later, it would look worse than it was. There really wasn't that much to it. The writers were right on it, of course. This was what they had been waiting for and the A's never let anyone down. Fingers started to tell them he and John had just been horsing around. When they asked him if there had been any laughing, he laughed and admitted there was no laughing. John was asked if any punches had been thrown. He said that if any of the writers wrote that any punches had been thrown, then there really would be punches thrown.

Dark said it was good for the club, because it loosened the players up. Well, I guess it won't hurt us. I know it's not going to bother the two of them as ballplayers. Maybe not even as teammates. We fight and make up. We're used to the fights and we shrug them off. I was asked about it by the writers. I am always asked about all that goes on in this club by the writers. I said this was the way we got going and the odds on us in Las Vegas should have shortened.

But John could be hurt by this. Let's face it, he has fought with almost all the players we've had since he's been in the ball club and Dark is determined to dump him. I think he helps us more than he hurts us, but Dark is determined to dump him. He believes he makes more trouble than he's worth.

Dark, himself, may say he's not sure if he'll be back, but he wants to be asked back. After the playoffs, he said, "It's up to God. If He wants me here, I'll be here." Well, everyone knows who God is around here. And when He was asked about Alvin, He said He would talk to him and announce a decision later. After we won the division or after we won the playoffs would have been the right time to rehire Dark, but Finley first wants to see him sweat through the World Series.

After the playoffs, Finley asked us, Sal and I, when the team wanted to take off for Los Angeles, but he told us he wanted to leave yesterday morning. He made it seem as though we had a share in the decision. We left when he wanted to. We were supposed to have a movie on the flight, but we didn't because he didn't want one. A movie might have relaxed us. Instead he tensed us up by insisting we read the scouting report. We had five hours on the plane and a four-page scouting report we could have studied in half an hour. When Finley passed the reports out, some of the players were so annoyed they refused to read the damn thing. Vida tore his up in tiny pieces and scattered them around the plane.

Finley called Dark and the coaches and Sal and I up front to go over the report together—to be sure we realized what a great report Al Hollingsworth had put together. It *was* a great report and we might have gotten something out of it if it had been given to us at the right time. I left after a while and so did Sal, but Finley, his manager and coaches spent three hours or so studying that report, which reflected a lot of respect for the Dodgers.

We didn't screw around on the plane. We were strictly business. We talked baseball. We were subdued. One of the stewardesses later told a writer we were one of the best-behaved ball clubs she's ever had on a plane. She said we acted like we had business to attend to in Los Angeles, which we did.

When we landed, there were many, many newsmen waiting for us, television cameras and all. But we got right off the plane and right on the bus and went on our way to a team meeting. Those of us who did speak to the reporters simply said we respected the Dodgers as a great ball club. If they weren't, they wouldn't be here. We also said things like: But we are a great ball club, too. We expect to win, but we expect it to be a tough fight—and all that bullshit.

The fact is, I figure we'll beat them in four straight. I just wanted to be businesslike about it. I think a lot of us were trying to play it straight. What with all the hassling that always goes on around our team, no one takes us as seriously as they should. It's something that sticks to us like a stain.

When we left, Finley lingered to talk to the reporters, especially the TV crews. We laughed about it, saying there was good old Charlie O. jumping on the glory wagon. But I suppose you could look at it another way and say he took the spotlight so he could take the heat off us and let us escape to some sort of privacy. One of the things he said was that I wouldn't play unless I was 100 percent ready, which annoyed me when I heard about it. It put me on the spot to prove I was ready. It pressed me.

I had been getting by as designated hitter in the playoffs, but I'd have to play in the field in the World Series or not play at all. I missed the meeting so I could go to the doctor's office—Dr. Robert Kerlan. His staff is supposed to be the best in the business at handling athletes' injuries. They took care of Sandy Koufax, Jerry West, Elgin Baylor and Wilt Chamberlain.

Before I went up, Herbie Washington warned me against getting a shot of cortisone. He said it deadens the pain of an injury like mine, but it is dangerous because without feeling in your leg you run the risk of pushing it too far. He confided in me that Finley and Dark had asked him about it. Running was his specialty and he'd dealt with muscle pulls previously. He had warned them about cortisone shots the way he now was warning me.

I saw a Dr. Vince Carter, who works with the hockey team in town. I explained why I was hesitant about taking a shot. He explained that he would give me only a small shot only in the affected area and assured me it would work out fine. I agreed, and he searched for the sore spot, found it and shot right into it. I went to another part of the office and spent half an hour in a whirlpool. Then I spent another half-hour getting rub-downs on each leg. Then I spent half an hour getting ultra-sound therapy.

I was in that doctor's office about three and a half hours. When I was finished, I felt fantastic. I went to the hotel and visited Finley, telling him how I felt. He said that was good to hear. Next, I went to see this lady who had come in from Phoenix to be with me in Los Angeles, a lady by the name of Traci. A fine lady, and I had a fine evening.

Then, today, I got to the ballpark and saw the fight. Later, the trainer, Joe Romo, told me they weren't going to let me play until I was 100 percent ready. They wanted me to test my leg. I was furious. I felt it would be foolish for me to extend my leg on a day when I didn't have to play. I felt if I loosened up a little and took some treatment and rested I was more apt to be ready than any other way. I've been around enough to have earned the right to say how I'll handle my own leg. I went out on the field and Dark started to speak to me right in front of the writers who were there to watch the team work out.

I said, "Alvin, look, I'm not gonna risk my leg by rushing myself, but I am gonna play."

And Alvin answered, "Mr. Finley wants you to run and I'm here to see that you do what he wants."

"Well, I'm not gonna run."

"If you don't run, you won't play," he said.

The writers were starting to move closer to listen in, so he asked me to walk with him into the outfield so we could talk privately. We did and I repeated that I thought it was ridiculous to subject my leg to any unnecessary strain. He agreed. But he said he was on a spot because that's what Charlie wanted, and I was putting him on a spot by not giving Charlie what he wanted. I told him I was sorry about that, but I didn't give a damn about what Charlie wanted, because no one gave a damn about what I wanted.

I said, "Look, give me a little respect. Give me a little Aretha Franklin. I'll tell you when I can play, and, when I do, you can applaud."

"I want you to play if you can walk fifty percent. But Charlie doesn't want you to play unless you can run one hundred percent." He added, "You know how Charlie is."

"I know. And I'll play if I'm fifty percent. And when I play, I'll run. But I'm not going to run until I have to play."

We were both pissed off. He said, "Look, you go back to the doctor today and no matter what the doctor says, you say he said you were one hundred percent."

I said, "Oh, shit!" I started to run. I ran about 80 percent speed and I was all right. I did some stretching exercises. I took some batting practice. People said they hadn't seen me hit the ball like that in three or four months.

When I left, the writers asked me about the situation. I said I would decide if I could play or not, not the doctors and not anyone else, and I had decided I could play. I went and iced up my legs awhile. Then I dressed and went back to the doctor's.

Kerlan was there this time. I told him our team doctor in Oakland, Harry Walker, didn't believe in shots. But Kerlan said he did, and he was sure the shots would work. He also turned me over to a physical therapist—I think his name is John Miller—and he really did a job on me, massaging me, supervising some stretching exercises, and so forth. I felt super.

When I got back to the hotel, Traci wanted to know where

I'd been. She'd missed me and she was upset with me. I checked at the desk. I had three letters, four telegrams and nineteen messages. Just about all of them were from people who wanted tickets to the World Series. A month back, when you have to order your tickets just in case you get there, no one's ready to commit themselves. Now, the day before the Series starts, everyone I know in the world wants a couple of seats or more. I feel it is so fucking unfair, it is unbelievable. With all that I've got on my mind at this time, they have to heap this sort of problem in my lap.

I'd put out $1800 to order 30 seats for the games in Los Angeles and $4500 to order 100 seats for the games in Oakland. I'm prepared to take care of the people who take care of me all year. I'm not going to worry about the rest of them. Some of these people will give me the money for these seats and some of them will forget to give me the money. Others think they don't have to give me any money, because I can afford it or I get tickets for free or I owe it to them or something. That's the way it is and I don't know what the hell I can do about it, except not let it get to me.

I invited my father to the Series. I told him I had tickets for him and if he got on a plane and came out, I'd give him back the money for the fare, put him up at my place, of course, and be happy to have him. The truth of the matter is, I'd just as soon not have a lot of family around; I don't have the time for them and I don't want to be distracted. I don't want the hassle of hearing how I'm spending my money on everything else but them, and how wrong it is if I'm dating a white girl, and how the white guy who is my business partner is screwing me for sure.

I always invite my partner, Gary Walker, and he never comes, but this time he surprised me and came. And I'm glad he's here. He understands. He and his wife, Connie, showed up at the hotel. He stuck out his hand, wished me well, gathered up Traci and took off to leave me alone to get my stuff together.

I went up to my room and now I am here, alone, laying on my bed, resting, trying to sort out my thoughts, get my head

straight and get ready to play a World Series. It starts tomorrow and I expect to show up.

Saturday, the 12*th.* We won, 3–2. We won the A's way.
One big hit for one run. A squeeze-bunt sacrifice for another.
An error resulting in another. We only got five or six hits,
but we made the most of them. We played good defense and
we got great pitching. In fact, we used our two top starters
and our top reliever. I mean, we had to go to our best to beat
them. They are a good team and they kept it close. But our
best beat them.

It was very inspiring. I was moved afterwards in talking to
the writers to remember Dick Williams. I said we were still his
team. I said we won with the fundamentals he drilled into us.
This is true. It was not meant to demean Dark. It was put out
to praise Dick. He deserves it. It was an inspiring day and his
inspiration was in us.

I didn't sleep at all last night. I was worried I wouldn't be
up for the game. That may seem silly. I've been here before.
It's nothing new to me. Sometimes it seems they make too
much of it. It's a ball game. It's our business. I'm bone tired
and mentally worn out. I was worried my leg wouldn't let me
perform well in right field.

I got up out of bed early, about 7:30. I wasn't hungry and
couldn't eat much. I got a cab and got to the ballpark early,
about 8:30. It was four and a half hours before the ball game,
but I didn't want to wait at the hotel. The papers were full of
headlines:

REGGIE WILL PLAY
REGGIE WON'T PLAY
WILL REGGIE PLAY?

I didn't want to rap with reporters. I didn't want to sign any
autographs for fans. I wanted to work on my leg. I sat in the
whirlpool about half an hour and got rubbed down for another
half-hour. I got some ultrasound treatment and sat in some ice.
I got another rubdown and did some stretching exercises. I
lay down on a table for a while. The time passed slowly.

We had a couple of team meetings to talk about how we were

going to play this team. How were we going to play them? Hit the ball hard. Pick it up cleanly. Throw it hard and straight. It comes down to that, doesn't it? I went out and took some batting practice. My leg felt fine, but I didn't put it to too much of a test. I was swinging the bat pretty good, but may have been favoring my leg a little, swinging a little late, hitting to the opposite field. There were a lot of writers around on the field before the game, so I went back down to the dressing room after a while and sat down and tried to rest up.

When I went back out to start the game, the crowd had filled the park. This is a city which fills its park and supports its team. And this was a record crowd for this city of more than 55,000 fans. It was inspiring to see that crowd and it turned me on, even though I knew most of the people were rooting for the other team. The press box was packed. They even had a second press box built into the stands. A thousand reporters I suppose. TV and radio crews, of course. The impact of it turns you on. I didn't feel nervous, I felt turned on. Center stage and a warm spotlight. There was bunting around the ballpark. It is a beautiful ballpark. Well laid out. Well kept. I hear it's an outstanding organization. It must be nice to play here for this team.

We stuck to our rotation. It was Holtzman's turn, so he went. Vida will work tomorrow, Cat on Tuesday back in Oakland. Andy Messersmith started for them. I knew him from the American League, as he used to be with the Angels. A top pitcher. A hard-thrower with a great change-up that keeps you off stride. He had a great record this year, so I expected great things from him.

They have a lot of great players, but I haven't seen most of them that much. Our scouts called Steve Garvey at first their "most consistent player and hitter." Jimmy Wynn in center their "most dangerous hitter." Bill Buckner is a spectacular left fielder. Davey Lopes, their second baseman, is a superrunner. They have two good catchers, Joe Ferguson and Steve Yeager. When Yeager catches, Ferguson plays right.

We were told in our scouting report that defense is their soft suit. Bill Russell makes a lot of errors at shortstop. Lopes, at second, makes a lot. Wynn, in center, is sore-armed and can't throw. Down the middle, where you should be strong, they are weak. We were told they make mistakes and give a team openings. We are a team of opportunists.

I got the big hit for us—my first time up, in the second inning, batting cleanup. Messersmith threw me a high slider on a one-and-one pitch and I swung a little late, but hit it real hard and sent the ball into the seats in left field. I felt like I'd put on an impressive show. It really felt good. It took all the pressure off me and a lot of pressure off my team. And I believe it deflated the big balloon of emotion the Dodgers had created for themselves.

In the fifth, Holtzman, who is a good hitter but hadn't had an at-bat all year, hit a double to the opposite field. It may have bothered Messersmith, who uncorked a wild one with Kenny taking third. Then, with a two-and-two count on him, Campy executed a perfect squeeze bunt back to the mound and Kenny came home. You don't bunt with two strikes unless you can really bunt. A foul is out. But Campy can really bunt and he is a confident player under pressure. It was a perfect play and I believe it amazed them. Execution!

In the Dodger half, Campy did bobble a ball hit to him by Lopes. Buckner bounced a ball over Geno's head at first and Lopes took off. I saw the man moving like the wind as I went for the ball. I rushed so I bobbled it, then threw bad and he scored. I don't like to make mistakes and I was sore at myself, but it was only 2–1.

Holtzman had been hit in every inning, however. He just wasn't sharp. Tough as always, but not as sharp as usual. When he walked Wynn, Dark took him out. I think Kenny could have toughed it out and Kenny thought he could have toughed it out, but it wasn't a bad move. The only thing was, it was a little early for Fingers. But Rollie, five stitches and all, was really throwing. He was throwing as hard as I've seen him throw. He struck out Garvey. He nicked Ferguson to load

the bases, but bore down and got Ron Cey on a fly ball to Rudi
to end the rally.   They got a lot of runners on in this game, but
left a lot on.   They were not an opportunistic team and it hurt
them.   They couldn't get the hit when they needed it.

In the eighth, Campy singled.   North sacrificed him to second.   Bando bounced to Ron Cey in front of third, but the
young third baseman held the ball, deciding where to go with
it.   When he threw it away at first, Campy continued on home,
Bando went to third and it was 3–1.

My main concern was to hit the ball up to right or center to
bring Bando in.   I did just that.   I hit hard and deep to right-
center and I knew Wynn would never throw Sal out.   But, at
the last moment, Ferguson cut in front of Wynn and threw as
well as a man can throw and beat Bando at home.   It was a
fantastic throw.   Bando bowled Yeager over, but he held onto
the ball.   It was a super play.   It cost me an RBI and us a run,
but it was something to see.

Running to first, my leg hurt.   When Alvin asked me in the
dugout, I admitted my leg was beginning to bother me, so he
sent Claudell in to play in my place in right field in the last of
the seventh.   I hated to leave, but I had not told the truth
about my leg the other day and lucked out on it.   I was not
going to press my luck in a World Series.   I had a homer.   We
had the lead.   I wasn't about to hobble after a hit in the late
innings that might give them the game.   I stayed on the dugout steps to direct Claudell to where he should play the hitters.
I stayed in the game that way.   I rooted.

With one out and one on in the eighth, Willie Crawford singled to center to put the tying run on third.   But Van Joshua,
batting for Messersmith, grounded out and they were out.   I
have seen Messersmith better, but he showed me he had developed a change-up that is as good as any I have seen.   The
best I have seen!   Pinch-hitting for him enabled me to see
Mike Marshall.   He came strutting to the mound as if he
owned it.   I was impressed with his cockiness.   It stuck out all
over him.   And he retired us in the ninth.

In the last half of the ninth, Fingers got two outs fast on fly
balls.   Then Wynn hit a fly ball a little harder than the others.

It went to left-center and I thought either Rudi or North might catch it when they jumped for it, but they bumped gloves and the ball jumped into the seats to make it 3-2.

In the dugout, I got a little tense. I could see Rollie was wearing out. I don't think he's pitched that long more than once or twice all season. When Garvey singled sharply, I was glad Alvin lifted him. He had asked Cat if he could pitch for an out or two, since he was not going to work for three days. Cat had said he could, so he went to the bullpen and now he came in. Ferguson came up acting cocky and the Cat struck him out. And that was it.

It's funny, but afterwards Ferguson continued to be cocky. He said Hunter hadn't shown him as much as he expected from him. The Cat can fool you that way. You think he's not throwing anything, but he's throwing everything and right where he wants it. Hell, he struck Ferguson out and Ferguson should have respected him for it. Respect his record, man. Respect our record.

Even before the game Ferguson was saying they were gonna do this, they were gonna do that. Do it, man, don't talk about it! Do it if you can, then talk. I'm convinced this is a cocky club and it will kill them. Ferguson isn't the only one popping off about how they can handle us. Going into the game, they were putting us down—and after being beat by us, they were still putting us down. Ferguson is a fool and so are the rest. They'll learn.

I sat for more than an hour after the game talking to the writers, giving them the good lines and whatever they wanted. I didn't put the Dodgers down. I said they no doubt were nervous in their first World Series game and I said I believed we'd have to be even better than we had been to beat them. But I don't really believe we will have to be.

Before the game, Finley came into the clubhouse and told us Odom had a severely sprained ankle and should have been placed on the injured list so he could bring in another player. But the move required the permission of the Dodgers, and they had denied it. A Mike Andrews all over again, although I believe Charlie has learned his lesson and will not make that much of this one. He said the Dodgers were doing us dirty and we should do it to them good. Well, we sure as hell didn't need a pep talk at that time.

Afterwards, he came around giving out congratulations and accepting them. I picked up a bottle of soda pop and he snatched it out of my hand and posed for a picture by my side. Well, it's his pop. He owns it all. But fundamentals won this one, not Finley.

I am back at the hotel now and I am tired of talking. I am going to turn this fucking thing off because I am looking to relax. I have only one more thing to say. I believe we will beat the Dodgers in four straight games.

Sunday, the 13*th.* Did I say four games yesterday? Well, make it five. We got beat today. By a super pitcher. Don Sutton has tremendous stuff and he can put it right where he wants it. He's sort of like Ferguson Jenkins. Not that tough, but tough. Capable. I understand he had a lot of hard luck this season, but has been outstanding since they got into the stretch run. Well, he was outstanding today.

He beat Blue and Blue took some beating. It was 3–2 again, only the other way this time. It wasn't a matter of Blue blowing a big game. He just got beat. We just got beat. We're all in this together. But I don't believe they can do any better than they did in this game. I don't expect them to win another one.

The Dodgers got a run in the second on a walk, a bloop single and a solid single by someone . . . Yeager. They got two more in the sixth or seventh. Garvey bounced one up the middle. Campy made a super play on it, but he couldn't nail him. That fucking Ferguson then followed with a hard-hit homer to center, about 400 feet. Well, he hit it so he rates it.

Meanwhile, Sutton was stopping us smoothly. Campy got a double in one of the early innings. And I singled in the seventh. But those were our only hits up to then.

Sutton started to tire about then, though. With one out in the eighth, Dark sent up Jim Holt and Claudell to pinch-hit and each hit a single. Claudell is cool, like he's been here before. Campy hit to short, but Russell butchered it. That loaded the bases and we were ready to strike. But Billy North bounced the ball toward second and Russell scooped it up, stepped on the base, and threw to first for the double play. The only thing was he threw low and in the dirt, but Garvey put his glove down and gobbled it up. It was a great grab by Garvey and it saved them the game. If he hadn't got the ball, we'd have had two runs and another in scoring position with Bando, Reggie and Rudi coming up. Forget it!

In the ninth, Sutton hit Sal with a pitch. That brought me up in a tight spot. He fooled me on a pitch. I started to swing, checked and punched the ball into the left-field corner. It went for a double and sent Sal to third. We were back in business.

Alston took out Sutton. Sutton had a shutout, but the way Alston has used Marshall this season, you'd think he never made a mistake. He strutted in and made one right away. Rudi ripped a single to center that scored both Bando and me. Rudi is real. After Tenace struck out, Dark sent in Bambi to run for Rudi. Or Finley sent him in.

It was a tough spot for the kid to be in. He was supposed to steal to put the tying run in scoring position. Marshall knew that. I knew it. The people in India knew it. And we had been warned Marshall had a marvelous move to first. Herbie just doesn't have the experience for this spot. Marshall stepped off the rubber two or three times to freeze Herbie. He threw once and almost got him. He threw again right away and got him. Herbie was leaning the wrong way and lost. It was embarrassing and I felt for him later, but he stood up to the writers in the dressing room beautifully. He didn't alibi. He blew it and he said it.

Well, it was a mistake. We don't make many. I'm disappointed, but not depressed. I said so to the writers. I said it was a good game and I hope they enjoyed it. I said I still think we will win and I still do. I didn't say it, but I think we will win three straight and wrap this up in the fifth game. I really believe that.

L.A. bounced back and it boosted them back up, but that

may be bad, because they could regain their overconfidence.   I sense that they are not ready.   Sutton saved their skins today. Tomorrow is another day.   Tomorrow is Tuesday night for us.   Back at the mausoleum.   We are headed home and I do not believe we will see this beautiful, full ballpark again this season.

Tuesday, the 15*th*.   It was 3–2 again and we won again, which makes it two out of three with two to go.   The Cat cut them down with help from Fingers and we took advantage of some mistakes they made in the field.

It was a wild day which started with a call from Los Angeles from a friend informing me of a story in the *Times* there on an interview in which my dad bitched because I hadn't brought him to the Series.   The story was read to me and it depressed me.   It was headlined "Jack the Tailor" and it made my old man sound like a braggart, which he isn't.   He brags on me, but he's not a braggart.   He said I had given him some money, but he suggested I hadn't given him much.   He admitted I had invited him to the Series and he said he had made plane reservations for him and two of my brothers, but when I didn't send tickets and didn't call again, he didn't come.   He said he was waiting for a call.   Well, he ain't gonna get it.

I told him I had tickets for him and anyone else in my family who wanted to come.   I told him I'd reimburse him for the fare when he got here.   What was I supposed to do, fly up there and hand him the tickets?   He is my favorite man, but he is human and he was taken advantage of by a writer.   If the writer had been fair, he'd have called me and I'd have set the story straight.   I can't worry about it.   I have a World Series to worry about and my family should see that it comes first.   If someone was sick or something, that would be another thing. I told my mom I'd rather have her here later and she understood.   It was the hardest thing I had to do, but she was super about it.   She was really super.

From now on, I don't believe I'll even stay at home during a World Series.   I'll go into hiding in some hideout where no one knows I am.   I am tired of the telephone ringing and the

doorbell buzzing. I am tired of giving interviews and of talking on this tape. I am tired. I have not slept more than two
or three hours a night since the playoffs started. I get to bed
at midnight or twelve-thirty and get up at seven or seven-thirty,
but all I have done is lay in bed in between. I have been taking
sleeping pills, though I don't want to take too many or any that
are too strong. I don't want to be groggy.

Susie is staying here and she helps a lot. She is a lovely lady.
We are seeing each other again. Forgive and forget. I got to
have someone I can talk to besides this machine.

I was edgy at the ballpark today. At batting practice Blue
brought around Murray Olderman, the writer who wrote that
story in *Sport* that turned me off. I had about decided to
forget it and had just about forgotten it. I hadn't seen him
around and hadn't thought of him. But weeks ago, I told Vida
and other players what I was going to do and he didn't forget.
So when he saw the writer he thought of bringing him to me.
As I understand it, he told the writer I wanted to see him and
all but pushed him in front of me. That's the Blue Boy's sense
of humor. Well, all my teammates were watching and it sort of
put me to the test to back up my threats. There was no way I
could back down. I told Olderman off.

I am not apologizing. I don't know what I would have done
if I had seen him among other writers in an interview situation,
or if he had approached me and spoken to me. I do know that
seeing him made me mad all over again. The way he was
shoved in my face made me make my move. I was so mad, I
don't remember my words, but I used the words I always use,
which ballplayers use, which are not the nicest ones in the
world. I told him I thought he was a hypocrite who had made
me look like a hypocrite. I told him he was a horseshit writer
who had written a horseshit story, and I didn't want to see him
again—not in the clubhouse and not anywhere else. I suggested if he wanted to put me to a test, I'd punch him in his
fucking mouth. Well, it wasn't poetry.

I'm not sorry. Maybe it made me look bad, but I'm not sorry.
I have this book now, but I don't usually get to write about
other people. If he can write about me the way he did, it

seems to me I am entitled to talk to him the way I want. Fair is fair. I am sure the sportswriters will rally to his defense, and I will be made to look like a bad man to the public. But if I don't stick up for me, I don't know who will.

Joe Reichler, an assistant to the Commissioner, got him away from me, then came up to me and told me that if I threatened Olderman again or laid a hand on him, I wouldn't play again in this Series. Well, that is a bunch of bullshit and it doesn't scare me in the slightest. I am not such a slave in this system that I can't exercise the rights of a free man. They are not going to do anything to me, and they know it and I know it.

Maybe I'm used to rhubarbs, but I felt like a load had been lifted off my shoulders. There were about 50,000 people packed into the old Mausoleum tonight. The joint was jumping for a change. We had Hunter ready to roll and they were down to Al Downing. Al is a talented veteran, but he has not worked regularly for a couple of seasons. They don't have a third starter, much less a fourth, and that has to hurt them. I guess they have one who is hurt, Tommy John. But he wasn't here, so he couldn't help them. We got three runs before they got a run. Hunter shut them out for seven innings and they were in a hole by then.

With one out in the second or third, North singled. Campy grounded to Cey at third and he threw to first, but Bill just kept on running and reached third. It was good going by Billy. Bando walked. I came up and topped a pitch in front of the plate. Ferguson came out for it and fumbled it, and a run was scored. Dependable Joe Rudi singled and we had our second run. Geno walked to load the bases, but Fosse grounded out and we wasted most of our opportunity.

In the fourth, Green bobbled one and they got a couple of men on, but then Greenie made up for it by turning a line drive into a double play. The next inning, Greenie walked, Hunter sacrificed him to second and Campy singled him home. That did it for Downing. The next inning, I walked, stole second and took third on a wild pitch, but Jim Brewer retired Tenace and Fosse and I was stranded.

In the seventh, Hunter walked someone and gave up a single to someone—Russell—but pitched out of it. In our half Marshall fanned me on a fastball. I was swinging for the downs. In the eighth, Dark replaced me with Claudell in the field. I wasn't happy about it. My leg no longer was bothering me and I thought he saw that when I stole second. The way I was running, I didn't think I had to tell him. Claudell lacks my experience in the field. It wasn't wise.

Buckner homered with one out and Dark yanked the Cat in favor of Fingers. This wasn't wise, either, and the Cat was bitter about it. If Fingers had failed, it would have hurt, but Fingers doesn't fail. He was a little lucky this time. He has pitched in every game of the Series so far, but he has been struggling since he went so far in the first game. He has admitted his arm is tired and it is hard for him out there. But he is tough.

Wynn singled. Then Garvey singled, only Greenie grabbed it and turned it into a double play. They said later that Greenie was lucky to be where he was, but Greenie is always where the hit is. He is smart, not lucky. That took a lot of starch out of them. I wonder if we won't look back on it later as a sort of turning point.

In the home half, Geno singled and was taken out for our designated runner, Herbie the Bambi. Geno didn't like it a lot and was popping off a lot later. The eighth was a typical A's inning. A lot of moves by the manager we could bitch about, but they didn't beat us.

Fingers was still struggling in the last of the ninth. Willie Crawford cracked a homer to make it 3-2 and I thought Dark would lift Fingers, but he didn't. Campy fumbled a ground ball. Rollie had to show his stuff. He struck out Cey. Russell ripped a ground ball, but it was right at Green and Greenie turned it into another double play and they were turned away again.

There's a lot of talk that we are lucky, but you cannot be lucky all the time, and we win all the time. We have them thinking they are unlucky now. There is no way they are going to win thinking that way. I have come to the conclusion they have a lot of talent, but they are not showing it. I believe they have the best-balanced ball club I've seen since the 1969, 1970, 1971 Baltimore ball club. But that was a better team, and more experienced.

I doubt that the Dodgers have the poise to get back into this Series. From the way they talk, I suspect they are an emotional ball club that can roll right over you when they are rolling. But we have held them in check and they have allowed us to take command. We have the lead now and we will not lose it. I feel completely confident now. Maybe I will even be able to sleep tonight.

Wednesday, the 16*th*. Buckner blew it! He smeared himself all over the daily press saying they were better than we were and we had only three players who could play for the Dodgers. He named a good three—Reggie Jackson, Joe Rudi and Sal Bando. But he didn't name enough. If Campy isn't a better short-stop than Russell and if Greenie isn't a better second baseman than Lopes, I'll retire. Doesn't defense count in that man's mind? And what about pitchers. The Cat couldn't pitch for them? Or Kenny? Or Vida? Or Fingers? Forget it.

He is stuck on statistics or something. He doesn't know his own game. We have the guys who will not blow the big play when you need one. We have the guys who will get the big hit when we need it. It is all there in the records. Read them, man! Not the stats. Read the wins and losses. Add up the championships. Respect the records. Man, you're just a baby. Don't be putting down the people who have done it. Admire them.   Do it, and then they'll admire you.

I respect them more than they respect us and that's wrong—we've done it and they haven't. They'll do something before they're done. I can see that. I'm not afraid to admit it. I admire people who play my game the way it should be played. In the third game, when I got to first, I told Garvey I thought he was great and I was learning a lot from him. And he thanked me and was grateful for it and I don't hear him popping off. I mean, this guy is a go-getter. He really goes after the ball and attacks it. He is an excellent hitter. He is a fine fielder. He executes. He has a lot of poise and plays like a pro. He is going to be one of the greatest players in the game and I told him I really respected his style.

I think Ron Cey plays with a lot of poise. At bat and at third base. Very professional. He made a big error, but who hasn't? He's going to be good. They've got a lot of going-to-be's. That's just not enough yet. Buckner looks like a lot of ballplayer. He's got guts and a smooth stroke and a great glove. Ferguson is a powerful player. Yeager is a great catcher. A great catcher! Sutton is something else. Messersmith is marvelous. Marshall is marvelous. I'm not afraid to admit it. I think we're better, but I'm not boasting to the world about it while a World Series is going on. I'm not putting down their weak points.

Guys like Ferguson and Buckner lack class. I understand Marshall treats people like dirt. It's too bad, because they got too much going for them to give it away. Well, Finley cut out the story and pasted it to a file card and waved it in our faces before tonight's game. He read it to us and stressed the fact that since Buckner had said only three of us could make his club, what he was saying was that our other 22 weren't worth shit. He waved it in our faces and walked out.

Well, hell, we already knew what the boy had said and a lot of the guys didn't like it. Billy North was burning. The Dodgers said some things about Billy being a bad ballplayer. He didn't deserve that. He's a lot better than they think. But the pep talk didn't turn us on. When Bando was asked what he got out of it, he said he got a little rest. You won't win with newspaper clippings. You win by behaving like professionals on the field, which the A's do, even if they don't do it off the field.

We did it on the field again tonight. We did it with handicaps, as usual. Finley had Dark bench Tenace, bring Rudi in to first and put Washington in left. We've gone this way before and it weakened us defensively. It did in this game. In the first inning, Buckner doubled off Washington's glove. In the second or third, Yeager got a double on a ball Washington hesitated on. These were balls Rudi would have had. An inning or so later, Garvey singled off Rudi's glove. This was one Tenace would have had. We were lucky these things didn't pay off for them. And Washington did get a couple of hits, where Geno hasn't been hitting. Claudell's going to be a good fielder. He just needs experience.

Tenace was steaming. He said Finley doesn't treat players as people. Which is true. But maybe he shouldn't. The thing is, if I was managing, I'd play Geno. He's helped us win two World Series and I'd figure I owed him the right to try to help us win a third. I know he's been a big player for us for a long time. I knew he would bust his ass to win. I like him and I hated to see him taken out. Which is why Finley is managing and I'm not. I'm swayed by sentiment and that's wrong. Claudell has had a hell of a season. He helped us get here and he deserves to play, too. He's young, but he's behaved like an old pro at the plate, so there's no need to be nervous about him.

The moves Charlie made Dark make were not moves I would have made, but looking at them objectively they were not necessarily bad moves. And the way they worked out, they were all right. Finley doesn't favor defense the way I do, but he is not always wrong and he is sometimes right. He won't let friendship interfere with business, where I will, which is why I am not suited to be a manager—at least right now. It's easy for Finley. He doesn't have a lot of friendships to worry about.

I told Dark before the fourth game, I definitely did not want to be removed for defensive purposes again. I am a good defensive player when I can run, and I can run now again. I do not want to be embarrassed by being lifted from World Series games and I do want to be in a position to contribute with my glove and my arm, as well as with my bat and my legs. I could see it coming and I wanted to cut it off before Charlie could set it up with Alvin. It was all right for a game or two. It may have saved me reinjuring myself and it improved us in the field. But I don't need to be saved now. There is no one with a better glove than mine on this bench.

The fourth inning . . . was it the fourth? Yeah, the fourth.

It started with a helluva play. Wynn hit hard to Holtzman. It was over the mound and Kenny had to twist to get it and it put him out of position to throw to first, so he just flipped to Green for the throw to first, and Greenie got the man. I mean Kenny has to be thinking and Green has to be thinking and it was just a helluva play. When you make plays like that, you win. Then Garvey singled and someone walked. Then someone struck out. But with two out, Russell hit the ball to right-center and it went for a triple. I guess it looked like I wasn't running right. Or lost the ball in the sun. But it just went over my head and over Billy's head. Winkles was running the outfield and we thought he had us too deep on Russell in L.A. when he blooped one in, so we had moved in. And now we were too shallow. We ran all right, but it was too far for us. It was legit. And it brought in two runs.

It was 2–1. Holtzman had hit a home run earlier. Hey, Holtzman hits if he gets to bat, but this was a bonus. You don't expect doubles and home runs from your pitcher in a World Series and it takes a lot of pressure off the big bats. You say, "Man, there's one the easy way." So we were one down. Messersmith was throwing hard and throwing that terrific change-up, but we were starting to time him. We wasted a couple of singles in the fifth. We got him in the sixth. North walked and worried Messersmith until he threw wild trying to pick him off. That brought Billy to second. Bando brought him in with a single.

I walked. I've been getting walked a hell of a lot. I've struck out only a couple of times. They see I'm swinging the bat good and they're pitching scared to me. I can only count on one good pitch per at-bat, so I take a big cut at it. Then I'll get three or four bad ones before I get a good one again. I'm not getting much chance to hit, but I am getting some hits and a lot of walks and I am getting on for guys to get me in. Rudi sacrificed me to second. Claudell walked to load the bases. Then Holt hit for Fosse and singled Bando and me in, and we were ahead. That little trade Finley pulled off earlier, in which he swapped Pat Bourque for Holt, paid off here. This one hit was worth it.

Yeager bitched about my run, but I think he did it out of frustration. He thought he had me. The throw had me beat, velocity-wise, and he had me beat, blocking-the-plate-wise, but he never tagged me. The throw was a little off-line and he had to reach to his right for it. Instead of sliding right into him, I made a good hook slide to the left. He made a pass at me, but he missed me as I stuck my right leg right through his legs and over the plate. I made a good play. He made a good play. He's a good catcher. He just missed me.

He called the plate ump, Don Denkinger, a liar, but I got to give a lot of credit to the ump, because he was in a position to make the call and he waited until the play happened to call it, instead of calling what looked like was going to happen. This has been an excellently umpired Series and the television people told me that when Yeager sees the films, he'll see clearly how he missed me. Well, hell, we had 'em anyway. Green bounced out and that brought in the fourth run of the inning, and we had 'em, 5–2.

It was a great feeling knowing we had the game won and with it we had the World Series. There is no way this team is going to lose a three-run lead in a game like this and there is no way it is going to lose a three-to-one lead in games in a Series like this. This was the big game of the Series, the fourth one, because either they win it and tie the Series or lose it and lose the Series. Even if they win the next one, they have to go home knowing they need a sweep there, and there is no way they are going to get it. Maybe an experienced team, but not a young team. And it doesn't matter if it goes seven games like last year's Series or five games like this year's—it is all the same. We are going to win the one we have to win.

This Dodger team is a better team than the Mets were, but they are not going to take us as far. Buckner says if it goes 162 games with us, they win 160. He's blowing smoke. If it goes 3 or 5 or 7 or 107 or 162 or 262, we win the odd one, the one we have to win. He knows it now.

In the eighth, they got a walk and a single from Garvey and Fingers came in. Fingers was always coming in. Kenny had done his job and he could have cut them off, but you don't take chances at times like this. He was still struggling but he was still surviving. He struck out Ferguson to get out of that inning, but then he had trouble in the next inning, the ninth. I singled off Marshall to start our half, but was left there. Cey singled to start their half. Russell struck out. Then Joshua rammed the ball, right over second. Greenie dove for it and smothered it. A sensational stop. He got to his knees to throw. He had to hustle to make the play but he made the play. He always makes the play. He made a double play out of it and we were back in our clubhouse taking it in stride and raving about how good Greenie was. They were back in their clubhouse beginning to bitch again about how lucky we were. I spent an hour telling the media how lucky we were to be this good and went home.

I drove a lady friend to her home and hung around awhile. Around midnight I went to my own home where a lady friend was visiting. Susie. We relaxed. I relaxed as much as I could. I mean it was a good feeling knowing we had it won, but we still had to win it and I was still worked out. I'm going to sleep now. To bed, anyway.

Friday, the 18th. Before the last game tonight, a broadcaster taped an interview with me and asked me if I was happy about Blue going for the clincher against Sutton. I said, well, hell, I'd rather have Hunter, but I'm happy with Blue. I mean anyone would rather have Hunter in a game like this. It's like saying Seaver is going today, but I'd rather have Koufax. Well Koufax could do it when it counts and the Cat can, too, just as well. Look at the record. I don't care what team it is, even if it has a Seaver or a Sutton, I'd rather have a Hunter. But the Blue Boy will do. He's not going to be alone out there, you know. And if he needs help, Fingers will be making that daily walk. And he may not need help. When that Blue Boy is right, they can dig Ruth outta his grave, or Gehrig, or any of those cats, and ain't anyone going to hit him.

Sutton posed a problem. I didn't figure we'd hit him a hell

of a lot, either. He's a professional pitcher, I can see that. But I figured if we made the plays we'd win, because with the pressure and all, I didn't think they'd make the plays.

Before the fifth game, when Finley walked on the field, Dark excused himself from the writers. He smiled and said, "Pardon me, but I've got to go see what the lineup is gonna be." At that point, he was able to have fun with the situation. Well, Charlie is not only the owner of the ball club but the general manager, so he's got two rights to meddle. I don't want to manage a ball club when I retire. I want to own one. Then I can own as well as manage. And then I can't be fired. The only reason Finley hasn't been fired is because Finley does all the firing.

But the old boy is smart sometimes. Before the game he came to me in that gruff way of his, with that deep, slow-speaking voice of his, and he said, "When we win tonight, there'll be television in the dressing room. They'll put up a platform there and the Commissioner will present the trophy. I don't want to take the trophy from him. I don't even want to be seen with him. I've given orders for Dark to send Bando, Hunter and Campaneris up there to represent the team. Now, they'll be looking for you, because they'll want you up there, too. You find me first. I'll have a bottle of champagne for you. When they call for you, go up there and spray that whole fucking bottle of champagne over that sonofabitch."

I looked at him and I started to laugh. "You mean it?"

"You're damn right I mean it!"

"Dynamite! Outasight!"

"You'll do it?"

"I'll do it, dad."

I forgot about it for a while after the ball game began. We got a run right away. Campy singled. North forced him at second. But then Billy stole second and, when Yeager's throw went into center, Billy went to third. That brought Bando up. I went into the on-deck circle and prayed for Sal. He hadn't been hitting a hell of a lot and I wanted one for him in the worst way. I knew they wouldn't walk him with me coming up next, so I knew the job would get done. And ol' Mr. RBI knocked the run in. He lifted a long fly to left, just what was needed. But Billy manufactured that run. He had made a great move getting to third. He was really running. The Dodgers put him down and he was burnt up about it and it cost them. Fosse homered in the second and it was 2–0. A big breaking ball that just hung there. You could see it from the bench. He enjoyed it and we enjoyed it with him.

Blue was blowing 'em down. With one out in the second, Ferguson and Cey singled, but Blue just bore down and got 'em out of there. An inning or so later, Campy made a hell of a throw to get Wynn after he hit a hard shot that glanced off Vida's glove. And Ferguson hit a foul homer. I remember that. But they tied it in the sixth. They had a pinch-hitter. What's his name—Paciorek? Spell it for me, man. I'm a superstar, I don't have to spell. He hit a double, hitting for the pitcher. It was one way of getting Sutton out of there, anyway. Blue walked one. Buckner bunted to move the runners up. Wynn's fly ball brought one of them in. Then that good-looking Garvey hit a single to bring the other one in. Steve stroked it real nice. Ferguson came up with a chance to put them ahead, but he put them out of the inning with a fly ball. All that talk!

In the eighth, Vida got a little wild and Dark sent for Moon, which surprised everyone. Vida had walked one on and gotten two balls on the next one and Moon threw the next two balls. I guess Moon was as surprised as anyone. He got a ground ball out of Lopes, however, to leave both base-runners on base. They left a lot of base-runners on base. That's baseball. You bring 'em in or you lose. Blue Moon got one out and he won the game.

We really won it in the seventh when Rudi hit a home run and we just saved the lead after that. The circumstances were strange. When Buckner took the field, the fans in left started to throw a lot of garbage at him and he was gonna walk back off the field. The fans were wrong, of course, but fans threw stuff at us in both cities. I threw a frisbee back to the fans in one game. Just sailed it back, cool. But Buckner blew his cool. He brought it on himself by blowing off at the mouth. It caused a delay and during the delay Marshall, who was pitching, didn't bother to warm up. I was waiting with Rudi by the on-deck circle and we both saw it and we agreed if he wasn't staying warm, he was going to have to come in with a fastball.

Rudi said, "He's going to come inside with it, try to move me back, intimidate me. And I am going to hit the hell out of it." Which is what happened.

Now, I admire Marshall's style. I told him that when I ran into him in the tunnel before the fifth game and he thanked me for it, but he was short with me and went right on his way. I wanted to talk a little, but he didn't want to talk to me. I mean I'm no slob, but the motherfucker won't even talk to a fellow player! I understand he won't talk to the writers. He's a college instructor in physiology or something and he tells the writers there's no sense his telling them anything because they wouldn't understand it, anyway. Well, that's bullshit. He may be smarter than me and he may be smarter than you, but he is not smarter than everyone—and if he was smart enough he'd see it. And if he was really smart, he'd see that there is no point to putting everybody down. It makes him small and there is no way he can cut everyone down to his size.

I put some people down. But I am nice to those who are nice to me. Or have never messed on me. I figure if I can leave a fellow with something, whether it's a nickel or a dime or a kind word or simply a smile, it's better than nothing. I figure every friend I make puts me one up on where I was yesterday. Maybe Marshall don't need friends. Maybe he likes it alone. He's entitled to go his own way. But it's a hard way to go.

I have to admit I admire his style. He doesn't give any ground. He doesn't give anyone anything. He is so sure of himself he makes more of himself than there is. I wasn't impressed by his stuff. He didn't seem to have anything anyone else doesn't have. He has a good fastball and a better slider than I expected, but I didn't see his screwball. He didn't overpower us with his pitches. He must overpower people with his attitude. He says he can pitch every day and he pitches every day. He swaggers out there and he gives you a look that

says, "Fuck you, I'm Mike Marshall," and then he throws the
ball and defies you to hit it. If you're awed, you're not going
to hit it. Only the A's aren't awed. He has complete
confidence in himself, but against the A's it's misplaced.

Anyone can pitch every day. It's not how often you pitch,
but how well. I suspect if you study the record you'll see he
didn't pitch so well the second half of the season. He didn't
pitch so well in the World Series, when the guys who have
really got it put it on the line. I suppose he's still swaggering,
but he has no right to, because he cost them the last game of the
World Series. He stood there and refused to warm up while
they were quieting the disturbance in the outfield. I saw what
he was doing. I dug it.

He was saying, "I'm a bad motherfucker and I don't need a
warm-up to wipe you boys out."

I laughed at it. I told Rudi, "He's gonna go to the heater.
We've been waiting for the screwball and he's been feeding us
fastballs."

And Rudi replied, "He's going to crowd me and I'm going to
hit the ball up into the crowd."

Marshall was saying he didn't need it, but he needed it.
Hey, man, get off that pedestal, this is Joe Rudi you've got to
pitch to. This is a man who's been there and done it and if
you don't pay him respect, he'll ruin you. That was what was
wrong with the Dodgers this whole Series. They didn't pay us
our due respect. We respected them more than they respected
us. So Marshall came in with the heater, crowding Rudi, and
Joe just inched back and belted that ball 400 fucking feet, almost out of sight into the left-field stands, and we were ahead
again, 3–2, and that was that.

I thought Rudi won the MVP award and the free car that
fucking magazine gives away every year with that home run, but
they gave it to Fingers. Rollie took his evening stroll and
finished up for the fifth straight game. Oh, yeah, Cat bailed
him out on one batter in the first game, but Rollie was in them
all and worked well in all. It was work for him, too. Rollie
wasn't right, but he was ready to work.

They had a shot at it in the eighth, but we took it away from them. Buckner led off and singled to center. The ball took a bad hop and bounced past Billy North. Buckner saw it and kept right on running, right past second toward third. They say it looked like Billy loafed, but I can't see him loafing on a play like that. I was just drifting toward him to back him up, because it's the sort of thing you're supposed to do, but when I saw the ball take a funny bounce and get by Billy, I broke into full stride and went for it.

I saw everything happening in front of me. If you're baseball-wise, you see the whole scene developing. As I went for the ball, I saw Buckner going into second. I knew instinctively what he was thinking. He was human and he was thinking third. I was saying to myself, "Where the fuck you going, man? Hey, man, don't run on me, don't disregard me. Respect me. At least hesitate. Break stride. Wave at me. Holler, 'Hey, Jack.' Something. Anything. Let me know you know I'm there. Don't pass go. Don't collect no money."

As soon as I got the ball in my glove, it was up in my hand and thrown and headed for Greenie all in one motion. He was a long way away, but he had come out deep to get the throw and it hit him chest high where it was supposed to hit him. And as soon as he got it, he had turned and thrown to Bando at third. And as soon as Bando got it, he put it down and Buckner slid right into it and was out and what might have started the tying rally was ruined.

It was instinctive on my part. I can throw a long way. I can throw hard and accurate. But I never even thought of throwing to third. I have been taught to throw to the cutoff man for a relay throw in that situation and that's what I did, instinctively. I made the fundamental play I was supposed to make and it worked. I knew if we worked it right it would work. I never even took a look for Greenie before I threw. I threw where he was supposed to be and he was there. I know he didn't look for Bando. He threw where third was and Sal was there.

I was very, very happy, but Billy North was happier. I had saved his skin. As soon as he saw it, he turned to me, we dropped our gloves, held out our left hands and slapped each other there hard with our right hands. He laughed and said, "Right on, brother, right on!"

I guess Buckner felt bad. Well, hell, he made the right play. Not the right baseball play, but the right human play. I'd have done the same thing, because I'm human. If you're human you're gonna go for third. I don't give a damn if your name is DiMaggio or Mays or Aaron or Clemente—and they're the best that ever did it—you're gonna do exactly the same thing in the same situation. If you're hustling. If you're hustling, you got to go for the base. If what I do, if what Green does, if what Bando does isn't executed fundamentally perfect, you're safe. Then a fly ball can tie up the big game, and you got two batters behind you who can hit a fly ball. He's hustling and if he makes it, he's a hero. He doesn't make it so he's a goat. That's baseball. He talks too much, but I feel for him because people have to say he blew it. But he was just playing baseball and playing hard, the way you should play.

Fundamentals. Execution. That's what won for us. He was out, so he was wrong, but that's second-guessing. If he holds up, people are gonna say he should have gone, he would have made it. They'd assume that, not knowing he wouldn't have. They say now if he stays at second he'd have brought in the tying run on a hit. Maybe. They didn't get the hit, but they'd have had one more out to take a shot at it. Wynn walked. Garvey and Ferguson hit fly balls and they were finished. Ferguson hit another foul homer, but fuck it, it was foul. That play on Buckner sapped the last of their spirit out of them.

In the ninth, Cey hit a fly ball to me. I was nervous on it. It was easy, but it's amazing the things you think about at a time like that. You think about what life would be like if you drop it. I didn't drop it. Russell popped to Greenie. He didn't drop it. Then Yeager—no, Joshua, batting for Yeager—bounced back to the mound. Fingers took forever to throw it. I watched him holding it, moving toward first, aiming it. Finally he threw it. And it was all over.

After I caught the first out of the inning I started to think about the celebration and I remembered the way I had told

Charlie I would douse champagne on Bowie Kuhn. I started to get a little nervous about coming on to the Commissioner that way. It was one thing to say you'd do it, but something else to do it. I'd put up the big, bold front and I would have to back it up. Unless Finley forgot. Fuck it, Finley never forgets. If the situation developed the way he said it would, I'd have to do it. I felt kind of funny about it. I realized then that everyone would assume I was doing it because of the threat from the Commissioner's office over my rapping that writer. Which is what it has turned out to be today. I knew no one would know the real story. I figured, fuck it, I'm gonna do it. People will say it's my personality.

After the second out, I motioned to my bodyguard Tony Del Rio to come down by the field so he could come on the field and get me off afterwards. There had been no new death threats, but I just wanted to be sure to get off safely when that crowd of kids came on the field. Fingers fielded the ball and the crowd came on and Del Rio came to me and helped me off. It was a madhouse. I was happy as hell. You know, we'd done it. I'd expected to do it, but now it had been done. I didn't think about three straight World Championships or anything, just that we'd won again. I got into the clubhouse and everyone in the world was there. It was wild. I suppose there have been wilder celebrations. Some of our cats were cool about it. But it was such a relief to finally be finished with it that we did holler a little.

The TV people were there and the press and I have to give Finley credit, the stage was set exactly as he said. He was there and I got my bottle of champagne and they were calling for me to move up in front of the cameras. I was shoved up on stage with the other players right alongside the Commissioner. I sensed he was uneasy next to me because of what had gone down the day before, knowing me and not knowing if I was going to say something nasty or punch him or something. Maybe it was just my imagination, because he's the most ill-at-ease man I know. He's a nice guy, but he's never easy around players. He was born ill-at-ease and he always stands stiff and awkward in spotlighted situations. He had that frozen sort of smile on his face and he was saying all the things he was supposed to say: Congratulations. The best team won. The A's are an extremely deserving team. They are a credit to the game and to the nation. And he looks forward to seeing us here again next season. . . . You know.

I popped the champagne cork and he could see it coming. He tried not to let on, but he put his hand on my arm and he pressed down with all of his strength to try to keep me from raising the hand that held the bottle. He held that forced smile on his face and he was forcing himself physically to stop me. I had to force my arm up. It wasn't easy. It may have looked easy, but it wasn't. But I am stronger than he is, so I could do it. I got my arm up as the champagne erupted out of that bottle and I sprayed the stuff all over him—all over that man and his forced smile and his conservative suit—and everyone started to holler and laugh and I knew the nation was watching. He didn't know what to do or say. It really bothered him, but all he did was keep smiling and keep his mouth shut. He was angry as hell, but he wouldn't show it. All of a sudden I sensed that if I kissed him on the cheek it would show it was all in good, clean fun, so I leaned over and did it, and it did ease things. Everyone hollered louder and laughed harder and that was it and I got the hell off camera.

He didn't say anything to me. Finley said, "Job well done, Champ." I shrugged. I thought he was gonna give me a hundred dollars or something, but he didn't come up with a dime.

They had a victory party upstairs. I don't drink, but I drank. I drank three bottles of champagne and two six-packs of beer. I remember that much. I don't remember much else. I vaguely remember tearing the place up. They tell me today I tore curtains down, turned over tables of food, just wrecked the room. Most of the people had gone before I got to the point where I went wild. I remember thinking I wanted to have some fun and let off some steam. It was just such a relief to finally be finished with the season and to have won it all again that I got drunk and tore things up. I didn't hurt anyone. No one was offended. There were no fights. Just good, clean fun.

Tony told me he didn't dare drink because he knew he'd

have to drive me home. He did. I started to sober up a bit by
the time we got home. It was a little after midnight. I was
supposed to meet my partner and his wife and Susie at home,
but I guess they got tired of waiting and went out for some
food. Tony and I and another guy, Rich Foley, went out on
the balcony and sat in the cold air and sipped some stuff and
shot the bull and I fell asleep. They helped me to the couch
and I sacked out there. Some time later the other people came
back and woke me up and put me to bed.

I woke up this morning at 8:30. I felt beaten and bedrag-
gled and all let down. I am sitting here now trying to take it all
in and wrap this up, because I guess we're about at the end of
it. The season is finished, isn't it? I don't know what more
there is to say. I've said it all. By now, I don't know what I've
said. I haven't censored it. I just said what I thought. I
guess I'll get to read it over before it becomes a book. I figure
I'll find myself in here somewhere.

I feel like I had a good season. Not a great season, but a
good season. I can be proud of it. I contributed to a tremendous team effort. Not many teams have won three straight
World Series, so we have to be regarded as one of the rare
teams, one of the great teams of all time. If Finley doesn't
fuck around and bust us up because he thinks he can win any
way he works it, we can win another one or two. We can get
the five in a row he's always talking about, if he doesn't mess
with us too much. I feel I had a good World Series. Not a
great one, but a good one I can be proud of. I hit .280 or .290
and executed some good plays in the field. Considering that I
was hurting, I held up.

I have nothing left for now. I will try to get through the day
and then I will take some strong sleeping pills and try to get
through the night. I have got to catch up on a lot of sleep. I
have got to catch up on a lot of living. It is always a long
season. Living with Finley is exciting, but exhausting. Living
with our guys is exciting, but exhausting. When it is over, I
never have anything left. I want to go beyond baseball and
look at the rest of life all winter long, and I hope it lasts a long
time. The spring will be here soon enough and with it another

season. There may not be many seasons left, but I think I still have my greatest season ahead of me. I will have to take care of my legs and stay healthy and then I can let it all out.

I feel as though Charlie can't say I didn't earn my money and do a decent job for him and his team. I feel friendly toward the man now. I feel friendly toward every player on my team. I am going to have to call him and tell him not to trade Moon or Billy. Keep us together, my friend, and we will do the job for you again. I suspect we will see the Dodgers again and I suspect they will be tougher next time because they will have been through it this time. They are where we were three years ago. And they have learned some hard lessons we had to learn. I told that to them in their dressing room after the last game. I went into their clubhouse to congratulate them so they could see I respected them and had no hard feelings if they didn't give us our due respect. I consoled them, because I know what it is like to lose.

I said, "See you here next season, same time, same station."

I hope it turns out that way, but a man never knows what life holds for him.

10 ☆ NOVEMBER

Wednesday, the 27th. Tomorrow is Thanksgiving, but I don't know what I have to give thanks for. Finley says he wants to trade me. He has told the press he wants to trade his pop-offs, Bando and Jackson. It is very disappointing. I am disappointed in Finley. Every time I begin to believe in him a little, he lets me down. We have done a job for him and now he's spreading it all over the papers that we are pop-offs. And to show he doesn't need us, he is going to dump us as if we were trash.

I don't believe he will trade us. He realizes that if he lets either of us go, he will not win the World Championship again. I believe he is just talking trade to try to beat down our bargaining position. He knows we are going to want more money than he will want to give us and he knows he is going to have to go to arbitration with us and he wants to better his bargaining position by pretending other teams don't want us.

I don't know about Bando, but Baltimore supposedly offered Bobby Grich and Don Baylor for me and refused when Finley asked for Ross Grimsley instead of Baylor. If Green retires, we could use Grich. Walter Youse, an Oriole scout I've known since I was eighteen, told me if Finley would take Grich and Grimsley for me, the Orioles would give them up in a second. He called, representing the team, to find out if my leg was all right. He said I was just what they needed and with me they could win it all and they'd give a helluva lot to get me.

Finley was quoted by several newsmen as saying he'd take a million bucks for me or Bando. So Ewing Kauffman, the Kansas City owner, said he'd give a million. So Finley said he'd said two million. So Kauffman said he'd give two million. So Finley shut up. I think he is putting up a smoke screen as he does so often to suit his purposes. I don't think he'd find it hard to make a good trade for me with any team, but I think it would be bad for his team. At this point he has helped this team by picking up Billy Williams, a distant cousin of mine, to be our designated hitter.

There have been times I wanted to be traded from Finley and times I didn't, but I never really liked the idea of leaving this team and my teammates. It is not always easy among us, but we have learned to live with one another and to win with one another. And I am proud of what we have put together. I am settled in Oakland now and I would hate to leave the team when it has won three straight and may win more.

I think he might trade me if he thought I didn't want to be traded or if he needs the money, which he may, or if he finally is going to sell the team. We did not even draw a million fans in town this season, which is a shame, and he may be forced to sell. If so it will kill him, because it is all that is left in his life. He might strip it of its stars before unloading it or moving it.

If he doesn't trade me, I will take $160,000 if he offers it to me. If he keeps talking of trading me or doesn't offer me a fair sum, I'll ask for more. And the way the arbitrators feel about Finley, I might get it. If I went to a city like Baltimore, I'd have to get $200,000 or think about giving up the game. My real estate business is booming in Arizona. Living in Oakland I can commute to Tempe. It would be impossible for me to keep control of the business while I was in Baltimore, and the business is my future. My partner can operate it all right alone, but if I'm not playing my part in it, there's no point in my being part of it.

I'm selling land out of Oakland this winter instead of returning to Tempe. I still have my home there, but I have one here now, too. I visit there now, but I live here. I've taken a couple of trips there. I took a trip to Pittsburgh to be part of a promotion for Willie Stargell's sickle-cell-anemia program and I'm doing some things like that. My image has held up. Some writers rapped me on the thing with Olderman, but a surprising number defended me, including Dick Young in New York.

I shaved off my beard because I got tired of it. And because my partner suggested I should, since he felt I might scare some of my middle-class white customers. If I still liked it, I'd have kept it, but I got tired of looking at it in the mirror. I look a little younger now. I've lost a little weight. I'm dieting to ease the load on my legs. I have to do different to survive.

I'm living easy, sleeping nights, enjoying female companionship and traveling a little. I got two speeding tickets near Bakersfield on my way to L.A. The cops may have recognized my license plate, "MVP 73," but they didn't give me a break the way they do here. One of them is supposed to have said, "You're in Dodger country now," but I never heard it. It made the news. Everything I do makes the news.

I was surprised to hear Dark is returning. I thought he had the credentials now to go somewhere where he would be more respected. But Finley asked him back and he came running. He said after the season that Jesus was spit on, crucified and so forth, so why not Alvin Dark? I say we didn't treat him quite that bad. I told him he had held up and earned my respect.

Well, I would like to be back with the A's, too. The Cat won the Cy Young Award. Marshall won it in the other league. Burroughs and Garvey won the MVP awards. I can't complain about Burroughs, but I'd have voted for one of the winners. Not me, but Rudi, or maybe Bando. We all finished in the first five or six. Fingers should have been there, too. And Hunter. Cy Young Award or no Cy Young Award, the Cat probably was our MVP. Fingers won the World Series MVP, where I thought Rudi would. But I'd have voted for Green. I know he didn't get many hits, maybe he didn't get any hits, but he dazzled them defensively. He took more runs away from them than we scored. He may have done the most to win it for us and it was worth more than $20,000 to each of us.

The A's are a great, great team, colorful, controversial and successful. I would like to stay with them, but if I wind up with another team I will give them everything I have.

11 ☆ FEBRUARY

Friday, the 28th. After the loss of Catfish, I wasn't so sure I wanted to be back with the A's. But, then, I had no choice in the matter, did I? I'm not a salesman who can go to work for the store across the street if I want, can I? I'm a ballplayer and I have to play ball where they tell me to play ball. I could quit being a ballplayer and become a salesman, but that would be throwing away a lot, wouldn't it? So I'm a slave to the system. A highly paid slave—but a slave, nevertheless. Catfish escaped the system. He's the first who ever did. I would if I could. More power to him. Even though it hurts the A's terribly. A man has to look out for himself. If Finley is looking out for you, look out!

The one thing they've always said good about Finley was that he was a smart businessman. You call losing Catfish smart? It was the dumbest thing that's ever happened to a baseball man. He thought he had Hunter at his mercy. Charlie offered to pay him his money, but not the way the contract called for. I'm sure he thought the contract was unbreakable. I'm sure most baseball men thought they could break the terms of contracts without breaking contracts. Well, a court has ruled otherwise and, unless an appeal is upheld, the establishment will have to conduct itself more honorably from here on in, which will be good for the game.

Hunter had told me he was going to have a go at it, but I was surprised he won. The A's lost. They may not lose their championship without him, but there was no way they were going to lose it with him. They still have a lot of players who know how to win, but it is going to be a lot harder to win without the best pitcher in the game. If Blue becomes the pitcher he was becoming a few years back, it will take up some of the slack. The A's did not have to be at their best to win their division the last couple of seasons, so maybe this will bring out the best that's in them. It will be easier to win the division than it will be the playoffs and World Series. The big games are the ones in which you're going to miss your big pitcher the most.

Put in terms of salary, Catfish will collect about $700,000 a season for the next five seasons. To put it into perspective, I think there are a few other players who could collect that kind of cash if put in the same position. Johnny Bench, for one. Maybe me. Finley always said he'd sell any player he had for a million dollars. In Hawaii I approached Al Campanis of the Dodgers on the beach and asked if his club would pay a million to two million to buy me. He said he couldn't talk about it without tampering, but he hinted he'd sure look into it. But when I asked Finley to sell me, he said he'd have to be out of his mind to sell me. He said the fans would run him out of town on a rail.

I don't know why Finley said he was going to trade me if he didn't trade me, but he's always saying things he doesn't mean. He didn't trade me during the interleague trading period, then he hinted he'd have traded me during the second trading period if the Players' Association hadn't called it off. He didn't want to trade me within his own league for fear I'd hurt him all season, but he may trade me yet. I'd like to go to one of the Los Angeles or New York teams, but I wouldn't want to go to a bad team in a bad town. I suppose I could go to the Kinetsu Buffaloes of the Japanese League, as Mike Andrews is doing. I could do a lot of things, but The Man calls the shots.

He is amazing! A dozen or so A's were going to go to arbitration on salary, but he sweet-talked a lot of them into signing before they got to it. We won it all again and he offered us the same salaries or less and the guys were angry. But he got to them and upped the antes and got their signatures. I was surprised when guys like Vida and Rudi and Geno signed before arbitration, but when he got to arbitration with the rest of us, he won his share.

Circumstances put Catfish in another class, but I figured if $200,000 was tops, that's what I rated. I got the same $135,000 as last season. Bando wanted $125,000, and got the same $100,000 as last season. Holtzman wanted $112,000, and got the same $93,000. Maybe we wanted too much. I don't want to make a big deal about it. Times are tough. People are out of work. Families are hungry. I'd look like a fool if J complained.

So it's spring and training camp is opening and another season is soon to start. Lord only knows what this season holds for us and what the future holds for me. I still believe I am the best, but I believe I still have to prove it—and then go on proving it. I want to have a better season than last season, but I am just learning how to play and only now approaching my peak. If my health holds up, I believe my greatest year is right out there somewhere, waiting for me. Everything good in life is out there somewhere, waiting for me, if I can only find it.